T0307367

HOPE I DIE
before
I GET OLD

t-t-talking 'bout re-generation

RICHARD BONNETT

Book Baby Publisher

Hope I Die Before I Get Old, t-t-talking 'bout regeneration
Copyright © 2020 by Richard Bonnett

Printed in the United States
Book Baby Publishing
7905 N. Crescent Blvd
Pennsauken, New Jersey 08110

ISBN: 978-1-09835-179-3

Two natures beat within my breast
One is foul, the other blest.
One I love, one I hate
The one I feed will dominate.
- Tara Leigh Cobble

Author at age 17 (1972)

Dedicated to my late Mom who never stopped praying for me.
Her prayers were answered.

CONTENTS

FOREWORD

No names have been changed
April 1988:

The old man slumped into the passenger front seat completely relaxed with eyes closed and head resting back. The rest of the car was twisted, its passengers hurt or in temporary shock, but the old man...he was in total peace. Not the peace of natural sleep, there would be no awakening this time; it was more like the peace of surrender throughout his whole demeanor, like every one of his muscles had gladly let go the strain of many hard years of struggle. There was no smile to belay this peace, his mouth was closed. The only motion from him was a shock of gray hair gently flipping back and forth in the springtime breeze; the only part of him still influenced by this world. As I leaned in with one hand on the crushed dashboard and the other on his seat, I knew his body had expired...his lower torso was wet from the last act of a dying person; the bladder releasing when muscle control is relaxed. His life on Earth had just ended within the last 100 seconds, he was in transition. Bent over and leaning in, I wondered if his spirit was departing at this very moment. I looked intently at his surrendered face wondering what he was seeing at that very moment; wondering what he was experiencing, who he was seeing—A loved one? A bright light? Angels? Was he still aware of where he was or what just happened to him? Was he out of his body floating above me and watching? Could he see through those closed eyelids, could he see me, hear me? I had to try; leaning in, I whispered into his ear the only thing I knew could help him at this last moment of transition, if it wasn't already too late…then I ran to the driver's side to help the living.

I'm not sure why, but throughout my early life I have encountered these close proximities to death. By my mid-20s I had been to more funerals than most people attend by age 60, witnessed fatal car wrecks, only witness to a drowning, and a few near death experiences of my own. Most of these funerals were close friends. I believe God placed me close to these experiences for two reasons.

1. Force me to view my own mortality.

2. Time was running out.

I had come around a sharp turn on Rt 345 in rural Berks County that afternoon. A VW Rabbit was perpendicular to the road with the front end smashed into a cement culvert in an embankment. I probably would have driven past without noticing a car in the ditch if there wasn't broken plastic and dirt in my lane. I slowed in my lane and wondered why no one was around, why the cops hadn't cleaned this thing up. Then I saw movement in the VW back seat and jumped out of my truck, realizing this accident had just occurred. I mean, *five seconds* before I came around the bend it occurred. The dazed occupants were just beginning to stir, realizing they were in a bad accident. I looked around for a second car in the accident but there was none.

The driver was a woman in her 50s, her body was lying in the culvert with her legs still in the car near the pedals. Both legs were unnaturally draped into the car like bleeding rope. It was obvious they were broken in numerous places. She was trying to move, but couldn't pull herself away from the car. I wasn't touching her for fear I'd hurt her more, so I ran around to the passenger side old man and the scene I just described.

Now a young mother with her two children in the back seat had my attention. She was my age at the time and her three kids were the same ages as my kids. I was thinking, "This could be Lori, Steph, Ben and Josh...this could be my family." My heart went out. The kids were just starting to whimper. While mom was still pretty dazed, she was just starting to comprehend what had happened and began moving. I tried pulling the driver seat of the two-door VW forward but it was twisted tight. The driver started pleading for help; her initial lack of pain from shock was wearing off and she was now hurting. I told her I couldn't move her because she had some bad injuries; she already knew this anyhow, and she'd have to wait 'til an ambulance came.

It dawned on me now that someone better call an ambulance; this was before cell phones. I yelled to a neighbor running toward me, telling her to call for help. No cars had come by yet and I was still the only one on site. Turning back to the mother who now had gathered her kids off the floor and was examining them in the back seat, I could see mom growing frantic as her kids began crying. I settled her down and suggested she not move the children until an ambulance arrived. Once she was settled down, she asked me to check on her grandfather. I told her I already had and that he was unconscious and relaxed. I wasn't about to tell her he was rejoicing with the halleluiah choir.

Smoke had been billowing out from under the hood, and moments later puffed into flame. At the site of flames Mom got hysterical so I told her to hand the children out to me. As she handed the smallest to me, a man arrived and said he had a fire extinguisher in his truck and ran off to get it. He got back about the time I was pulling mom out of her tight quarters. The fire was sending smoke into the car. I held two of the kids while mom held the other, waiting to see what happened with the fire. The driver, still lying half in and half out of the drivers' compartment, was pleading with me and her daughter to get her away from the car but her injuries made it too dangerous to move her. I handed off the children and sat on the ground with her to put her at ease. I told her if the fire gets too bad, I'll yank her to safety. The other guy on the scene quickly extinguished the fire as more neighbors arrived. Maybe two minutes had passed since I arrived. We could do no more than wait for the ambulance. Waiting, I learned from mom there were three generations in the car. The older man, her grandfather, had lost his life-long wife just six months ago and was heart-broken with depression over his loss. She said something to the effect that he struggles through each day since her passing. I remember thinking those worries were over for him. I never got their names or phone numbers and left once the ambulance crew and fire department had everything under control.

That Sunday my Pastor asked the congregation to pray for the Mulvenna family, who had been in a fatal crash. After the church service, he brought me up to date on the injuries. Pastor Bill Parks knew nearly everyone in the area and even though the crash victims do not attend our church, he had visited Myrna (the driver with broken legs) in the hospital because he knew their family. She would be hospitalized for weeks trying to heal her legs back and then months of therapy to walk again if all went well. The older gentleman was DOA. The woman in the back seat would be okay and the kids had no serious injuries that he knew of. Pastor Bill said he would pass my name on to them. That was the last I heard of it other than a few passing updates from Pastor Bill on Myrna's progress.

Then one spring a few years later, at little league sign-ups for High Point Chapel where I was assistant coach, I saw the name Nick Mulvenna on our team list. As soon as I matched the name to the face, I knew it was one of the two kids I pulled out of the back seat of the wreck. His Dad, Mike Mulvenna, whom I hadn't met yet, had also volunteered as assistant coach this season. Mike was by his son's side, so I went up and introduced myself and apprehensively explained how I knew them, knowing the old man who passed away in that crash was probably Mike's dad.

Mike is a very down to earth, born again, burly, blue collar kind of guy who is not shy with his opinions. He and I would share many good times coaching baseball games over the next several years. Later, because Mike and I got along so well, Coach Lou assigned me to keep Mike away from the umpires during games before he got thrown out. Mike took little league seriously and had humorous umpire opinions he was unable to restrain at times.

I remember one game when his son Nick was pitching and getting a lot of called balls, which Mike thought should've been strikes. He went behind the batter's cage to see how the ump was calling the pitches. He would criticize every other call as if the umpire couldn't hear his comments. At first the ump glared at Mike a few times, then warned him. I was standing nearby enjoying the 'Mike & Umpire' show when Coach Lou decided it was time for me to go rescue Mike. As I approached, I heard his last comment to the ump concerning how he was calling the opposing team pitcher now on the mound, "Yeah, sure…if that was *my* kid on the mound, you'd 'a called that last strike a ball'!" And with that he was thrown from the game. Mike turned to me in shock with his hands out as if pleading for justice, astonishment all over his face, asking in all seriousness, "What did I do?" The more innocent he pleaded, the harder I laughed. That was Mike.

Well, when I introduced myself to him that day of sign-ups, he stopped in his tracks, put his arm around my shoulder and proceeded to tell anyone listening that I was the guy who pulled his wife and kids from their burning car. Before I could stop him, he had bestowed genuine American Hero Status upon me and couldn't thank me enough. That's Mike, he is lovable from the get go. I explained there was no bravery on my part and anyone would have done as much but Mike wouldn't hear it. More importantly, the best news he could share with me was that the older gent in the car accident, was a born-again believer in Jesus Christ. That was the best closure to my wondering about that accident day.

Funny thing about heroes, there are none. Just ask any 'hero' and they'll deny what they did is heroic even if they pulled 50 people from a burning building. 9/11 firemen don't consider themselves heroes, neither do soldiers. "Just doing our job" is what they'll say. Other people have the right to hang the hero title on you, but most folks would perform the same hero duty if in the same circumstance.

However, the truth is, deep down, everyone wants to be *someone's* hero. Not in the *rescue* hero way, but in the, *"I will never let you down or fail you"* way. That's why we have kids. Seriously! If you're lucky, for a few years that little bugger looks up to you as their hero like no one else ever saw you before, as you always wanted to be seen in the eyes of others—perfect and without fault. For a short time in your life, while they're very young, you can do no wrong in their eyes. It works that way too, in some degree, when we meet our life partner and fall in love…then a gasket blows or something. Someone falling in love with you is the same as being a hero to them, for a period you can do no wrong. Get a dog? You're reaching for hero status, buddy. I'm telling you; I know this stuff! Dogs can't see your faults. We look for a relationship with anyone who can't see our faults.

Well, now that Mike officially declared me a hero, I would also like to add my opinion to all heroes before me. If I'm anyone's hero, that person is in for a big chocolate mess. But like I just said, deep down, all my life, all your life, WE have been trying to meet permanent hero status to at least one person. Heroes are good people, and that title bonafides your existence, perhaps even stamps a golden ticket to heaven at the end of your days. If you're a hero, no one will remember the bad things you did. Hero status sort of wipes the slate clean, or at least eliminates a lot of bad moral debt you've accumulated, if even for a short time.

I guess if I've ever really been a hero to anyone it was my wife, kids, dog, the IRS, and now my grandchildren. The dog croaked so my grandchildren are the only ones presently holding me in hero status. Lori and my own kids have seen me run from enough fires. Like I said for the third time now, deep down, we are all striving to be perfect in *someone's* eye, anyone's eye, in order to clear our slate of bad debt. Keep this in mind as you read these stories.

Our lives are the attempt to meet other's acceptance and expectations. Boy, do we disappoint. Even heroes disappoint.

PREFACE

Italicized names have been changed

About five years ago, my wife Lori and I went to a dinner meeting for officers of the local Daniel Boone Optimist Club. It was held at the home
of Maureen and Dan McCarthy, two doors up from our house. Maureen was
president, Lori was VP; the meeting was well attended by club members,
many of whom were other couples from our neighborhood. Before the meeting officially commenced, we were helping ourselves to the buffet dinner and
mixing with those gathered around. There was a regional big wig up from
the Philadelphia suburbs to officiate the induction of officers in this newly
established Optimist chapter, or something along those lines. His face was
familiar but I just couldn't place it until he was introduced to someone in the
room as Bernie Romic, retired Haverford Township Police Officer.

Right then the meeting shifted gears. I introduced myself to Officer
Romic, my name drew a curious stare as he studied my face; then I added,
"from Manoa Lanes." His mind adjusted back over 30 years and immediately
remembered me, then warily shook my hand as memories stirred behind his
gentle eyes. From there, the two of us went into the camaraderie of two warriors who had once stood firmly against each other but were now on the same
side. To both of us, Manoa Lanes was not a neighborhood or a bowling alley,
but a street gang that had very few surviving members, of which I was one. He

started out with, "I'm sure I arrested you a few times…didn't you one time…," and he went on to cite a battle story from my past. He remembered all right. Matter of fact, I still had one of his arrest citations in my 'ancient papers pile' at home. At the "Lanes" I knew him as Officer Bernie. Though slim now, he was a bit portly back then and was known as the cop that wouldn't leave his Cruiser to run us down. One after another we reminisced about events, individuals, court hearings and fatalities, which marked that time of our lives. Tonight, we would each hear the other guy's point of view for the first time. Bernie would tell me how crushed Mr. & Mrs. *McNicol* were when he first arrived at their house minutes after their son Mikey put a shotgun to his heart and ended his life, then I would tell him *why* Mikey was considering taking his life before he did it. We learned a lot that night, for the first time hearing and understanding the other side's perspective.

After a while it dawned on us that most of the Optimists members had gathered from other rooms to listen. None of the people present knew any of this stuff from my past and probably thought they knew me pretty well. They knew Rich the good neighbor, Rich who goes to church every Sunday, smiling Rich ready to help. This *other* Rich in the living room was blowing their minds. Lori was familiar with it all; we had dated through most of the "Manoa Lane" years. As much as we needed to get on with the meeting we just couldn't stop asking each other what *really* happened the night of such and such, or other 'wondered about' happenings from 30 years earlier.

Before the evening closed, I went home to look up the citation to see if it had Officer Bernie's name on it. Some of the Optimist members, curious about the nature of the arrest, urged me to check if I still had the citation since I couldn't recall the violation for which it was issued. Sure enough, I found it in my pile of historic papers; it was signed by Officer Bernie so I walked it back up the street to show him. Ironically, it was the **only** citation I had kept for posterity since it was the last I ever received. We both had a laugh, then he flipped it over to write, "Years later - did not turn out too bad, Officer Romic, badge #104." He handed it back to me and said, "Looks like your debt has been paid, I'm glad there's one happy ending." Officer Romic hit the nail on the head; my debt had been paid, but not in a way either of us had figured it would ever be paid.

Bernie died six months later of cancer. Tonight was one of those chance meetings that in no way happened by chance. Bernie had known some broken-hearted parents because of our gang and he needed some questions answered. I answered some of those questions. It was closure for him from a troubled time in his career, of that I am sure. For me, he opened up how much pressure the Havertown Police force (and he) was under at that time to rein in this fledgling street gang.

That night, several Optimist folks told me I should write a book about my experiences. It wasn't the first time I'd been told this and had always brushed it off. However, since I turned 50 I started to take on a different perspective of my time on this transient spaceship and questioned whether a book about my life might have any positive value to readers. What good would these stories serve if I did tell them? Most of it I'd rather leave in the past. But then I remembered, "To whom much is given, much will be required." And after this chance meeting tonight, I questioned if writing this book was a responsibility I have been shirking. Perhaps this effort has been required of me, to put it down on paper so others can benefit from the path I took to get to the Rich Bonnett they know today. If you read the book all the way through, I'm sure you will benefit from it. If I didn't think so, I wouldn't have bothered. Hopefully, it will prompt you to face some questions about your own life.

In order to tell my story, it has to be told in its proper chronology. I couldn't just jump in the middle and cover the gang days, people might think I was born with a mental defect. The correct chronology will help the reader understand *how* I arrived at different mindsets throughout my youth, and understand why I would do the stupid things in my stories. So while it may seem unnecessary to the reader to go all the way back to childhood stories, I believe it helps set up the later years. Also, stranger events have happened since my 2+ years at Manoa Lanes. This book is not about a gang kid. The gang kid was just a small part of my life but the part most people seem captivated with. Or perhaps the real fascination is: How does one get from there to here?

The format I chose is a series of short stories, starting as early as I can accurately recall, events that had profound influences on me. This is *not* a biography but glimpses of a day here, a week there, or a summer somewhere else. These short stories present events that established a morality that allows someone to do things that most folks' conscience would not allow. I've tried to keep my opinions to a minimum until the final chapters and let the stories speak for themselves with minimal explanation of why a particular event was included. Each story is picked for a reason; they are an insight to my character and characters that influenced my thinking.

I'm sure some of my old friends will be surprised that certain 'famous' stories concerning them are missing. The reason is because the book is not a 'Best Of" or 'Greatest Hits' compilation of stupid things I've done. Also, some of those stories have no purpose other than shock value, which is not the intention of this book. Some may argue certain stories that made it into this book are not good reading, but hey, it's my book and I can write what I want, you can skip what you want. And you can't beat the price either! I tried to keep it readable for ages 15 on up; that turned out to be one of the more difficult challenges of this effort. I'm sure some parents will disagree it meets that criteria. Try to get your money back! HA! The stories are as sanitized as I could allow without losing their realism. It is my hope that mature readers would put this book in the hands of a young person dear to them, who may be on the path of serial bad choices. However, this book is not solely targeted at the young wayward son or daughter. It is for all who have wondered out loud to God about the fairness of life and the hypocrisy of justice. To all readers, it will certainly make you examine your own life, and we all need to do that from time to time.

Now, what do you think of the chances that 30 years later a retired Haverford Township Police officer would drive over an hour to our little town of Birdsboro (pop 5,000), show up two doors away, six months before he died, to expose me to my neighbors and get his questions answered? That my wife Lori and her friend Maureen would be voted VP & President respectively in the Birdsboro Optimist Club to unknowingly set up the meeting. That Lori would finally talk me into attending the only Optimist meeting I ever attended (I am not a member). And that meeting would launch this dinky book. Life! What a trip! There are no coincidences.

Richard Bonnett, Birdsboro PA
written shortly after my 50th birthday, autumn of 2003

INTRODUCTION

All of the stories in this book are true and there are many witnesses to this fact. There are, however, some descriptions in the book that may be unintentionally in error due to the passing of time. Each story has been reviewed for accuracy by a principal participant(s) from that story other than myself. Those story participants and permission to use their names are listed in the *Acknowledgements*.

The dialogs are reconstructed from actual events or impressions left. They are re-constructed in the vernacular of that period as others and myself would have conversed, but cleaned up enough to be presentable in print without vulgarities. The gist of the conversations is fairly well remembered by myself or friends; enough so that accurate dialog could be reconstructed from joint recollection.

i.e.: I remembered John being too frightened to step into the next room. The dialog becomes: "There is no way I'm going into that room," John said while retreating.

I am sure there are some errors due to faded recollection but those involved who have read it before going to print attest to its accuracy. Nobody's perfect.

Names in some stories are changed for obvious reasons. In most stories I had permission to use original names. Some deceased individuals with untraceable family were also left as original names. In general, if a person's name is *italicized* at its first introduction, the name has been changed. Non-italicized names are actual names. In most cases, I will state at the beginning of the story whether the names are original or fictitious.

If some of the early stories seem strange and you're ready to put the book away, bear along a few more stories. It will all make more sense as you continue. Each story is included for a specific reason. Much of who we are is the result of the company we keep and the experiences encountered in that company. By our early teens, our character has pretty much been formed by the friends we choose, the authority we respect (parents, teachers, etc.) and the degree to which we decide to follow True North on the universal moral compass. Whenever I read about a young person found guilty of an outrageous crime, I immediately think, "How did they ever get to that point?" My stories are intended for the reader to see how one gets to that point and back again because in this day of moral relativity, we all know that True North can vary widely for each individual's moral compass.

I also feel obligated to issue a Warning: My life is not really "book-worthy" when compared to the lives of folks who went through some great feat of courage, catastrophe, survival or adventure. With that being said, it is really for you to decide.

CHAPTER ONE

We Three Friends

*No names in this chapter have been changed
unless italicized.*

A best friend is our most valuable possession throughout life. Some of us don't find that person until high school or college, or even later in life, as a workmate or neighbor. In a society that is so mobile, where it is difficult to know someone long enough before they move or change schools, some never find a best friend until they meet their wife or husband. But I'm not talking about spouses here, your wife better be more than your best friend! I'm talking best buds, your other half before you met your better half. I was one of the lucky kids to find my best friend at age four, living a few doors down. We grew up together and stay in touch to this day. His name is Joe Peca, JP, or 'JoePec' said as one word. He played an important role in forming my confidence and better character.

We really don't remember when we met because we always knew each other. Probably found each other when we were four years old and allowed to wander a few houses away. Over the years, many have tried to divide our bond. At times we even tried to drive each other away, but we have stood the test of fire and are solidly bonded at the heart.

Defining what makes a friend "best" is hard to pinpoint, but I'll venture. First there is love, a sustaining love that grows from trust and shared adversity. Second is their loyalty in the face of your failing them. Third, there is the test of time. Over time you learn all there is to know about that person and accept it without question or examination. Long-time best friends have a chemistry of knowing each other's thoughts and moods without speaking. Best friends nurtured together from so young an age have the strongest bonds because we haven't learned to build defenses yet. You innocently give yourself to each other before you know enough to judge each other. You just naturally grow up being a big part of that other person.

There was a third wheel that fit into this friendship. His name was Steve Sisca, the Sisco Kid, Bruin, Sneedsley and a few other nicknames. I say 'third wheel' because he wanted what Joe and I had in our friendship but never quite got there, though he was very close to us. Steve was the reluctant mama's boy who wasn't allowed to get his sneakers dirty, while Joe and I were the trouble makers. The three of us were a trio that moved in and out of each other's lives, living on the same street and forming alliances over the years as we matured into our late teens. After Steve's mom died in our early teens, the formula flipped dramatically. Then Steve and I were always in trouble, while Joe was forced to struggle with a disabling illness that threw him down hard. But the three of us always stayed close no matter what new friends floated in or out of our lives. We three formed the core among our other friends over the years. The brotherhood of those early years stitched us together for a lifetime as only time can.

From ages five to 15, JP and I were inseparable. Then a long bout with bad health and hospitals turned Joe into a bit of a recluse due to fatigue, but we still saw each other for weekly catch-ups. This drove Steve and I closer, especially through the dating and adventure years of 16 to 19. The doctors had Joe back in shape by 18, but by that time Steve and I were hanging with guys Joe wanted nothing to do with. By 18, the three of us would start paling around together again. So in the early years you'll read more about Joe, the teen years more about Steve. That's it for chronology.

Joe and I invented our own language of communicating around others so they couldn't understand what we were saying, had secret signals, started more secret clubs than we can remember, and instinctively knew what the other would do before they did it. Probably the worst talents to couple together are two kids that are both very imaginative and adventurous. "I've got a great idea!" would be the seed of many a regretful venture that would end in trouble or hilarity. Often, carrying "pretending" too far would garnish the same results. The following stories come to mind when I think of "pretending" and will give you an insight to our imaginations.

"And in those days, there will be wars and rumors of wars"

Approximate age when this story occurred is 10 or 11 years old (1963)

Playing Army was serious business in our neighborhood, with after-school combat games of a dozen kids being common. Mushy rotten apples from local apple trees in the fall made for ideal hand grenades. To detonate a grenade, you had to explode it on the body of your enemy. It was grassroots paintball before paintball guns were invented. As good soldiers, Joe and I regularly patrolled the turf around our neighborhood with diligence; too much on a few occasions.

While out on patrol one morning, we came upon two newcomers in the hood playing too close to our ammo dump (the apple tree) on JoePec's back lot. After sneaking up to watch them, we saw they were playing Army too. Joe and I came to the same immediate conclusion…"Germans!"…and went into action. Upon charging and shooting them, these newcomers did not fall and die per all rules of pretend Army engagement no matter what neighborhood you came from. No, these Krauts tried to run away. This violated all rules of backyard Army and demanded serious discipline. You *had* to fall dead for at least 10 seconds before coming back to life. We had no choice but to capture one prisoner while the other (his brother) got away.

We tied our prisoner tightly to the apple tree so as to face us and started interrogating. Name was Lowry (sounded German to us) and had just moved in two streets away. After intimidating and accusing him of swiping grenades, we told him we would let him go after teaching him never to set foot on U.S. soil again. The penalty: Face the grenade launcher. It was human target practice from close enough range so we never missed. Once the adrenaline got pumping, we continued to pelt him with rotten apples until he was screaming bloody murder.

Just as we thought we were getting our message across; I heard a crackling noise coming from the inside of both of my ears as my feet left the ground. Someone of great strength was hurling me to the ground BY MY EARS! Turns out, the brother that got away had fetched the Gestapo (his Dad) for an insertion rescue. We didn't see him coming. When I looked up from the ground, an enraged man in his late 30s was dragging a wincing JoePec by the ear toward me. The man pried me up by my ear again and got in our face. Herr Lowry turned the interrogation on us, while his free son untied his bawling brother. "You've got a choice of *me* dealing with you or taking me to your parents," was the extent of his questioning. If we hesitated just two more seconds, he would have relished the opportunity to twist and rip. Up to this point in my life, I had never seen an adult (other than my dad) so out of control and ready to throw all reason and law to the wind. Mr. Lowry was so hot that even being under the scourge of my Dad's flailing strap looked a heck of a lot safer than where I was now. I was scared stiff this guy would rip our ears off before getting his rage under control.

Joe made a futile attempt explaining we thought his kids were Germans but that made matters worse since as it turned out, they *were* of German descent. Fortunately, it drew attention to Joe who blurted out, "That's my house right down there!" before Mr. Lowry would've ripped into him. We were promptly marched by ear to Joe's back door where the maniac pounded 'til Joe's mother answered in alarm. "These two yours?!" he asked accusingly, then spilled the beans on what we were doing to his son. Mrs. Peca assured him both of our dads would beat the tar out of us. Nothing new there. This seemed to satisfy him enough to cool down, so he left with his sons who were whimpering from their ordeal in the background. Mrs. Peca lectured me and told me to go tell my father what I did. Joe got the typical Italian slapping around your mother gives you as a warm-up for the belt you'll get when Dad gets home. I never let it get to my house. Reasoning that I already had seriously aching ears, I wasn't about to invite my Dad to balance out the pain to the rest of my body. No sir, silence was the order of survival for this one.

Let me state here that JP and I had fathers who believed a strap or stick were the best way to get their point across. Many a time, Joe and I would compare body welts from a good whuppin' after a hairbrained scheme went awry. Occasionally, when going to knock on the other guy's door, we could hear our buddy pleading for mercy as our respective dads laid into us. Joe loves to tell of the time he knocked up for me and my brother answered the door saying I couldn't come out because I was getting beat. My brother held the door open wider for emphasis so Joe could hear me crying. Joe quickly slinked away fearing he might be somehow implicated. So you couldn't blame soft parents for the way we were. Nope, it was just a fact that we had too many lousy ideas that needed to be tried, without ever considering the consequences. Act first, think later.

"And I will pour my wrath upon them"

On another war-torn occasion, Joe and I encountered two more new victims our age walking up the street. They had some of the finest looking weapons we had ever seen. We always had 'beater' guns, homemade guns, or pieces from our last two guns duct-taped together to make one. The only time we got a new toy was our birthday or Christmas; other than those two occasions we had to buy our guns out of our own pockets, which were usually empty.

These new guys looked like rich kids whose parents bought them whatever they wanted. That was enough reason for JP and I to stop them for questioning, even though we were not involved in a game of Army at the moment. I remember them being polite and answering our questions without an attitude. We asked to examine their guns, so they handed them over trustingly. Never surrender your weapon!

I really can't say why (without going off on a tangent about subliminal psychology) but I knew I couldn't let these guys go scot-free. Perhaps their politeness was a sign of weakness or fear that I had to capitalize on. Probably, it was my prejudice that the best soldiers (Joe and I) should have the best guns, and we didn't. So I smashed one of the shiny new rifles on the stone wall next to me with such force that the kids started to take off. I ordered them to freeze with some threat and they did. Joe followed my lead and destroyed the other rifle. We handed back dangling plastic with twisted gun barrel, then warned them they got off light. The "got off light" line is one my Dad always used after whacking the tar out of me. The saying left an impression on me because I'd think he overdid it when Dad thought he metered out a 'get off light' whacking. I had to figure I was lucky. I'm sure these brothers felt they were lucky to be let go without bodily injury. I yelled after them "We coulda' stole those from you, ya' know!" trying to emphasize that we were fair in our punishment.

A week or so went by and Halloween rolled around. While out Trick or Treating, we knocked on a door in the newly constructed 200 block of Glendale Road. A pretty young mother eagerly invited Joe and I into her new home. The house was busy and she was really into the festivities of the evening, maybe she saw this as a way for her new family in the neighborhood to meet the local kids and learn a little about us. This was typical of the '60s with new home construction and new families exploding all over into new suburbs. So we came in and took off our masks as she requested. When she didn't recognize us, she called in her two sons who were in the kitchen getting their costumes ready. Four jaws dropped...then the brothers pointed at us yelling, "THAT'S THEM!" Mom's pretty face went from Halloween joy to stone cold ice. Joe was behind me, closest to the front door engaging the 'feet's don't fail me now' retreat, and muttering "Oh Brother! Can you believe this?" It did seem like our luck to encounter these two under such circumstance. The enemy walked right into their camp! Word got back to us in a day that other Trick or Treaters saw us running from the house and gave our names to the woman. At the same time, we learned that Ralston was their family name.

Once again, Joe and I lived in fear every time the phone rang or when we stepped into our house, wondering if Mrs. Ralston had caught up with us. Neighbors calling my folks happened often enough that I had developed a few defensive tactics. First, was to sneak in the house and ask my brother Charles if I was in trouble for anything. This was risky, as it gave away the fact that I *was* in trouble and usually had to confide the problem to my brother who could use it against me in blackmail. At best, this defense only provided a warning. Second, and best, was to intercept the phone call. This, however, involved staying home for a day or two answering all calls without making it look suspicious. If I was lucky enough to intercept, I could say my parents aren't home and offer a heartfelt apology. This worked a few times. Sometimes, if JoePec's parents got called first, Joe would receive his punishment then call me as soon as he could get to the phone, warning me to stay by the phone. The worst calls were the ones that came during dinner because my mom sat right next to the wall phone. On those occasions, she would answer, look at me while silence buried my fate, look at my Dad, then apologize to the party on the line and promise the problem would be strictly taken care of. By the apologize part, my Dad would have already cracked me upside the head and asked me what I did. But on this occasion it was all for naught. Mrs. Ralston never called and we figured we were home free. Right?

For a while we *were* home free…until I got my newspaper route a short time later. Sure enough, the Ralstons are on my delivery route. No way I was going to collect their newspaper bill (you collected in person each week back then, no 'mail in' bills) and was content to deliver their paper fast and free for as long as I could afford to. Well, eventually you have to face the music and in this case the music, being Mrs. Ralston, turned out to be a compassionate soul who wanted to talk it through with me.

This was a new concept to me, who thought all parents wailed on their kids. Mrs. Ralston was a refreshing reproach after the norm of witchy nun whackings, long-term groundings, and my Dad's justice. I truly believe the fact that my being a responsible paperboy persuaded her I had redeeming qualities. I apologized and offered to pay for the guns. She saw this as admirable but refused my money, instead asking me to promise to treat her sons with respect. I promised.

I don't know if this was a smart mom who saw an opportunity to win over a local bully to protect her sons, or if she just got lucky bringing her sons under my protection. No one ever bothered the Ralston boys while I was around, and I even became friendly with them, actually liked them. Sometimes, they would even help me out on my paper route. Turned out they weren't rich kids at all, except for the nice mom whom they were close to. Mrs. Ralston demonstrated true forgiveness, which I never forgot.

———————————————

This book starts out with Army stories for a specific reason. Life is a battle. We all fight back differently. Some fight back by *helping* others through their battles, other fight back creating another battle. Subliminally, we are all afraid of losing the battle. There is no real 'scale' to tell us how we're doing in this battle; seems like we wander through our years wondering if we're winning. Where is the fine line between those that win and those that don't? With seven billion people on the planet, do those that place in the top 20 percentile get certified 'successful' as winners and the other five billion are losers in life? At some point in our lives, most of us learn that money, things and power are not the measuring rods in this battle. They merely make our lives more comfortable and secure. That is not success. So that leaves love as the front-runner for success. All right then…when do you succeed in love? A whole new set of measuring rules for love?

My love quotient was dismally flawed. Somewhere, somehow, I developed a cruel streak that would sometimes creep to the surface. I wasn't proud of it and knew 100 per cent when I was over the line. Mostly it stayed manageable, but I occasionally thrived on the fascination in seeing people frightened at my hand. Joe was by nature a gentler person, but fed his curiosity by following my lead and thrilled to these occasions. The older I got, the more dangerous these occasions became. New kids in the neighborhood presented a threat. I saw myself as the designated protector of the hood. Neighborhood hero?

'Fear is the mother of violence, and it makes me fret to see the way she breeds'

– Peter Gabriel.

Real War Heroes

Both of our dads served several years in Europe during WWII, so naturally they were war heroes in our young eyes. My dad served for almost three years in England and France in a support capacity, which kept him behind the frontlines and out of harm's way. However, being fluent in French, he was an interpreter to different officers while in France. He had interesting stories of watching London bombed night after night from the safety of the hills on the outskirts of the city, of the terror of V2 'buzz bombs', of telling French families his officers were commissioning their homes for their headquarters and the war effort. Three years out of your life in a war on foreign soil makes anyone a hero in my book.

Joe's dad saw the worst of humanity during that war. He was a medic in the frontline infantry fighting in Germany and saw many men die. His unit was one of the first to liberate Dachau concentration camp. Being a medical aide-man, he was given a camera and told to record (photograph) the condition of the victims he treated. He actually lived the scenes out of *Band of Brothers*. As kids who loved to play Army, we would ask him about Germans and the war. To our confusion, he would never discuss it with us because we were too young to understand. The most we ever got from Mr. Peca was an abrupt "war is no good, boys", or when asked what Germans were like responded, "Germans are just like you and me," which puzzled me for years.

Joe's dad brought back all kinds of war treasure. He had a complete German infantry uniform with helmet, rifle, and a German Lugar. From the abandoned Dachau offices, he had prison stationery and letterhead pages. But the thing that held our undivided fascination was a shoebox of about 40 black and white curled photos he took of naked corpses and skeletal survivors from that concentration camp. Joe wasn't allowed to see the photos, but once in a while he'd sneak them out and we'd go over each one trying to make sense of what they were. These pictures were legend in the neighborhood and many of our friends didn't believe us when we told them about the pictures. Remember, this was only 18 years after the camp was liberated and the holocaust *was not* being taught in school or shown on TV documentaries, certainly not common knowledge to kids under 12. All Joe could tell me about the people in the pictures was that they were Jews. It was a big mystery to us. What was so wrong with Jews that people would treat them this way? We didn't know it was the other way around.

One evening a few years later, when Joe's parents went out for the evening and I was sleeping over, Joe got the box out and we sat at the table by the back door going over the pictures again. They left a permanent impression on our young minds the few times we saw them; our only reference to real-life horror at that age. Now at 13 years old, we had some vague understanding that these camps existed, mostly because of the questions I asked my folks, never mentioning the pictures.

That night, we forgot to put the pictures away. Joe's folks came home late, his dad saw the box on the kitchen table the same moment we realized we forgot them. I thought from the look on his face he was going to send me home and lay into Joe but instead his demeanor relaxed as he pointed to the pictures with his ever-present cigarette and asked us what we thought of them. He sat with us for maybe 15 minutes, chain-smoking while telling us how sick in the mind men can be, that sick minds did what we saw in the pictures. He told us the people in the pictures were being gassed and burned in masse like diseased cattle because they were Jewish. He talked about Hitler being insane, how war is not a game but a horrible job that had to be done, that good men died so sick minds could be stopped, that war is more terrible than we can imagine. No details, I don't think he ever gave Joe any details of the war; he had put it all behind him. We didn't ask him any questions that night. We were too shocked at what he said and the adult way he treated us. Up 'til now, Mr. Peca had been this mean guy that always looked pissed-off and wailed on Joe. Tonight, he treated us as we were unaccustomed and I learned another side of the man. He got up, told Joe never to show those pictures to anyone, then went upstairs leaving Joe and I at a loss for words. It was the first time he ever talked to me that he didn't treat me like I was a pain in the ass. Mr. Peca figured we were old enough to understand and he knew someday he'd have to explain the pictures. After that, I saw some warmth in Joe's dad. With years, Joe and I grew mature enough to talk with and enjoy each other's dad…even laugh about the dumb things we did that they *knew* about. Neither dad would ever bring up the war years until we got older.

I mention this about our dads and our exposure to those pictures because both left an enormous impression on us. Keep in mind that horror pictures available to our generation at the time only played at the movies and the worst I'd ever seen was King Kong vs. Godzilla. There were only three channels on TV, no Netflix or violent X-Box games to desensitize us. Those pictures rocked our world. We admired our dads' war duty even though we knew little and understood less about it. I wondered if the way we treated those neighborhood kids was confused emulation of how we perceived our dads would have handled things in real combat. We understood firsthand they both knew how to wail on their own kids with no visible remorse.

Other Turf

In other neighborhoods roamed other kids like me. Visiting their neighborhoods would eventually mean confrontation. Usually, they were Public School kids we didn't know. Attending Catholic school, the nuns had taught us to cross to the other side of the street and bless ourselves when we walked past Manoa Elementary School because it was full of heathen kids doomed to purgatory at best, hell most likely. According to the seven sacraments I was taught, the nuns were telling the truth.

Ric Freilicht was one of the kids who would always start a fight whenever I was on his turf. Manoa School had a big playing field, this was his turf. He'd just walk up like he was waiting for me and say, "You think you can take me?" or "You wanna fight?" So we'd fight. Mostly, these confrontational bouts would come to a draw, which resulted in our respecting each other. Later in our teens, we became good friends, a bad combination. Eric never lost his love for fighting and eventually ran out of local challengers.

I mention these neighborhood fights because of the momentum it creates and the friendships they forge. Ric and his friends would tell kids in other neighborhoods I hadn't visited, that Rich Bonnett could probably kick their butt and I'd spread the same about him when his name came up. By the time I entered Junior High, I had this gauntlet of kids I never met who wanted to see if they could take me. So the fights followed me to Junior High in the form of after school "callouts". If someone 'called you out' you both agreed on neutral ground to meet after school. By the end of the school day, a bunch of kids would've gotten wind of the 'callout' and there would be several dozen kids showing up to see the fight. I had three such 'crowd' events. Before that, there were a dozen or so neighborhood fights. I mention this in no vain context; I was knocked out cold twice by age 14 and lost my share of fights. But even those you lose gain you respect for never backing down. Also, rarely did these fights originate over an offense for something I did. They were simply a social righting of the order of peer seniority in my age group.

On rare occasions, I fought out of rage. When I got fed up with Bob O'hara stealing my paper route collection money, I sent him to the hospital with a dislocated shoulder. He was too embarrassed that a kid smaller than him did this, so he never told his parents (or mine) how it really happened and I was too scared of the doctor bill to brag about it. The neighborhoods were teaming with kids from the post-war baby boom, and it seemed to me like everyone got in fights. The final point about this fighting nonsense… there was an unofficial brotherhood of respect for those who fought, both among the fighters and those that watched. At the time we didn't know it, but that brotherhood would later start hanging with each other and become a street gang known as Manoa Lanes after the bowling alley at which we would meet. But I'm way ahead of another chapter.

The Fire, age 11

If you play with fire… As I mentioned earlier, Joe and I had creative minds and often invented new games, stupid games. Next to Joe's house stood a mature wooded lot that would eventually accommodate four homes. It was a favorite spot to build forts. Glendale Creek originated on this parcel. On a dry sunny Saturday, we sat bored on two shopping carts we had dragged into the woods. The carts were turned up on their push handles with nose skyward. We had filled the carts with as many dry leaves as we could jam in the basket and were sitting on the front end facing each other five or six feet apart. Both of us turned up a book of matches from our pockets. Spontaneously, all the materials for a wonderful new game were at hand. No instructions needed to be given after the first match was flicked at the opponents shopping cart full of dry leaves. The obvious goal was to ignite the other guy's leaves so he jumped off his cart before he did the same to you. Last man standing on his cart wins. Matches were flicked as fast as we could light them, laughing in anticipation of getting the other guy's cart cooking under him.

Most of the matches were going out as they were flicked through the air but we didn't wait to see if one match took. We were assailing each other in a flurry of sparks and sulfur as fast as one could flick. Absorbed in the competition and laughing, there was no consideration of how to deal with the fire after a victor was declared. With match books now empty, we waited to see whose pile would start up first. We both had smoke, and where there's smoke there's...Wump! The leaves ignited and standing on the cart was the only way to get further from the heat.

To this day neither of us remembers who won. That was quickly forgotten in the scramble to put the burning leaves out. One of us ran to the nearby creek to lug out a water-soaked box that had somehow found its way there. By now the fire was in a 10-foot circle and spreading fast. Throwing the flattened wet box only succeeded in spreading the burning leaves further outside the circle so we tried to kick the leaves on the outer perimeter into the circle in an effort to keep the fuel supply in the inner ring. That was a waste of time. In desperation, Joe said, "Dirt!" and we tried scraping dirt together to throw on the beast but that method too was useless. I remember looking at my pitiful handful of dirt, then at the moving fire. The shrub line was now leaping 10 feet high so that Joe and I had to yell above the cracking flames. Time was of the essence and we had to discuss our options. "We better get the hell outta here before someone sees us," I yelled to a frantic JoePec scraping dirt doggy style between his legs with his hands. But it was too late. Mrs. Kenworthy, a neighborhood busy-body whose property adjoined the wooded lot, had been watching us from her backyard boundary after seeing smoke from her kitchen window. "Don't you two try to run! I know who you are!" she yelled at us in a shrill voice from the edge of her property.

We were caught. Not only did the woman know us, she was our school-crossing guard and I'd have to face her every day, twice a day until school let out in eight months. This was bad; I wasn't ready for worse but it was coming. Totally frustrated at being trapped by this town gossip, I was ripe to lash out at her next suggestion. "I'm calling the police!" she yelled at us shaking her head up and down in agreement with herself as if that would teach us a lesson.

"That's a great idea, Mrs. Kenworthy, but if you want a house to sleep in tonight, I'd call the fire department first!" I snapped back in the only satisfaction I would get this day. At this she took her focus off us to survey the rapidly spreading fire and ran off to the phone, just as frightened as us. In no time, the fire was half an acre in size with big trees on fire. No firehouse siren could be heard in the distance yet.

Joe and I used to sit on our bikes outside Manoa Firehouse on slow summer days in hopes the siren would go off. Then we would pedal like maniacs to follow the trucks to the fire. Just about the time one fire truck siren would get out of range another would round into view and we'd pedal our little legs off again, repeating the sequence until we arrived at the fire. We loved fires. We also knew how long it took firefighters to respond and this fire was approaching the Becker home faster than the fire trucks would get here. Now we were petrified of homes catching fire, as were the Becker's, Saccomandi's, and Kenworthy's who by now had their garden hoses trained on their houses. Joe's house was at the far other end of the woods and safe because the wind was blowing away from that direction. The blaze was now two acres and roaring like no animal we had ever seen.

'My Dad is gonna whip me raw' was the thought going through my head. While waiting for the fire departments to come, Joe had time to run home and get a shovel and rake to fight the fire but they never saw any duty. Our final effort to fight the fire was Joe's doing. Mr. Saccomandi told Joe to run and get the other hose on the side of his house and turn on the water. Mr. Sac was a dominating figure on the scene, being the largest man in the neighborhood. Joe came flying around the corner of the house, water spouting as the hose unraveled. Just like in a cartoon, when he got to the end of the hose at full run, the hose stopped while Joe went flying. The hose went whipping around spraying water on Mr. Sac who looked double pissed now. If we weren't so scared, it would have been as hilarious as it became in future tellings of the event. Joe jumped on the whipping serpent and trained the spray towards the woods, which it wasn't reaching anyhow. To this, Mr. Sac stated the obvious through a puff on his cigar, "No use botherin' with that shit, kid, put the water on the house." This line would for years be repeated infinatum whenever one of us was clearly missing the obvious. It became one of those trade mark sayings within your circle of friends, but you had to be puffing on an imaginary fat cigar when using the line.

The fire trucks came in time. The fire was extinguished after a production the likes of which has never been repeated on Glendale Road during our time there. Firemen with water backpacks, trucks with long hoses, Chiefs and cops all over, neighbors lining the street; for 15 minutes the horizon looked like a Vegas Fountain Show. We sat on Becker's open patio awaiting our fate. Our faces were streaked with soot and sweat as were our clothes. Both of us were black from head to toe. My mouth was never so dry in my life. Fighting the fire had drained us of everything as we sat there spent, too fatigued to care about our fate. The Fire Chief approached, inquiring how the fire started. Every finger under 16 in the assembled crowd pointed to us with contained glee. Society loves a hanging. Joe suggested we cry to look repentant as the Chief approached but I was too drained to pull it off. Instead, I stared in a daze at my reflection in the Chief's aviator sunglasses as he lectured us on the possibility of loss of lives and homes due to our actions. He never asked us how we started it but got our name and address, telling us it would be our responsibility to tell our parents and apologize to the folks whose homes we put in jeopardy. Since this event would have its own legs among the neighbors, the Fire Chief saw no need to visit our parents, word would get there.

Ironically Mr. Peca and my dad had been watching from Joe's driveway on the other side of the woods ever since the fire trucks arrived, not knowing their son's involvement. My dad remarked to Mr. Peca, "Probably started by some juvenile delinquents, hope they catch them." Dad always knows best. So I started home to acknowledge my dad's statement. On the short walk home, I had enough time to fabricate a better explanation on how the fire started so our parents might go easier on us. The real reason would get us punishment for being stupid on top of punishment for playing with matches, starting a fire, and embarrassing my parents again. "Joe, tell your parents we started the fire playing with firecrackers. They'll understand it as an accident and go easier on us." Joe readily agreed as we departed to our fates. It was a stroke of misdirection that would save our hides…literally.

When I came into my backyard, my parents were sitting on the back-porch barbequing chicken and relaxing as they often did on sunny Saturday afternoons. Upon seeing my black face and clothes, they looked concerned while putting one and one together. When asked what happened I simply said "Mom, Dad, I started the fire down the street," and started bawling, no act. The whole afternoon finally caught up with me and just gushed out. For the only time I remember on these sorts of occasions, my dad did not react with his temper. They heard out my firecracker story and told me I was grounded for several weeks and not allowed to see Joe Peca (our parents always thought the other kid was the bad influence and used these events to try and separate us). At dinner they announced I'd have to surrender ALL my fireworks for my dad to destroy. Unfortunately, they passed the judgment on to my brother too; fearing if the Fire Chief came around, my dad would be put on the spot for allowing us to have firecrackers, expecting him to pay damages or at least be prompted for a very generous fire company donation. This was no small punishment for my brother and I financially. My brother and I saved for months every year before our summer vacation to visit my mom's family in Canada. There, we would stock up on firecrackers for the whole year. We had just come back from Canada at the end of July. My brother was so angry and demanded I pay him for all his fireworks. I don't remember what came of that but my dad blew them all up in the barbeque with closed lid. Sounded like popcorn on steroids to supply an arena event. Dad never took the strap or stick to me for that one. Years later, my mom told me they figured I had been through enough that day and knew I learned my lesson before I got home. They were right.

Actually though, my *first* scare with fire was in Charlie *Morgan's* garage one winter day when we were about six or seven. Trying to get warmed up, we poured some gas in a bucket with rags and lit it. WUMP! The eyebrows on Charlie's face got singed off and we all ran away down the street in fear of being caught. When the fire trucks started coming up the street, we followed them back to Charlie's house as if it were all new to us. His house sustained some damage but he took all the blame for that one as evidence hopelessly pointed to him. The rest of us never told our parents and we stayed away from Charlie for a year, too afraid to knock on his door should his parents question us.

That's it for playing with fire. There are a lot of analogies that could be made here. The most obvious being: I was too often playing with the proverbial fire throughout my youth. *And if you play with fire, you are going to get burned.*

Steve Sisca, whom I mentioned earlier in our trio, is absent from these early stories. He was around, just never got into trouble, having always to work at his dad's grocery store at 'Tent n' Taska' = 10th St. & Tasker Ave in South Philly. He would tell us admiringly of the street gang that was the bane of the neighborhood around his dad's store. He wanted badly to belong to anything other than his Dad's store on Saturdays, that was for sure. Fortunately for Steve, his mom and dad kept him busy and away from Joe & I.

Mrs. Sisca would often say Steven couldn't come out to play with us when we would knock up for him. He had to sneak away to hang around with us. But after an event like the fire, Steve was in high demand by Joe and I since we were not allowed to see each other for a while. In four years, Steve's mom would die of cancer and he would do his best to make up for lost time and missed adventures. In the meantime, he lashed back by swiping money out of his dad's cash register and stealing cartons of cigarettes from the store stock to sell. All thieves start small. You'll hear more from Steve.

CHAPTER TWO

Strange Brew

The three stories in this chapter progress in time from ages six to 16 as I describe three families from the street I grew up on. All family names have been changed.

Note to my Christian friends: You may find the Baritz family story offensive if you view it from a sexual point of view. The story has little to do with sex (we were ages 6–11). It's about discovering the differences in how our close friends and neighbor lived and raised their children; that others have very different morals from what I'd been taught, yet they still seemed to be good people.

The Baritz Family. Age 6-11 Rated PG 15

"And he made them male and female"

Growing up on Glendale Road, I thought our neighbors were typical. As I look back, I wonder if other neighborhoods had the likes of our Baritz, Riechstadt, and Heckler families. I'm sure they must have.

Living next door to JoePec was the Baritz family. They were the youngest, hippest, richest, and handsomest couple on the block by far, and my introduction inside a Jewish family lifestyle, since they were the only Jewish friends we had. Joe and I were close friends with *Robby*, their son who was our age, and *Cindy* his sister, a year younger than us. The big scuttlebutt among our moms who were all in their mid-30s was that Mrs. Baritz had Robby when she was only 17 and her parents gave them everything. If it was new and cool, Baritz had it. While our folks were driving Galaxies and Impala sedans; they had Barracudas and Corvettes. Robby got anything he wanted because his dad worked at his grandfather's Hobby Shop. They had Go-Carts, mini-bike, pool table, any athletic equipment for any sport, games, gadgets, you name it. When I needed my first good baseball glove, I saved my money, gave it to Robby, and his dad brought me home a mitt worth twice the amount I gave him. For acts of generosity like that, we all thought Robby's dad was great. But the Baritz family had more than gadgets. They had family values that contradicted so much of what we were learning in Catholic school. They were my introduction to the fact that we don't all live by the same set of rules.

The Baritzs were free spirits all right. They slept in the nude. Yeah…I know, that's normal to many, but in the mornings, they walked around their home naked too...while WE were there! Rob and Cindy thought nothing of it because they grew up that way. Joe and I thought it was the wildest thing since the Crazy Foam! We'd go to Robby's on Saturday mornings around nine before his folks got up and be playing a board game on the living room floor. Mr. B would walk by on his way to the bathroom or kitchen in his full birthday suit, nonchalantly stop to say hi to Joe and I, whom he liked, and think nothing of it. We'd be holding our breath to choke back the laughter. It took maybe a year before Mr. B figured it might look bad, because one Saturday while offering a customary hello, he noticed our chuckling and added, "Robby, from now on, don't let your friends in the house until your mother and I are dressed." Up until then, Joe and I were the only kids allowed in their house.

Well, we weren't there to see Mr. B. swinging in the breeze. Even at seven years old we knew *Fay* (Mrs. B) was a blonde knockout in a petite frame. The vision of seeing her jigglin' to the bathroom got etched into my young mind as the standard to judge all future female figures. However, she was more discreet and wouldn't come out of the bedroom naked if she *knew* we were there. It was those times she wasn't aware of our presence that were most amusing. Sometimes, we would tell Robby we needed to use the bathroom so we could sneak upstairs and spy the angle into her bedroom where she'd be watching TV in the buff, clicking the remote (first on the block with color TV and clicker remote). All that exposed womanhood prostrate before us stirred thoughts that were supposed to be dormant for years far off. She was probably about 24 at the time.

A few years later, Joe and I developed a snooping routine when we knew Robby and Cindy were sleeping over their grandparents. Knowing the kids were away and dad was at the store; we would ring the doorbell in the morning for Robby. Fay would answer the door while standing behind it naked. One of us would play the stall man, asking as many questions about where Robby was, when he'd be back, is Cindy home, etc. She would sometimes peek her head around the open end of the door with one of her headlights hanging in plain view. This only worked once or twice before our scam became so obvious, she just laughed at us, then shut the door saying, "You two are bad, go home". A good thing for us was we didn't have to worry about her calling our parents for playing Peeping Tom. We were just curious.

Naturally, Cindy adopted her mom's 'au naturelle' freedoms. Good 'ole Cindy thought nothing of flinging her clothes to the wind. And Joe and I thought nothing of asking her to! By the age of 10, we were past playing Doctor and had moved on to post-med studies. Let me clear something up first before you get the wrong idea. We hardly saw Cindy as a sex object; we didn't understand what sex was yet. Our fascination at this early age was still about the difference between boys and girls; not really knowing yet what that difference was all about or what to do about it. She was the local tomboy included in our play while hardly thinking of her as a girl for most of the time. She was often included in our games simply because she was with her brother. When she took her clothes off, we noticed the difference, but it was more curiosity than being lewd. Joe had the good fortune of sleeping over their house often. Rob, Joe and Cindy would take their evening bath together with the blessings of Fay. They invented more things to do with Crazy Foam than you could imagine! As kids, we weren't sure what to make of the moral contradiction between our Catholic school puritan standards and the Baritz freedoms. Joe and I questioned whether it was wrong but weren't about to ask our parents opinion. The Baritz Family saw nothing wrong with nudity, that it was much too hyped and no big deal. We weren't about to rat out our friend's parents, plus we enjoyed the show.

Every fort we built from ages eight to 11 had more than one purpose in mind. Cindy was always our first member and we always provided a place for her to hang her clothes. Once she passed the club initiation, we'd start on another fort with a new and wilder initiation.

We could talk Robby into some pretty lame ideas too. One time, for him to join the fort, we told him he'd have to 'pinch one' out his bedroom window. He didn't get his butt far enough out to clear the house and left a long brown skid mark down the white siding. I'll admit we were sickos, laughing like mental patients over that one. The wall faced Joe's house and every time I knocked up for Joe, (until new owners painted the house) I'd notice the faded skid mark and chuckle.

There was another thing we learned from Robby and his dad—every swear word under the sun. This is a rite of passage many children learn from some impressionable person in their early years, hopefully outside their own home. Robby was our instructor but his dad was a true pro who brought cussing to the level of prose; we never heard Cindy or her mother swear. We'd play backyard catch with Mr. B just to hear him call us 'f-n A holes' for throwing the ball over his head. When he realized our overthrows were on purpose to hear him cuss (we couldn't hide our laughing), he tossed his mitt in disgust, resigning to Robby that his friends were all !@#$%s. Nope…never found any of those words in our Catechism.

Of course, word got around that Cindy would strip if Joe and Rich asked her too. This really impressed some of the 5th grade boys I was trying to impress when transferred to Manoa Public School after an abrupt dismissal from Catholic School. Though on one occasion when I asked Cindy to strip for my two new public-school friends, whom she also knew from school, she said, "No way." These two friends were also Robby's friends and he promised Cindy his allowance for a few weeks if she'd strip, so finally she agreed. Was that pimping?

However, after school when the four of us stopped at Robby's house for the show, she got cold feet. The Baritz were the only family we knew with a maid, a nice young black woman from Philadelphia named Glenda whom we liked for her kindness. Their parents were rarely home and the maid stayed with the kids after school and cleaned house. Robby told us to wait in his bedroom while he went and persuaded Cindy, 'The show must go on'. She came giggling into the bedroom, but when Robby locked the door behind her, she panicked and wanted out. The room broke into bedlam as Robby took matters into his own hands by wrestling her pants down while Cindy laughed and fought back. For them it was just another sibling wrestling match—only with spectators. Please keep in mind these are nine- and 10-year-olds naively hoping for a short flash at best, no touching.

The four of us were chanting, "Strip her, Robby, strip her! Strip her, Robby, strip her!" while holding the bedroom door shut because the maid heard the commotion and had retrieved the key to unlock the door. We were laughing because the maid was on the other side of the door pushing with all her might, which was about equal to the four small boys against her. So there we were, the door bouncing back and forth a few inches with each thrust, us chanting "Strip her, Robby, strip her", while the maid is yelling in her ethnic drawl, "Robby! Now you quit strippin' Cindy, ya hear! Robby! You stop that now? Open this door! What's Mrs. B gonna say when she hears about this?" So Robby had to cut a deal with the maid and his sister to cease all his she-nanigans if she kept quiet.

A year or so later, the Baritz family divorced and then moved away. It was for the best. At 12, we were approaching the age where we were passing from naïve curiosity to sexual interest. Their moving away is one of life's fortunate twists that often had me wondering 'what if?' Imagine us maturing into our teens with Cindy next door? I can imagine the trouble on top of trouble that may have emerged. Joe visited Robby and Cindy at their new place in Philadelphia a few times but I lost touch.

A year or so after their move, Mr. B was found tied up, gagged, and murdered in his apartment mob-style, allegedly for drug deals gone bad. I guess he had more hobbies than the hobby shop. The neighbors always wondered how such a young couple could live the lifestyle they did with one Hobby Shop income. The murder of Robby's dad explained a lot. Our parents learned about it through the newspapers and told us. So passed the Baritz family from our lives but what a splash they made, what impressions they left. They were certainly the best early example of moral contradictions we were exposed to, which is why I included this mildly sordid account. The nuns taught me one thing, and my parents didn't always agree with the nun's or the church. Then Manoa Public School threw in a few more contradictions to both, and the Baritz family was contradictions to everything. What's right or wrong was starting to fall into the vague category of one's own interpretation as I approached 12. And my interpretation was leveling towards the lowest common denominator.

The *Reichstadts*. ages 12-17

"Forgive them for they know not what they do."

Next door to our house lived *Levi* and *Ida Reichstadt*. She was a dominatrix, he was her short, frizzy haired, nerdy, professor husband with a lisp who lived a Spartan existence and had no friends. If you mixed Mr. Peabody's confused academics with Sherman's looks (talking Rocky and Bullwinkle here) and stuck a prayer-cap on his head, you had Levi Reichstadt. Fortunately, (for the kid) they had no progeny. Levi was one of these guys who would watch our back yard wiffle-ball games from inside his back door, waiting for the ball to cross onto his property. When that happened, he'd storm out his back door to confiscate our ball, then come at us stuttering and tripping in his haste to lecture us on property lines while we stared blankly back at him wondering how horrible it would have been to be born like *that*! It wasn't like he had a garden or something to protect, it was just a dumb weedy lawn. Our parents would explain to us that he was a frustrated man, and for the sake of peace asked us to patronize his request…which we did…for the most part…sometimes…once in a while? Nahhh! We picked on poor Levi 'til we drove him to move away. It was constant war with him, with never a victory on his part.

He'd put wooden stakes and rope up to divide our properties because he was too cheap to buy a fence. My friends would wrap the sticks and rope around his front door and railing so he couldn't get out of his house in the morning! He'd be huffing and struggling to squeeze out his door when just then, I'd use that moment to leave for school, shaking my head as I walked by. Levi would freak out at me while half stuck in the door and I'd just shake my head and laugh, driving him ballistic. The one thing that made him madder than a loon was laughing at him, and we had his number. He'd come to my parents and stutter over what we did; when my Dad turned to my brother and I to ask if we did, I replied, "Dad, I can't control what my friends do to Mr. Reichstadt." Levi gave up any hope of my parents intervening, so from then on we had free rein to teach him proper neighborhood etiquette.

His house, lawn, shrubbery, car and person took more sustained abuse than any person should have to experience. It was always a favorite of mine to come to the high school bus stop and tell the guys to check out Levi's house when the bus goes by. If the night before we saw Ida and Levi leave the house, we'd go into action and "do Levi's house". The bus would go by and there'd be lawn furniture on his roof, an azalea bush in his mail box, trash cans high in his trees, a Stonehenge of shopping carts tied together on his front lawn, and other such property improvements. If he was out front admiring our handy work when the bus went by, we'd call to him imitating his wife's nasal voice, "Levi! Oh Levi! Are you bothering those nice boys again?" And poor Levi would go off to his lab to invent Malox…he really was a professor. My brother and his friends also had Levi's number and free rein to *educate* him. So the barrage on the poor guy was relentless.

The final straw that sent Levi packing was a spontaneous event that knocked him cold for at least five seconds due to our teasing and his own clumsiness. We didn't foresee this, but probably wouldn't have change a thing after seeing the final outcome. Let's jump to our teen years for this story.

Steve was fueling up at a local gas station while three of us sat in the car waiting. Across from the gas station I saw Levi appear, walking toward the bank directly across from us. "There's Levi!" I sounded. We flew out of the car like firemen who knew the drill and started beckoning in unison, "Levi! Oh Levi! Are you bothering those nice boys again"? at the same time approaching him by exaggerating his distinctive walk. When he saw us, he shifted into a hurried walk to get away, going as fast as he could go without running. He was so focused on us that he never saw the low stop sign in his path. He hit that thing so hard it sounded like someone threw a brick at it. The sign whipped him off his feet and flat on his back, knocking the back of his head on the pavement. That had us howling into next week while yelling the likes of, "Walk much, Levi?" but he never heard a word of it. He lay there long enough for us to realize he was cold conked. After a few tense moments, he slowly sat up and stumbled off, trailed by our enthusiastic advice and encouragements, "Hey Levi! Only the cars have to stop!" He was defeated. Shortly after this episode, a FOR SALE sign adorned his front lawn. We didn't put it there.

Never treat the neighborhood kids unreasonably; they'll grow up to return all you gave in spades. There were other neighborhood wackos but I'll stop here. Those times were much different than today. There were no video games and only three channels on TV. *All* the kids played outside and in doing so, knew every family for a dozen homes on either side of us and on the next streets over. All the kids knew each other and regularly played neighborhood tag or street games together with no respect for backyard boundaries. Only a few of the neighbors (without kids) took property lines seriously…Levi drew the misfortune of living next to the Bonnett children.

I'm sure in retrospect I would handle things much differently. Fifteen years later, I passed an aging Mr. Reichstadt waiting for the bus on West Chester Pike. I couldn't mistake him as I drove by, same face scrunched up in permanent frustration. I had matured, married, was raising children and often felt guilty about the way I treated that poor man. He was so outnumbered and outwitted back then that he never even had a sporting chance. I made a U-turn, intent on pulling up to the bus stop and introducing myself since I'm sure he wouldn't recognize me. I wanted to give him a ride to his destination while I apologized for the hurt I caused him. But the bus got to him first and I sat there wondering, "You know best, Lord." Maybe I would have given him a heart attack? More likely he would have tried to run away. Either way it wasn't meant to be. I'm sorry, Mr. Reichstadt.

Is *Gabe* Home? (age 14)

"Ye shall enter into their lands and take full possession"

He better not be home. Often when a family went on vacation the local kids would take advantage of their open driveway or lawn for wiffle-ball games, kick ball games, tag, etc., and then there was that one week we borrowed the whole house. Let me introduce another neighbor, the *Hecklers*.

Booker was a friend I knew from my paper route. He had a friend we all knew from our school bus stop, but was out of our loop, poor at sports, frumpy, and a bit odd. I'll call him *Gabe Heckler* for this story. The Hecklers were the wealthiest family on our street after the Baritz family moved out. They had a Lincoln Continental, belonged to a country club and tipped better than anyone else on my paper route. Before leaving on their vacation one year, Gabe told Booker to keep his eye on the house. Book told Joe and I what Gabe told him; now there were six eyes on his house. Well, this information was much too valuable to let sit idle for a week. Gabe had the best model car racing layout and other gadgets of any 13-year-old boy in the neighborhood, but we couldn't bear hanging out with him in order to play with his cool toys. Now all that fine stuff was sitting idle in his basement, a pure waste from my industrious point of view. We, on the other hand, would love to be using them as intended. So we came up with a plan to balance things out. You've gotta have a plan.

Booker unlocked a kitchen window while he was visiting Gabe a day before they left on vacation, hoping they wouldn't check. They didn't, and that was the extent of our plan to get in. After checking to verify the window was unlocked, Joe and I had to extend our plan for entry and concealment. Booker, Meatball, Paul, Joe, and I were the guys in on this challenge. Getting one person in would be easy enough. A woodlot bordered one side of their house and we all knew the house on the other side of them had working parents. What we needed now were the fine details that can foil simple plans. Things like if the mail was stopped, will neighbors be checking in? Since I had been their paperboy, I knew what time the mailman came by and Booker was confident no one would be dropping by to check the house since they weren't close with any of their neighbors. Our plan wasn't just to sneak in and out; the plan was to have free rein in the house, set up a country club atmosphere for the week, live like the Hecklers!

I snuck in the kitchen window while the others waited on the street. They waited 15 minutes, then came knocking on Gabe's front door like they didn't know he was away. The knock told me they were looking up the street, down the street, across the street. When they were sure the coast was clear, they rang the doorbell. I then acted like Gabe, being glad to see his friends and let my buddies in. Gabe was never so popular as he would be this week! It was a good plan as long as we didn't get lazy or over confident, which we didn't. Well, maybe we got a bit overconfident.

On the first day, we limited ourselves to hanging out in their nicely finished basement. This was just until we knew if their mail was stopped, even though the mailman, or anyone else for that matter, couldn't hear us in the basement. It was a fine afternoon of race track tournaments and civilized playtime, but there was a fully stocked bar down there and by the second day Booker was mixing us drinks with fancy names, which he learned from his folks. I found a few magnum-size old-style seltzer water bottles, the kind that are under pressure. Pushing the top mounted dispenser shot seltzer water 10 feet if you shook it. A seltzer water fight broke out and lasted as long as the seltzer.

By the third day, with the race car set shorted out from the seltzer fight, we figured it was safe enough to hang out upstairs watching TV, play records, card games, and whatever pleased our fancy. On this day, a knock came on the door and everyone freaked out and scrambled to the basement. You never saw kids jump so fast! I headed for the back door because the basement would be a trap. Hesitating, I quickly ran to the front door window to see if it was just some salesman or the like… and there stood JoePec. He hadn't been with us earlier when we all entered. When Joe couldn't find any of us hanging around the neighborhood, he figured we were at Gabe's. So he knocked up on his own, unannounced, scaring the boogers out of us. After that we came and went as we pleased with individual signals for entry. Joe remembers coming in late again the next day and seeing me sitting in Mr. H's Lazy-Boy, sipping one of Booker's mixers, smoking one of Mr. H's expensive cigars. He fell apart laughing when he saw me sitting there addressing him in the character of Mr. H telling him to "take his friends and get the heck out of my house".

Such were the shenanigans of that week. By the last day we were inviting trusted 'guests' to visit and the whole deal had become ridiculous. It was a good thing for us they didn't take a two-week vacation. We had all agreed at the outset not to take anything from the house and we all (we thought) honored that pledge. We prided ourselves in not being thieves on this occasion, neither had we 'broken and entered'—'entered and broken', yes, but not intentionally broken. The technicality vindicated us in our own eyes. We honestly felt it fair for the 'haves' (Gabe) to involuntarily share with the 'have nots' (us). On our last visit, we all helped clean the place up, which wasn't too big a chore since the Hecklers were not the best house keepers to begin with.

Several summers later, while down the Jersey shore with friends for senior week, one of the guys was rather flush with cash, especially in light of him not working. When pressed where he got the money, he admitted to lifting a small item of jewelry when we 'borrowed' their house (she had boxes of jewelry). He held it until now and sold it to pay for his week at the shore. We were more upset that he didn't split the proceeds with us than breaking our pledge not to take anything.

It is difficult to leave this chapter of my early neighborhood years with such a shallow description of growing up on Glendale Road. These stories were selected to reveal some of the events that had strong influences or set up early patterns in my life. They offer an insight to help you understand what I thought was acceptable if not caught, and how I arrived at the philosophy of 'anything goes', which I adopted by age 15. Joe and I had a very rich and cherished childhood, despite the trouble we brought on ourselves; and trouble seemed to be the norm. For some of us, it just follows like a cloud, albeit one of our own making. These three stories are a short cross sample of events that formed our young minds and established our own code of ethics, contrary to our Catholic upbringing. Which brings up those crazy Catholic Schools days of the 1960s...

CHAPTER THREE

Farewell My Sacred Heart

"Hinder not the children to come unto me"

Most of you have heard the atrocities experienced by those of us who endured the Catholic Gulag's back when **The Nun** was the body of that institution. I'm sure most of what you heard is true, but now it's time someone finally told it the way it *really* was. In other words, it's my turn. But you can rest assured, you never heard these stories.

I attended Sacred Heart Catholic School until the 5th grade. The baby boom was breaking the sound barrier, which translated into my first-grade class having 45 kids and one frustrated nun. The class was actually 88 kids split into two classrooms, one nun per classroom, no teacher aides because they weren't invented yet. You might find this hard to believe but I was schooled in a two-room schoolhouse, which is only one step up from the traditional one-room schoolhouse. At the time, a spanking new elementary school was one year from being completed, but until then, I attended the last class in the last two-room schoolhouse in Delaware County. From the get go, there was little hope of getting a good education with a class so large; it was about discipline and obedience to the church as much as it was the 3Rs. I had a big problem with authority. Yesireebob, me and those nuns were going to be the best of friends. My (paternal) sister Lillian informs me I punched Sister Joseph Regina, my first-grade nun, in the stomach and told her I hated her on my first day of school. We hit it off great. The class was so big kids would sneak away to play hooky at morning recess. Back in the classroom, Sister Joseph would freak out when she realized two of her precious cargo were unaccounted for. The police would come to get a description for a search… yup, it was a well-oiled machine that first-grade class.

In order to graduate each year, I had to plead with my mom not to let them make me repeat. The nuns would suggest I repeat the grade but were easily talked out of the idea in order to keep their class size smaller and be rid of me. They'd adjust a Math or English grade and push me through the mill. I wasn't stupid; just had a problem sitting still, listening, following instruction, getting bossed around, taking any of it seriously, or caring. I just wanted to be outside. I loved to daydream and had a problem with authority, other than these minor flaws I would have been a stellar student!

Instinctively, I had a strong dislike for all nuns; I just didn't trust them from day one, probably because they always smiled when someone did something deserving of punishment. Some nuns actually welcomed the diversion from teaching by disciplining some sorry kid who messed up in class, like someone delivered them a pleasant distraction from the drudgery of teaching. I never saw nuns as people. Don't get me wrong, I knew they were humanoid, just not like the rest of us. I was on my guard concerning these black cloaked mysteries; not like the rest of the human race, that much was for sure.

By the third grade, I had established a pattern for habitually being in trouble for one thing or another; like shooting off my blank gun in class or fighting with patrol guards. Patrol guards were kids with "stinking badges" that had the authority to report school yard violators. They were always honor students beyond reproach; it was like 'being made' in the Mafia, their word got you whacked. Whether you did anything wrong or not, if they reported you, there were no negotiations with the nun; the Patrol Guard word was beyond reproach. They could report someone on a trumped-up violation just because they didn't like the kid. On one occasion, one of these 'Made' guards reported me for some minor infraction, which could have easily been overlooked. Warning me he was on his way to "tell Sister", I became so enraged I threw an empty glass bottle at him with all my might as he approached the yard nun. He ducked as the overthrown bottle, which instead hit the nun hard in the chest knocking her back; I really winged it. Man, you should have seen the hatred in her eyes when her gaze fell upon me. At that moment, all her humanoid features departed as she descended on me like a Ring Wraith on Frodo.

For this and other forgotten deeds of civil disobedience I found myself always having to stay after school. When I say always, I mean *always*. My fourth-grade nun told me in early September, after my third strike, to just stay after school with her every day until the Christmas break. They would send me home with letters to my parents explaining my actions and requesting meetings. I'd read them to my friends, crumble them up el macho and toss them over my shoulder stating flatly, "That letter ain't makin' it home".

But the nuns got around that by sending any future letters home with my brother who was two grades ahead of me, an obedient good student. Then along with the after-school punishment, came the double whammy from my Dad: either *no TV* or *no going out on Saturdays*, or both. I was dying; a free spirit stuck in a cage of my own making. When I *was* able to be with my friends, I would make up for lost time and do even more outrageous things that got me into further trouble.

Under these downward spiraling circumstances, I had two choices. Straighten up…I tried that route with all my resources but it just wasn't within my constitution. So that left the second choice, lash back…all-out war. I knew I couldn't win a war against my dad, so that left the nuns to strike back at. I had brought them to the point of tears on a few occasions; I figured I could crack their habit blue armor enough to just leave me alone. That plan didn't work either and eventually they won.

I have to say though; I learned some valuable lessons from my punishments:

- Don't curse at the nun while she is close enough to hear you.
- Don't curse out 'goody two-shoe kids' who immediately rat you out to the nun.
- Don't beat up the kid who ratted you out while still on school property. Wait until after school and off property to get even.
- Don't trust just anyone at school with your schemes, they may rat you out, only trust your proven friends.
- Avoid nuns.
- Avoid my father.
- Forget about ever earning a shiny patrol guard badge.
- Forget about ever getting into the heaven the nuns spoke so highly of.

By following these guidelines of avoidance, I started to get around these cloaked servants that claimed to be wedded to Jesus Christ; they even wore a wedding ring to prove it. If nuns were married to Jesus as we were taught, that put *him* in my "people to be avoided" list too. But I wasn't worried about Jesus; he was just a ghost in a book from a subject I barely passed. As you can see, I developed a strong dislike for nuns. That distrust did not come from the punishments I received; I always knew enough to understand I deserved what I got. I knew the rules and understood how the whole program worked. What I hated was the glee they displayed over the public humiliation I and others received at their hands, often while the whole class would be encouraged to laugh. Even *my* flawed standards told me this was no way to treat a kid, especially being whom these nuns claimed to be—brides of Christ. Here's an example of actual punishment I received under 1960s Nunnery justice.

I missed the trash can with a crumpled piece of paper. The deranged nun made me stand in front of the class for half an hour with the trash can over my head, dumped trash at my feet. She'd continue teaching, occasionally asking me questions about the lesson I could not see on the chalk board. I'd have to answer from within the confines of my trash-can lampshade, making me yell louder because she pretended not to hear my muffled reply...a regular drill sergeant tactic, "I can't hear you, Mr. Bonnett!" Since I didn't know the answer because I couldn't see the lesson, she would whack at the trash can with her pointer (a three-foot oak rod) and the class would roar as I flinched. After a while my temper was so cooked under that helmet of humiliation, I had no control over what was about to come out of my mouth. The old Blue Meanie was about to get the shock of her elementary school career with the next reply that knifed out from under my trash can.

"Perhaps Mr. Bonnett can help us with this question?" she asked teasingly to the class as she whacked the can once more.

"Yeah? And you can go straight to hell where you belong, Sister!" I yelled as loud as I could so as to be sure she got it the first time. It's one of those perfect replies that rolls around in your head building up momentum until there is no holding back; it finally has to burst out to set you free. Liberty at all cost, no matter how short-lived. I was standing there blindly waiting for her to break the pointer across my legs (routine). Oddly, she didn't whack me, she didn't whack the can, and she didn't ask me to repeat myself. Time was suspended for a moment, two moments. There was dead silence from her audience as they were watching her stunned face. For 10 seconds I was no longer humiliated, I was in charge, I had silenced my accusers no matter what the cost. I couldn't see them, but there had to be a lot of dropped jaws in the room. Next, she instructed me in a very dead tone to remove the trash can from my head and go directly to Mother Superior's office and tell her exactly what I had just said.

I went to Mother Superior's office, which at that time in my life was the closest thing to 'The Great White Throne Judgment' of John's Revelation, and explained everything that happened, just as it happened, leading up to the "go to hell" comment. When I told her what I said, the poor old woman's face went white and I thought I'd need an ambulance for both of us before it was over. It was truly one of those "Jesus, Mary & Joseph" moments for her as she protected herself with the sign of the cross at mach 2 from what was just uttered. She quickly recouped, then calmly wrote another letter to my mother as I sat there in painful silence. Methodically sealing the envelope, she stared at me through squinting eyes and said, "One more tiny strike and you will be leaving us for good, Mr. Bonnett, you are incorrigible and our patience is at an end. Have both of your parents read this and call me." She was referring to my being expelled. Well…that was only a matter of time. Of course, the note went home with my brother. I never knew the contents of that letter, in later years my mom said there were many letters all basically about the same theme; I don't think they gave details to my folks. They would write something like "Richard used foul and insulting language to one of our Sisters of Regal Flamboyance." When my mom would ask me what I said I would reply something like, "I called her a rotten egg or something like that" and that would suffice for Mom. Always be vague.

Just on a side note here. Nuns rarely struck girls that were bad, but they loved to lay into the boys with yardsticks, pointers, or their hands. Pulling our ears, hair, collar, whatever they could get a hold on. Personally, I believe a lot of them were frustrated women that had been jilted in romance or had some reason to be men haters and go into the convent…just one guy's opinion though. In fairness, only a few Sacred Heart Nuns had the character flaws I described. It was just my rotten luck that I got three in a row, 3rd through 5th grade.

The Last Strike

That final strike was not long in coming. In December of 5th grade my mom started the process of transferring me to Public School, but she never made me aware of this. She apparently didn't tell the nuns either. Mom was fed up with their derogatory assessments of judging me incorrectly about my learning abilities and having few redeeming qualities. My mom was my only champion. Where there is a loving, praying mother, there is always hope.

The last day before Christmas break, each child in the Elementary School was given a box of colorful Christmas candy and gathered in the gym for our annual Christmas pageant depicting the birth of Christ. After the Christmas pageant, we would be dismissed early. It was a festive time and everyone looked forward to the pageant. I loved the choir singing those beautiful songs, the drama, the low blue lighting, everyone excited about Christmas coming. The joy of the season always seemed to be summed up in a good Christmas play. I was looking forward to enjoying this play. **Wrong**... unbeknownst to me, I was going to implement an unscheduled intermission during the play.

To accommodate all 600 kids in the gym, the bleachers would be rolled back, and the whole floor of the gym would be a sea of folding chairs with one central aisle going up to the middle to the stage. The 1st graders sat in the front and consecutive grades on back. This put the 5th grade in the middle of the auditorium. This same set up was used for Mass on Sunday mornings when kids were required to attend 9:00 Mass in the church, the gym being reserved for adult Mass. This was at the peak of the 1960s baby boom when there was difficulty fitting the masses into the Mass. I wonder if that's why they use that term for their church service. Anyway, all of the folding chairs had padded metal kneelers bolted onto the lower wrung of the rear leg support. These kneelers folded down so the participants in the Mass didn't have to kneel on the hard gym floor during Communion. For the Christmas play, all the kneelers were folded up.

Robert *Gillen* was sitting directly in front of me. I had pulled down the kneeler on the back of his chair to rest my feet upon. In the darkness of the gym and throughout the program, he would slyly drop his hands down behind his seat to untie my shoe laces, then knot them together. It was funny the first time and I tolerated it a second time. On the third attempt, I leaned up to his ear and told him if he tried it again, I'd twist his arm off. I guess he just couldn't resist. I was ready for him if he did try…and he did. I had taken my feet off the kneeler and placed them *under* the kneeler. As soon as he reached around again, his fingers feeling for my shoes, I slammed the kneeler up with my one foot, pinching his fingers between the kneeler support and the chair legs. Then I rammed my other foot into the back of the kneeler with all my might.

That kid let out a spontaneous scream of agony so loud the play screeched to a halt as every head in the gymnasium swung our way. I released pressure immediately and acted like nothing happened. Robert was bent over, rocking in his seat, holding his hands to his chest and bawling in pain. I hurt him worse than planned and he, naturally, couldn't contain his reaction to wail in pain. A few nuns ran up to him to see what happened, I heard my name and before I could run, one of the she-devils grabbed my hair and yanked me to attention in front of her. She grabbed my hand and started rag-dolling me down the aisle towards the back of the gym where Mother Superior and her entourage stood silhouetted like the Trinity against the outside daylight streaming through the glass gymnasium doors. They had been contentedly enjoying the play before my little intermission.

It was like the last judgment. These cloaked and hooded tall figures draped in blue and black down to their ankles, silhouetted before me, were waiting to pass final sentence on the damned. The judgment was swift and anticipated, I never said a thing. She didn't even require an explanation once she saw who the violator was. "Mr. Bonnett, I think you finally succeeded in getting yourself removed from Sacred Heart, gather all your possessions and go home, I **will** be calling your parents." A huddle of nuns whisked Robert past Mother Superior telling her they were taking him to the nurse because some fingers looked crooked; they were glaring at me. Ah! If he drank more milk his fingers would've been fine.

It was a very strange walk home that day, one I can easily resurrect from my library of emotions. I got my coat and things from my classroom, walked down the empty halls and classrooms where not a soul stirred, came down and stood outside the back of the gym, listened to the choir singing a closing Christmas song, wondering if I should go back in to let Sister know I was leaving. I didn't want to chance it, so started the mile walk home with my thoughts. What do I tell my mom, will my Dad ground me for Christmas break again, even worse, will they send my Christmas presents to the poor as they always threatened, or the worst thought…would I be sent off to reform school? Any and all were possible; I really stepped in it this time. I don't remember the final result; all the punishments just seemed to roll into one.

Also, I wasn't aware that my mother already had me registered at Manoa Public School starting after Christmas break. So my dismissal from Sacred Heart couldn't have been timed any better. However, if I had just made it a few minutes more through that Christmas play, I would have been *transferred* instead of expelled. What irony.

There's a point at which you start to believe what your dad and the nuns drill into your head along with your punishments. "You're incorrigible, you'll never amount to any good; "your future looks very *dim*, Mr. Bonnett," the nuns would say. As I look back at that point, even the 5th grade, I realize all of their assessments were only a matter of time to fruition because *even I* was starting to believe them. Eventually, a child will resolve himself to give up attempting to please those whom he can't possibly please. If you ever wondered how young people can go so far astray, this is the most typical pattern that sets them on their way. If you are always in trouble and being punished until you are 15, the dye has pretty much been cast. By the age of 16, you will have surrounded yourself with those like-minded and your future *is* dim. It will take a frightening wake-up call, a heavy dose of maturity, a brush with death, or a miracle to get out of the rut. If not, the rut gets deep, plain fact. My rut would get deeper with time.

I would like to say the transition to public school went smoothly but that wasn't exactly the case; nothing was going smoothly. I was lost in the new Math and failed it, having to be tutored that summer. That was nothing compared to the social challenges. The bad attract the bad and many of these public-school kids knew my reputation. So there were guys who wanted to see if they could take me in a fight, along with others who befriended me. I eventually managed to strike a balance. Robby Baritz and friends from my neighborhood told everyone to lay off me. I made good friends at Manoa, but it was a struggle to stay out of fights. My dad told me my next step was reform school for juvenile delinquents, which put fear in me because you were sent away for that. This new start was the best thing for me and I stayed out of trouble at school for the rest of my education. My grades always just got me by. When I moved up to Haverford Senior High in 10th grade, we were tested and assigned a roster between one and 19 (a roster of classes per your tested ability to handle them). The kids in roster one were the brightest, the kids in roster 19 only had one oar in the water. I was in roster 17 with guys that shaved and drove bulldozers at construction sites on weekends waiting to turn 16 so they could drop out. There wasn't much expected from us so little was given.

———————

There were a few things I took with me from Catholic School and The Roman Catholic Church:

- Based on the teachings of the seven sacraments I still had a slim chance at getting into heaven, having participated in the first four sacraments by 3rd grade (forced acceptance, I had no choice).

- Based on my lying by omission in every required priest confessional I took part in, my soul was still black as coal (as the nuns described it) and hell was my destiny if I died that day. But I had no intentions of dying that day, or next. Nobody does. Based on what I had been taught, I was very conflicted about heaven and hell, but was more convinced, based on being expelled by the very instructors knowledgeable of my chances, that I was more likely hell-bound.

- If those nuns and priest were God's representatives of Christ on earth, they (God and Christ) had bigger problems than me. I wanted nothing to do with God or Christ. By the time I was 15, I dismissed the Catholic Church, along with Christianity in general, as a bunch of spiritual screw-ups who changed the rules as it suited their whims. Simply stated, I believed we were all in the same boat and no one really knew where it was going or when they'd get off. Those in the churches who pretended to know were worse off for kidding themselves than those who thought as I did. Eating meat on Friday is a sin; now it's not. Mass in English is anathema so we had to learn the Latin. Oops! We changed our mind, English Mass? It's okay... and on and on... contradiction after contradiction. Basic Godhead 101 tells us all that sin is sin and never changes; even I had *that* much figured out. If the church couldn't get it straight, who were they to tell me what is or isn't sin? I'm in the clear, baby. If the great ecclesiastical minds of the centuries couldn't get the truth figured out, I was free to attend the church of "Dick Bonnett Says:"

The seeds of the new morality (relative morality) were planted by the corrupted churches (Catholic AND Protestant, Eastern and Western faiths) of the past. When the populace was failed by their own churches, they looked inside themselves for their own set of rules. And Viola! A new generation of church attendees that don't believe half of what their church teaches and are filling in the other half with their own belief system. Each man becomes his own belief system. Now *that's* the fox guarding the henhouse. Hold on, the world is being turned upside down, **moral relativity** has just become the new world religion.

My final conclusion by the age of 16 was: there is no God. Or…if there is a God he wrote this "human experiment" off for a lost cause, releasing us from the glories of heaven *and* the pains of hell, granting us unconscious oblivion instead; a non-existence when we die, like we never were. Maybe he's trying the experiment over again with a new and improved version of man on another planet since things did not go well on earth. This means God makes mistakes and what's the good of a God that makes mistakes anyhow? It is easy to see ourselves as cosmic guinea pigs or, at best, pawns. Anyway, these ideas were the early foundation of the church of "Dick Bonnett Says" (DBS) and I wasn't shy in sharing my thoughts on the matter. Actually, I enjoyed knocking holes in the faith of the next generation of church-goers in the early 1970s, the ones that only followed part of their church's teachings and didn't see their own hypocrisy in doing so. I loved to 'set them free' with DBS philosophy. Hey, my philosophy can't be any worse than those who preceded me. Who's to say I'm wrong, or right? Isn't it all based on our individual moral relativity? Then who's to say Hitler, Stalin or Pol Pot were wrong? They were following what they thought was a better plan for all of mankind.

Mankind…what a sticky mess.

Disclaimer: Today I hold no ill will towards nuns or priests. This chapter was written in the frame of mind of what I thought at the time, when I viewed them as my enemy.

CHAPTER 4

Devils and Angels

Summer 1964, 11 years old
All names and places in this story are original and have
not been changed.

Just about the time the nuns and my father had me convinced I was a no-good-nik, something ironic occurred. I turned into a devil…seriously.

To keep me off the street and hopefully out of trouble, my folks decided to send me to summer day camp. Friends of my parents sent their son Jay Sadow to Hunters Run, a predominantly Jewish day camp, so that was where I went to camp. Big Fat Mazziolli, a lanky Indian kid and three others were the only gentiles in my bunk of 18. There were maybe 50 other gentile kids in the whole camp. Having just been tossed from Catholic school where I was taught the Jewish race were all doomed to hell, I was feeling in good company. "So this is the crowd I'll be going to hell with" was my thinking as I arrived for my first day of camp. Seriously, that was my thinking. After the Baritz family moved away, Jay was my only Jewish friend. All of my friends were Catholic, most of our neighborhood was Catholic. By the end of the week I had decided it was far better to be in hell with this friendly, fun-loving crowd than go to heaven with a bunch of dried-up nuns, priests, and goody two-shoe kids. After my first week of camp, I had mentally defected to the dark side and secretly wanted to be Jewish. I learned quickly that the nuns had lied about these fine people and just as quickly, I was learning not to believe what any church or religious authority taught me, no matter how fancy their robes were.

At first, I hated the idea of going to camp and not hanging out with my friends, but after a few days I loved it. I was competitive, loved sports, and this place had me playing and learning all kinds of new sports from soccer to boxing. I knew some of the boys from school and the others I quickly made friends with. Jay and I were already close friends through our parents so the two of us stuck together on teams and schemes.

Most of the schemes revolved around raiding the girls' bunks. On my first day, Jay pointed to a long, flat, one-story building up on a slight hill where the girls bunked and told me that it was called 'Knob Hill'. The Arts & Crafts room shared a wall with three girls' bunks. This wall rose eight feet to open rafters, which viewed down into the girl's bunks. Picnic tables against the craft room wall gave us access to the rafters. With good planning, a stealthily run operation consisting of three guys could mount a successful panty raid while the girls were at swim session. The women counselors thought it was cute and harmless so they never made a big deal about it. This was a time-honored camp tradition established long before I arrived at Hunters Run. The highest honors were bestowed on he who snitched a counselor's panties and presented it to our own counselor. He would pretend to be a little upset, tell us not to do it anymore, and say he had to return them, asking to whom they belonged. But his real reason for confiscating the garment was so he could pull the dainty out of his glove box the next morning while pulling into counselor parking, then hang it over the rear-view mirror or antenna when he parked next to the panty owner's car. The rightful owner would spot them and the garment would disappear sometime during the day. It was always good for a laugh, but the ladies had their own ways of retribution.

These people knew how to enjoy a good prank and let things ride as long as it didn't get out of hand.

Even when we peeked over the wall when the girls were getting changed after swim times, they would just scream and cover up, then laugh it off as a good prank. We never got reported or in any trouble for it. You couldn't do that today.

An added bonus about going to camp was starting out on a clean slate. No previous reputations or stigmas followed me here. Being decent at sports, I remember early in the camp season one occasion when our counselor picked me to choose up two baseball teams from our bunk. There were a few jocks in our bunk who always wanted a guaranteed win. They expected me to load all the good players against the weaker players, but I refused; lopsided victories bored me after a few innings. Soon our counselor was designating me to choose teams more often; he got tired of being in the middle of the arguments over team sides he picked. This meant I could pick myself and another guy to choose teams or pick them myself. Most of the time, I would designate another captain to pick his own team by alternated picks. However, one afternoon while in a quirky mood, I loaded the uncoordinated, over-weight, and booger pickers on my team. The jocks were salivating and jumping around, boasting gleefully how bad we were about to get smeared. After they were done with their pre-victory dances and my guys were disgusted with me for apparently feeding them to the lions, I presented the challenge:

"Since you guys are so sure, that we'll be slaughtered…how about a handicap to make it interesting.""What sort of handicap you talking about?" the other captain curiously tilted his head at me?

"Your team can bat right-handed, but in the field you all have to catch with your right and throw with your left, even the pitcher." This meant wearing a left-handed mitt on your right hand. "No way," was his reply. I kept on calling him chicken and afraid of being beat while my band of misfits had gathered around and joined in the chiding. He had to give in…and NOW we had a ball game! We took to the field first.

When Counselor Steve returned and saw my team getting wailed on in the field, he stood there looking at me and my ship of fools through his sunglasses, wondering as the jocks at bat told him the new rules. I saw a broad smile spread across his face. Finally, the inning ended and we went to bat. It was great. Everyone on both sides was laughing at those guys missing easy hits and throwing wild left hand errors. The pitcher *had* to pitch underhand because he had no control overhand. The sight of Big Fat Mazz for the first time in his life rounding third on errors, running for all his oscillating might was priceless. Had we been able to lift him, we would have put him on our shoulders. The few guys who dreaded sports or had to go to camp because their parents forced them were having a ball. I never drove home so many runs. Everyone was hitting and having fun, not just the jocks. Counselor Steve loved it and umpired from the bench.

I don't remember who won the game, I just remember everyone having a good time. This new game style become popular until the 'The Ship of Fools' starting winning. Once we won a game, the other team wouldn't play handicapped any more. I heard left-handed baseball got around camp to other bunks too. I didn't think much of it, but apparently our counselor spread it around to the other counselors that it was my idea and why I invented it. To him, it meant I had leadership quality. This sets up what happened next.

Towards the end of the camp season, there is a sort of 'May Day" event in which all the bunks, some 250+ campers in all, are divided into two teams to compete against each other for three days in a series of different events. In the end, one team wins the grand prize. I have no idea what it was, probably ice cream and bragging rights.

Counselors select a few nominees from the oldest guy bunk and gal bunk and submit those names to campers to select a king and queen to represent each of the two teams. All of the campers are divided by bunk to create two teams within that bunk. There is also a theme for the games, which was the Devils (red) against the Angels (white) this year. A color guard would serve under the King and Queen chosen for each side, carrying banners and reporting scores. It was quite a production, at least I never saw anything like it. So I was really shocked when, at the large outdoor tent ceremony to kick off the games, I was voted king of (what else) the Devils based on skills demonstrated for leadership, fairness, and friendship. It seemed like in one fell swoop my past sins were swept away and society had welcomed me back with open arms saying, "Rich, how could we have been so wrong about you in the past?" It was like I was finally handed the proverbial 'Patrol Badge' I yearned for at Sacred Heart. Wow! I was the chosen one from among the Chosen People. Bright beams of light came down from the sky and blinded me...I fell on my face...there were angels singing...honoring me, and a loud voice came down from on high saying, "Rich, you're going to have to wear tight red leotards, horns, a silly tail, *and* ladies makeup on the final day of the event to lead your team". Wwwwhat!

It was true, I'd have to, along with my lovely Queen—Marsha Fein— dress in a devil's costume and deliver a speech before all the campers, staff, and invited parents. Well, it was the holiest ground I ever stood on, even if it was the wrong side according to my church. Hey...you have to support your team.

I never received so much *positive* attention in all my life. I was a camp celebrity overnight; everyone wanted to meet and talk to my Queen and me. There were couriers to come and go at my bidding, themed pep rallies where I had to stir up the team and put fire in their bellies! I oversaw events and was allowed to substitute players to plug a gap in a teetering sports event. It was really cool AND I had a long plastic pitchfork! The whole camp was decorated for the theme. Someone snuck red dye in the pool. I didn't do it! Girls with big noses and braces were kissing me unexpectedly. Strangers were reaching out to kiss my ring, I was blessing babies, marrying young couples, getting chauffeured around in an open top white Land Rover. Oh, never mind, that was someone else. It was a great time for three days, no matter whose side you were on.

All parents were invited on the final day of competition. I told my folks, but they were unfamiliar with these things. There was no way my dad would miss work for something like this and we only had one car at the time. It was one of those invites I told my mom maybe once while running out the door, just to say I did invite them. Probably told her something like "Mom, they voted me Camp Devil and you're invited to watch my team win," and I got a bad look from her, thinking I had gotten in trouble at camp too. Plus, I really didn't want them to see me in a devil's outfit; they may have fainted thinking that I sold my soul. Jay's parents were there and couldn't understand why my parents didn't come and later relayed the event to them. There were a lot of parents present that day under the Big Tent, making me nervous about the speech I was supposed to have memorized. I reviewed it a few times then tossed it because it was too long. The sweet counselor lady that took the time to write it was not happy about that. I was going to wing it. If I seized up, I could always just invite them to go to hell for a good time afterwards. (Forever the class clown, I actually had to bite my tongue to keep that line from popping out.) Heh, I'm the Devil, can't I say as I please?

For the grand finale ceremony, I had to don the full devil outfit, which the playful women counselors had gone way overboard preparing. Most of the female counselors were teachers in their 20s and 30s taking summer work. Their intention was to make me as cute as possible. My heart sank with each new piece of embarrassing garb they kept pulling out of that costume bag—red girl's tights, big gold belt and buckle, horns and mustache, crown, and then the tail…a get-in-the-way, drag-on-the-ground TAIL. They joked it was their revenge for the raided panties. It was a high price to pay, but now I had to play along. They had me strip down to my underwear and started to put the tights on me. Twelve years old in two months, standing there in my tighty-whities in front of these pretty ladies was humiliating. I tried refusing and squirmed, but I was outnumbered there on Knob Hill, the devil was being tortured by lovely angels. I hoped the Angel King was going through this in the next bunk-house! There must have been three 'she devils' buzzing around that sweaty bunk, dressing me to their artistic whims, changing their minds, trying new looks, discussing how each garb should go. It was hopeless. Then my Queen, looking hot in her red outfit came in and said I looked adorable, so I surrendered to all their feminine persuasions. They had their way with me like girls at a slumber party dressing their Ken doll with Barbie clothes. I felt sick to my stomach and almost ran out of there to the safety of the woods to hide. My undies showed too much white through my red tights, so the ladies spun me around while they stood back reviewing my look saying, "Well, that will never do, take off your underpants and we'll try two pair of tights instead." I was just about to bust out of there and start hitching home when one of the girls came up with some donated red panties to replace my white undies! Oiy Vey! I still get exci—I mean *humiliated* when I think of it!

I still wonder if that dress-up was deliberately planned revenge for being king of the hill for panties captured. It also took me years to figure out, but I often question if the lady counselors didn't intentionally swing the vote my way to get their chance at revenge by dressing me up. From the way they took such pride in putting me together that day, I don't think it was the case…but I'll always wonder.

With my face painted red, black eye-liner, tail in tow, and sporting red panties under my tights, I was put in front of the Red Team procession and marched with music down to the ceremony grounds where the winner would be announced. I tossed the mustache at the first opportunity before arriving at the big tent. For some reason, that made me feel less stupid. The ceremonies got under way with the speech from the Angel King and Queen, which I thought sounded just like the one I was supposed to memorize. Only they got to *read* theirs. Then I noticed the Angel King's speech was all crumpled up. That was MY speech! The disappointed counselor who wrote it must have given my speech to him when I told her I was just going to 'wing it'. My only consolation was that no one was listening to his words because they were giggling and pointing at him. He looked dumber than me with wings falling off, crooked halo…and white tights prominently displaying his little pointer (now I was glad to have the red panties and double tights). I don't think he had underwear on! Poor guy must have gotten it worse than me, probably had to tie him down to dress him like that. Compared to him, I was all tucked in and feeling butch.

I was impressed how perfectly Marsha, my Queen, gave her speech from memory. When it came to my turn at the microphone, I babbled a few short words about friendships, competition, and may the best man win, hoping it sounded coherent. Everyone looked at me at the end of my mini-speech as if to say, "That's it?", so I added, "That's it"! Applause and…phew! It was over.

For dramatic effect, to announce the winning team, the two camp owners, Uncle Morty and Uncle Milty (it's all true, I tell ya!) arrived in a helicopter to declare the winner. They carried a big army duffle bag from the helicopter and said the color of the team that was first pulled out of the bag would be the winner's color. If red was pulled out first then the Devils won, if white, the Angels. While the rotor blades wound down, Uncle Morty thanked everyone involved, parents for coming, blah blah blah, get on with it, man! Next came the scores from the first two days' events, but too fast for me to do the mental math. All the time Uncle Milty had his head in the duffle bag and was tossing different colored clothing as high in the air as he could, blue shorts here, handfuls of yellow T-shirts there, green bathing suits. Marsha and I were holding hands while black and grey socks delicately fluttered down around us…seems like everyone was holding their breath; I know I was. With the toss of each piece of clothing, the teams' stifled a premature cheer. Everyone was standing, anticipating the first red or white item to be tossed from the bag. The suspense was as thick as the August heat. When Uncle Morty got to the scores for the third day he stopped and looked at Uncle Milty. Uncle Milty reached down to the last item in the empty duffle bag and tossed high into the sky above us the most beautiful red T-shirt my sparkling hazel eyes will ever set upon. We had won! I had won! The Devil had won!

There was hugging and kissing and jumping and falling and yelling until we were too hoarse to yell anymore. Red tights and all, it was all worth it. It was my finest day on the planet in 11 years, 10 months. I never imagined they would let the Devil win. Angels are supposed to win. The irony of it all is that when I was finally recognized for my good qualities, I was dressed as the Devil.

Eight years later while at the AOB (Alma's Only Bar) in Alma, Colorado, I remember a drunken swaying Indian jumping up on the bar and declared to the heavens and everyone present "I AM NOT AN UGLY INDIAN WITH A BIG NOSE…I AM NOT A LOSER!" Everyone cheered. Never got his name but I loved that crazy Indian. He spoke for me and many others. He reminded me of my own sentiments at Hunters Run many years earlier while celebrating.

CHAPTER 5

The Legend of Nelly Broomall

*Age 13. All names and locations in this story are original
and have not been changed.*

At some time in most of our childhoods, in nearly every neighborhood sleeps a derelict home long forgotten, out of the way, boarded up at the end of a block. No one has occupied it for as far back as anyone can remember. The property boundaries are larger than the newer home lots built around it, a testimony to the time when it was one of a few original homes on the street from a bygone era, before the concept of mass-suburbia arrived. The home is always in a sad state of disrepair until the day it gets bulldozed for development. Often the windows and doors will be broken by local kids who have ransacked the contents and marked the walls with graffiti. The hedges are overgrown, scraggly branches are leaning out over the uneven sidewalks; that is if there is a side walk at all, or if you can find it below the years of accumulated weeds and leaves. Giant roots from big oaks heave sections of sidewalk enough to dent the rim on your bike wheel. You know this about the sidewalk because it's the only part of the house you ever take notice of while passing by. The house has architecture much older compared to the homes built around it, but no one really notices. Though the house has always been there; you routinely pass without noticing. The house is out of place. It doesn't belong. Its time is past. It is almost dead. But it has something special that none of the other homes in the neighborhood possess—a legend.

In this particular neighborhood, that house belonged to a woman now decades gone by the time I reached my teens. Her name was Nelly Broomall. Her house was tightly boarded up, its integrity still intact. In that sense, the house was rare. Across the street from her place was Williamson Field, an elementary school parcel of land that held four ball fields. Here we would play baseball with the local kids, no league. It was during a break in a game on a hot afternoon while gazing across the street at the derelict house that one of the older boys told us the Legend of Nelly Broomall.

For the rest of the ball game, I would look over at the house and imagine a frail elderly gray-haired woman hanging her laundry out on a breezy spring afternoon. She may have had a moment to react and turn towards the screeching tires of a car losing control as it rounded the bend. The story goes that sometime in the late 1940s, a car jumped the curb, sending it airborne through four-foot hedges, striking Mrs. Broomall waist high while spilling the contents of her head into the yard. Legend also has it that on certain breezy nights, people still see her out there in the yard hanging laundry, only to fade away as headlights approach around the bend. To a nine-year-old trying to cover second base, *that* will definitely put you off your game for the day. After asking around to our parents, who knew nothing of the story, I was content to forget about it. Then again, the home was a quarter mile beyond our neighborhood; how would my folks have known? Even if they knew, they wouldn't feed the imagination of their children with such a frightful legend.

Well, the subject got resurrected when I joined Mrs. Abel's Cub Scout pack that winter. Mrs. Abel's house was four doors down from Nelly Broomall so the local kids in her pack took the legend for granted. Naturally, we asked Mrs. Abel if any of the stuff about Nelly Broomall was true. Much to my surprise, she acknowledged that an elderly woman named Broomall once lived in the house, "but that was a long time ago, boys, she has passed on and we shouldn't talk about the dead". She said the ghost stories are phewy and not to bring it up anymore. I felt Mrs. Abel was being vague the way she cut us off. That was enough for *me* to call it true. Wow, think I'll walk pass the old house on my way home tonight after Pack meeting. The November night will be dark; maybe there's a chance her ghost will be out hanging clothes.

I stood across the street for about a minute trying to work up courage to peek into the yard. The hedges, now eight feet high were too tall to see over. Bare, overgrown tree limbs were casting shadows on the upper floor of the house from the one street lamp at the far corner of the lot. Below the 2nd floor, the whole property just looked like a black hole at the end of the block. I never really stopped to look at the place at night before. To a 10-year-old, it was intimidating. To step beyond those hedges was to disappear into darkness without a trace. I got the creeps and started freaking myself out, so I just went home, occasionally checking over my shoulder.

Three years went by before the subject of Nelly Broomall came up again. I was now an afternoon paperboy delivering The Philadelphia Bulletin. Joe Peca and I had decided a year earlier to take paper routes and had become good friends with a circle of five or six other paperboys our age. For me, a paper delivery route was a good way around the constant after school groundings or chores handed out by my father.

Our daily routine was to meet up at the 'Branch' after school to pick up our bundles, fold and stuff newspapers into our bike baskets, then clown around a bit before making our deliveries. The Branch was nothing more than a beat up two-car garage behind the pharmacy and Wilson's Corner Store. We would get a soda or ice cream at the pharmacy, then sit in a circle outside folding our papers, discussing the latest episode of Batman or the coming of The Beatles new movie. For any of you unfamiliar with folding papers, it was the simple chore of folding the newspaper tight enough to get a rubber band around it so when riding our bikes down the street, we could toss the paper on the customer's doorstep. Landing papers on the doorstep while riding was a talent all paperboys took great pride in. I say talent because it took a while to learn how to balance and steer a 50-pound load of newspapers with one hand, while aiming and tossing with the other (which is also why we all knew every heaved sidewalk crack along the Broomall property). If your aim was off, you would land it in the bushes and had to turn around, get off your bike, and fish it out. Most importantly, how close the paper made it to the front door usually reflected how well we were tipped. Breaking a milk bottle that was setting on the front porch was acceptable as long as the customer didn't hear it and you removed all evidence. Breaking a storm door window was a paperboy's worst embarrassment, but always brought on laughs back at the Branch.

Whenever you couldn't deliver your papers, you had to find a substitute to fill in. The best routes to have were apartment buildings. They were warm in the winter, air conditioned in the summer and out of the rain or snow. But best of all, you could walk through a large apartment complex and deliver 50 papers in half of the time it took to toss 50 papers on doorsteps, AND you didn't have to fold.

Terry Williams had the coveted 'Haverford Arms Apartments' route and made more money than the rest of us who had to work twice as hard. I think they gave him the route because he was the shrimpiest kid at the Branch and could hardly balance 75 pounds of Sundays (newspapers) in the large basket over the front wheel of his bike. Until meeting Terry, I was the skinniest kid I knew. Anyway, when asked if I would sub for him one October day, I didn't hesitate, it was easy money.

Finishing the apartment deliveries, I noticed Terry still had 10 single homes on the same street as part of his route. This brought me to the corner of Eagle and Manoa roads, the large wedge of real estate better known as The Broomall house. Of course, there was no delivery to her house, but I took the occasion to fake a puzzled face while going up to the house, pretending to be the confused paperboy looking for an address. Once I ducked through the overgrown hedges into no-man's land, no one from the street could see me. I was free to investigate as long and close as I wanted to. Being a bright afternoon and a brave 13 years old now, I had nothing to fear.

There were two rusty poles in the yard that would have supported a clothes line, so that much added up. All the bottom floor windows had sturdy boards across the shuttered windows offering no chance to peek in. The house was old and creepy-looking with pointed gables facing out from each side of the house. The front door was so overgrown with bushes that I could hardly get to it. But the back door... the *back* door... I must have stood there 10 minutes taking in every detail I could about that back door. Right then and there, an itch developed that would eventually just have to be scratched. Riding home that afternoon, I thought about that back door until I was sure. That back door, man, it is definitely accessible, I gotta think this through, but one thing was sure: we *are* going in!

A large sheet of plywood covered the back door. We could pull out the nails, pry off the plywood and be in without any problem. I couldn't believe nobody had done it yet! It's not like we'd be breaking and entering, no one lives there! And the person that did isn't around to vote on it. Yeah, we're in the clear, we're in. It *has* to be done. No way can I walk away from this carrot. Next item; who goes with me? Only trusted friends on this caper, we have to keep it hush. JoePec will be in on it for sure, we're besties. Terry too, it's his paper route and can keep an eye on the place while delivering papers. Then there is Rob Madonna, he's pretty big and strong, the door will be *his* job. No getting caught. I'll bring it up at the Branch tomorrow. Difficult sleeping tonight.

The next day I asked Terry if he ever saw anyone around the house; his answer was no. I sprung my idea to Joe, Terry, and Rob; immediately, the four of us were all psyched on the plan. Who could pass up such an adventure? Joe asked about ghost legends, Terry mentioned not wanting to get caught or he might lose his paper route, Rob and I got busy putting together a tool list to deal with that back door. Then someone asked what we would do once inside the house. This was an important question and I noticed wavering in the troops when I had no immediate reply ready. I never really thought about *what,* just the fact that it was doable and no one had done it yet was enough for me. Then years of conniving my friends into lame plans sprung to the surface and I said, "Nelly Broomall! We'll check the whole house out from top to bottom for any evidence of haunting, ya know—check things out, see if our being there brings her out." I saw Buckwheat eyes from that one, so I quickly came back with "and see if there's any old stuff worth keeping, she ain't using it." I guess that kept them on board, but I saw cracks in the team. I knew I could depend on Joe to see it through, and all I needed was one partner if the others backed out. This was my only focus now, nothing else mattered.

We swore to secrecy and picked a time. "Thursday night, no traffic then, 9:00 at the corner," I said.

"Night? Why night?" came wavering back at me.

"We need darkness for a lesser chance of getting caught, besides; it's always dark *inside* the house 'cause it's all boarded up. So it doesn't make any difference once were inside." No feedback from the guys, "Thursday night then."

Thursday night was warm for mid-November. With no rain, the leaves were dry and had accumulated in piles against the overgrown hedges. We swished back and forth through these leaves several times, past the back door before deciding what to do. There was a big 'ole tree with low branches touching the top hedges at the point where the path from the sidewalk led to the back door. All this provided good cover for us to stop and assess our courage. Only a few cars passed in the last five minutes. Rob and I were hesitant to pull the first nail out or even get close to the house so it was much to our surprise when Terry volunteered to go up and pull on the plywood cover to see how much work (and noise) was ahead of us. He strolled up the path and disappeared in the dark. I jumped when he popped back out of the shadows only seconds after disappearing, "Nailed tight," he said.

The four of us carefully approached the back of the house with Rob and I in the lead; it was our job to spring the door. I started to make a weak effort at the bottom with a screw driver, while Rob was more seriously prying with a crowbar. He was making good progress so I stepped back with the other guys and let him have at it with lots of "attaboy Rob" from the three of us. Rob was on a roll. He got the plywood off without much noise. Thinking we were in, all of us gathered tightly behind him, but he was still prying on the locked door. Getting along side of him, I could see the door was padlocked. The lock pried off easily too, but it seemed the door was boarded up from the inside or warped tight from many seasons of heaving. "We all need to push at the same time," Rob whispered. Joe heard him at the same time I did and we both rammed the door without a countdown to warn Rob, who was still prying the door latch.

The three of us fell through the door and onto the floor with such a crash that we were sure someone had to have heard it. Splintered wood and glass fell with us but we hardly had time to settle before we were hightailing out of there, having freaked ourselves out. I was so focused on getting in that I was no way prepared for what lay beyond the back door. For those brief seconds lying on the floor (Rob's back actually) in the tiny kitchen foyer, I only had a moment to flash my light around while struggling to get up. Two things struck me: OLD and CREEPY. And that's why I ran out, not because of the loud crash. We had fallen 40 years through a portal into the early 1920s. Etched into my psyche forever was a ragged curtain separating the kitchen from the next room. When we fell through that door, the curtain was blown away from us, probably the first time it moved in 20 years. The bottom of the curtain was shredded 12 inches from the floor by decades of mice or rats foraging for nesting material. I knew it wasn't a ghost as the wind caught it from our abrupt entry, but it still took me by surprise to see the curtain part as if someone was passing through the divide.

None of the other guys paused to see anything before running, or maybe their flashlights were off, I don't know. Safely across the street, they hung on every word of my curtain description then agreed unanimously, "Ain't no way we're going back in there tonight," and that was fine with me, I didn't have to pretend to want to go further.

"What are we gonna do about the door though? We can't leave it like that!" I said as our shaken crew looked into the blackness where the door had stood for decades, wondering if someone was looking back. So we came up with a plan; we'll run up, two guys put the board back in position while the other two tap a few nails in. Leaving the damaged back door open wouldn't matter once the big board was up to hide it. We accomplished the task with hearts pounding and trotted home champions, thrilled with our accomplishment. "We did it, we did it," Joe kept repeating as if our mission was accomplished. I waited 'til they were at their highest point and threw out the challenge. "So, who's up for goin' back in tomorrow night?" Terry bailed right then, Rob hedged without deciding, Joe quietly volunteered he'd go if I was going. Good old Joe, never passed up a hair-brained adventure, and we'd seen many together. All right then, Joe and I, we'll have to recruit two more; there is safety in numbers. Someone we could out-run. Always bring a guy slower than yourself to get caught if you have to run. That would be Larry; he was a year younger than us. Larry took a lot of undue ribbing from us since he moved into the neighborhood to become our lone Jewish buddy among all Catholics. Though easily scared and worthless in a fight, he was a good friend and lot of fun to have around.

That Friday night we were back, JoePec, Larry, Rob and myself. Once Rob heard Larry was coming, he came on board. Can't let younger Larry say he went in while Rob sat out, especially after doing the brunt work on the door. Once there, JoePec removed the plywood cover with his dad's tools he so proudly brought along. Crunching over the glass and splinters from last night's work, we all bunched up silently on one side of the kitchen, flashlights slowly scanning the room in unison.

No one spoke for a moment. We were listening, watching. Eyes, ears, noses were stretching every receptor to full capacity. Everyone was edgy and ready to blitz out at the first noise. Someone had to do something before we all ran out, so Joe walked around the kitchen table shining his light on the dusty cabinets nervously saying, "Cool, this stuff is from the 18th century." Joe had a poor concept of time. I remember telling everyone to turn off their lights. They did what I asked, not out of obedience, but because they thought I heard something. I kept mine on, but aimed it low, explaining that four flashlights blaring around the kitchen might be seen by cops driving by if they were looking close enough. "Look, only two flashlights on at a time, that way we'll have back-up if the first two flashlights go dead (alkaline batteries weren't invented yet). And aim them low, especially when near the back door." The guys were used to me bossing them around anyhow and would usually follow unless the request didn't agree with them. "Once we're further inside, the windows are all boarded up and our flashlights won't be seen from the outside. Also we…" But I was interrupted by Joe shouting, "Something moved in there!" meaning the next room. We burst for the door on wings. This time though, our exit didn't make it all the way across the street. Rob called a halt in the yard and asked Joe what he saw. "A shadow moved," he said in a forced whisper that lacked convincing as he realized he probably panicked too soon.

Slowly, we inched our way into the kitchen again. "There!" Joe said, shining his light on the curtain separating the kitchen from the living room. The breeze from the back door catching the curtain as a flashlight beam caught it cast a moving shadow on the wall in the next room. "It's *nobody,*" we said, expecting if it was anything, it would be a *some*body. This time, Rob and Larry shut the door and leaned boards or something over the door's four window panes (minus the ones we broke) so no flashlights could be noticed from outside the house. We held our lights on the curtain until satisfied it wasn't moving, like that would still the spirits of the house.

Joe was now on the other side of the kitchen table looking intently at something on the table. The rest of us were rooting through the cabinets excitedly whispering to each other what we were finding. "Look at these old fountain pens," (*) and "There's handwritten notes in this drawer," and "What's this for?", as Larry tried to figure the function of some kitchen tools before the era of electric everything in the modern kitchen. I was caught up with feminine hand-written reminder notes, probably penned by Nelly Broomall's own hand.

"Ho-ly smokes, you guys" Joe said in a slow metered warning as if to say, "Are you ready for *this*?"

"Whattayagot?" I asked, knowing he had something better than pens and widgets. All flashlights swung to Joe, who was on the other side of the table, but I couldn't make out what he was looking at.

Joe was still looking down, reading something with decades of dust on it. He wiped his hand across it while we waited in stone silence. He had something all right, I was reading his face and believe me, I knew all of Joe's faces and this one I never saw before. He stepped back from the table, swallowed a dry gulp and simply said, "It's true", and after a second of hesitation added, "We should get 'outta here now."

"Well, what is it?" we asked, unwilling to leave without some explanation.

"It's all true" he said again then quickly added, "Nelly Broomall, it's all true, the way she died, losin' her brains and all, the car comin' through her yard." "Listen," he said as he picked up a newspaper clipping and started nervously reading as fast as he could. We listened to every word in stunned silence.

It **was** true. A name similar to Nell Broomall, a widow, died as the legend says 20 years ago, of 'severe trauma to the head' while working in her yard. "Does that mean she lost her head?" Larry asked, being the most naïve of our little band.

"Sort of," I said, "It means her brains were all over the yard—only the paper can't say her brains were all over the yard." If she lost her head they would have said she was decapitated." I explained this with the authority of a paperboy who read the paper every day. Joe and Rob, both paperboys, confirmed saying, "That just how newspapers write things, Lar."

* Before ballpoints pens, fountain pens had a self-contained soft rubber bladder with a small lever on the side to draw the ink from an ink bottle into the pen. They were a mess but a required item for penmanship in Catholic schools until the mid-1960s.

Now we stood in silence around the table, thoughts wandering as Joe silently gleaned through the newspaper article for any other detail worth sharing. It was apparent to me now, as I thought about it, that some loved one had clipped these two articles and left them along with some other papers on the table and walked out to never return. Maybe hired someone to board up the house because they couldn't bring themselves to do it. Suddenly, I wasn't as afraid anymore, more in a state of wonder than fear. We never really thought we'd confirm the Legend of Nelly Broomall. And now being faced with the truth of it all, I was thinking what a tragedy it must have been for the person who clipped these articles, maybe a sister or brother. I felt a bit ashamed, filling our pockets with what were only trinkets to us, but articles of everyday life for a woman whose home had stood frozen in time since the day she died. Tonight, our vulgar intrusion had disturbed the peaceful memorial of a home sealed in grief until this moment. Without actually putting my finger on it at the time, I felt like I violated some age-old natural law; like grave robbing. There was no need to communicate it to each other. Like a mother gently scolding her children, I think we all felt like the spirit of Nelly Broomall had just chastised us for disturbing her home.

"She had one son," Joe continued, quietly looking up as he finished her obituary. Now all of us started to put it together and felt like jerks. The four of us loved our moms. Rob would lose his mom in just a few years. "Do you think that's who left this stuff (the articles) here?" Joe quietly asked.

"Yeah," we all shook our heads in somber agreement at the likeliness of that being the picture here. We were identifying with a son we didn't know, certainly a grown man now, who lost his mom in a horrible way, and we just broke into the house he probably grew up in.

Well, to say the least, the mood had changed from nervous fear to heel. "Joe's right, we should go," I said. "Put whatever you took back where you got it."

Joe said he wanted to take the newspaper articles to read at home and would bring them back. We all agreed to that because we all wanted to read them and assumed we would soon return to close the house up for good. Then one of us suggested we should all keep one small item but never show it to anyone or brag where we got it. Sort of a respectful keepsake as long as everyone agreed on it. We all liked that idea, like a membership into the Sons of Nelly Broomall. Joe took an old locket empty of picture, I took an ornate fountain pen she wrote with, I don't remember what Rob or Larry kept. We really didn't feel it was stealing. It was more like… belonging, like we were taking a keepsake to memorialize Mrs. Broomall.

I wonder if when Rob lost his mom to cancer a few years later, he came across that keepsake and remembered the son of Nelly Broomall. There was no skipping home that November night; each of us was resigned to his own thoughts. 'What if that happened to my mom?', 'If there **is** a ghost, she's not a bad ghost, she's probably looking for her son'—the kind of stuff young wandering minds imagine on their way home, walking in the cool darkness, kicking through the autumn leaves. My thoughts now turned to respecting the woman and her house, "We've got to keep all this quiet. If word gets out Nelly Broomall's house is open, the whole neighborhood would be holding a carnival in there before long." So before parting that night we agreed:

"OK guys, 'til we know how were gonna wrap this up and keep everyone from knowing what we did, I want everyone to swear silence or they'll hear from me." Yeh, I was that kind of a creep on occasion. They knew the situation and saw the comment as an empty threat that needed to be stated. We were all cool.

There was a lot to think about over the next few days. How were we going to keep one of the best neighborhood capers quiet? It's bound to leak, heck, we're kids! We didn't want the home of Mrs. Broomall ransacked or trashed. And if word leaks out, how do we keep the house from being raped and pillaged? Yep…a lot to think about.

Somehow, Larry's sister Eileen got wind of our adventure. She probably heard us talking on Larry's front porch where we often hung out. She pleaded for us to take her along next time. Eileen was a grade behind me and we were distantly sweet on each other in that awkward way throughout our teens. Later in our teens we would date, become good friends, and she would take me to her senior prom. Like a lot of girls, she was very emotional and easily excitable, but I did not know this yet.

My final venture into the life of Nelly Broomall would be with Joe, Larry, Eileen, and her girlfriend. I can't remember what happened to Rob this time around. I do remember it was a cold and windy night, at least a week since our last visit, and loaded with anticipation. We were also more afraid of getting caught this time because we hadn't been back for a week and we had read the newspaper clippings Joe had borrowed. According to the article, her surviving son was a policeman in a nearby municipality. That meant he may have checked up on the place and seen the jimmied board and door. Then he'd be checking it closely or telling his police buddies to keep an eye on the place during their patrols. I was more worried about this possibility than I let on to the rest of the gang. If the board had been re-nailed or even moved, we were going to bail for good, but that wasn't the way we wanted to conclude our adventure. After a lot of thinking, I had come up with an idea to keep anyone else from breaking in, while allowing us to let our close friends know the truth about Nelly Broomall.

For now, I just wanted to get through this last visit. We had guessed ourselves inside out over what might be in the other rooms and upstairs; now we had to know. So there we were, tucked in the sidewalk shadows again while I went up to check on the board. I hadn't dressed warmly enough and the nervous excitement of having Eileen and her friend (Joe and I can't remember her name so we'll call her Linda) had me shivering in the wind. "Everything looks the same," I told them when I returned. Eileen jumped and grabbed my arm in anticipation of going in. She never let go all night. A lot of "Oh my God, I can't believe I'm doing this" and "I'm scared - I'm scared - I'm so scared" was chattering back and forth between the girls. I wasn't real comfortable with their chatter, as we hadn't even gone in the house yet.

Joe and I paired up with the girls and stood in the kitchen again. Eileen was shivering worse than me so I figured she couldn't tell I was shaking. Joe opened a few of the cabinets to show them what we had seen so far. In a dish cabinet that was bare, Joe pulled out a few pages of old newspaper, thinking he might find more info. Turns out it was just used as cabinet liner but amazingly it was dated 1919. Joe's earlier comment on our first visit - "Some of this stuff is from the 1800s"—was only 20 years off the mark. It was time to move out of the kitchen beyond the shredded curtain. I volunteered to go first into the next room if Joe would lead the way up the steps to the second floor. Eileen and Linda were approaching whispered hysteria. The curtain was dusty and full of cob webs just like in a movie. I pushed it back with my sleeve to avoid touching it, while Eileen became part of my back to avoid it also, letting out a contained squeal as it draped behind her. I only moved into the room far enough to make space for the other three coming through, afraid to go any further without support. My arm was being squeezed so tight I had to ask Eileen to let up even though I liked having her near me. "Oh, right," she said apologetically, but it only lasted 30 seconds before the clamp was re-applied.

Our flashlights landed on antiquity. The house was completely furnished from a period spanning the 1910 to 1920, perhaps earlier. Dark wood furniture with mirrors and claw feet reflected our beams, making Eileen shriek and practically climb on me. After settling her down, we walked very slowly around the room in awe, doing our best not to disturb the dust while trying to evaluate what we were seeing. There were lots of adjectives thrown around concerning age, frozen in time, and life 'back then'. Stale air permeated the icy darkness. On the mantle were framed family pictures we took time to study, speculating who was who. The largest picture was of her son in his police uniform (probably a police academy graduation shot). The room seemed large with no other rooms opening off it. The girls had had enough, their nerves were straining their bladders and they needed to pee. Joe joked there should be a bathroom upstairs and that we'd wait down here 'til they were done. Finally, there were giggles to lighten the gloom. However, right about that time we had come full circle of the living room and faced the steps leading upstairs.

The stairwell was so dark that without a flashlight you couldn't tell if it led upstairs or downstairs. We were only using two flashlights, telling Larry to leave his off as a spare. He'd quickly flash it on though when someone gave out a "Wow! Look at this!" Shining my light up the stairs, I stepped aside for Joe to come along side, reminding him, "This is where you take over, buddy!" and slapped him on the back. I was glad to relinquish command. Twenty minutes of all your senses stretching every nerve to their max wears on you, even kids' nerves. Joe and I debated whether we should go any further. We were pretty freaked out, had proven ourselves to the girls, and had their pee excuse to bail us out gracefully if we wanted. Hanging in the back of my head, I still had the thought of the son in uniform coming through the back door and trapping us. Hate it when there's nowhere to run. But I knew I'd regret not seeing where she slept her last night. The girls and Larry wanted to bail when I shared that thought. Joe was feeling me out on whether to call it quits for the night. "Ya think there's anyone up there?" Joe asked, knowing it was a stalling tactic.

"If there is, it ain't warmed up to 98.6." I foolishly replied. Well… that set the girls off again and we had to settle them down once more.

Joe voiced a new concern that had us in debate loud enough to wake the dead. He noted the steps were really narrow and steep and we'd have to go up single file. There was no landing, just a skinny stairwell up to a blind corner then left turn down a hall, we guessed. Joe said he'd go first if I went second. Larry didn't want to be last and we couldn't ask the girls to be last. I said I'd go last, but that put Larry second. This shuffling went on to the point of ridiculous until I dictated the final marching orders. "Look, Joe goes first holding Linda's hand behind him, then Larry, his sister, I'll be last with my ears on the back door." That seemed to satisfy everyone. Joe got to hold Linda's hand, Larry felt safe in the middle, Eileen was between her brother and her beau, and I got to shine my flashlight on Eileen's derrière. So up we started, painfully slow, and yes the steps creaked from the ages. We tried to skip the steps that squeaked, but the whole stairway squeaked with the weight of five people on them.

Next thing I know there's screaming and shuffling to get down the stairs. Being last, I didn't know what was going on so I stood my ground in the steps blocking any stampede. By then Joe was giving the all clear to come back. I was still in the stairway when JP opened the door to the bedroom. Standing in the corner was a headless wicker female figure on a stand that could be used by a seamstress. Yep, a headless female form! Linda saw it and that is what started said stampede. In the second bedroom, we would get a final dose of the reverent creeps.

The order of march got shuffled exiting the first bedroom (which turned out to be mostly storage). Joe and I went first into the second bedroom, which was Nelly Broomall's. She was apparently good with needle and thread because in the corner stood a second wicker body form on a pedestal; this one had a dress on it. *That* was creepy enough representing a 6th presence in the room. Then we opened the closet. No one jumped or ran. Hanging there in the closet were her dresses, nightgown and wardrobe you'd expect in a woman's closet. But it looked like Nelly Broomall hadn't shopped for a new dress since the mid-1930s; it was our closest identification with her and I imagined her picking from that closet on that last breezy spring morning of her last day. She had no idea. I swept my hand across the hanging dresses and got a rush I will never forget. The girls were finally quieted by this personal confrontation and a few respectful comments were passed as they swung out a few garments to admire some lacing detail of that era. Someone sat on her bed and it sank too deep to invite more weight. It had been left as it was from her last sleep on earth.

We were finally satisfied. I felt I had a personal introduction to the lady of the legend. All of us were ready to close this chapter. So I left Nelly Broomall's house taking some long-lasting impressions, along with a tiny bit of her with me, enough anyhow to include as one of the wonderful memories of my life.

How many kids get to explore a time capsule with a legend? Why me? Exploring the Nelly Broomall's house and personal effects ignited my wonder about what happens to a person after they die and the fairness of the way they died. It was the first time my sub-adult mind actually stirred to consider what happens to someone after they pass from this life. Lord knows I'd be confronted with enough of it in my teens and twenties.

———————————————

Even though he and I told this story dozens of times, I called JoePec to verify my recollections and add his. We shared in different ways the same conclusion; that with maturity, our perspective of that event changed as we realize what we took from there. What started out as an adventure for thrill's sake only turned out to be our first confrontation for respecting the dead. Previous to this, we were the guys knocking over tombstones for fun. Without realizing, we treated this encounter with respect and reverence not standard for our modes operandi. As Joe said on the phone, "I'm still amazed we didn't ransack the place. We destroyed everything else we messed with! And that no one else went into that house after us." This brings me now to my plan to keep our house intrusion quiet.

Up until now, the word on Nelly Broomall's house was kept relatively quiet by a trusted few, but leaks were starting to get back to us that so and so might know we've been in because of overhearing Terry or Rob at the Branch. Two weeks had passed since our first night in the house and all of us were chomping at the bit to tell a few of the other guys. Terry and Rob returned to board up the door as close to the original condition as possible, even remounting the pried-off lock and shackle. They had re-used the original nails and within a three- or four-month period, the splintered board edges had aged enough to look natural by the time spring arrived and kids might be investigating. No one would be bothering to snoop during the dead of winter.

Up at the Branch, folding papers and eating donuts, I shared my carefully thought out idea to keep the Legend of Nelly Broomall alive. It generally went like this:

"Go ahead and tell a few close friends we were in her house, but make sure you tell them you'll deny ever going in if asked in front of others." I started to explain. "I figure you won't have to tell too many 'cause rumor will start to spread on its own from those few you told. When asked by people hearing it third hand if we broke into her house, **never** admit you did, you could get in big trouble if the wrong people blab it around. Instead, ask them where they heard it from; laugh, be vague, let 'em guess, tell them to ask Booker's or Paul, or that *you* heard *they* went in, send them on a wild goose chase." Then I followed with, "You can look obvious you went in but deny it if you're smart, her son is a cop and will eventually see someone was in there and the sooner the better for us, then he'll board it up even better. But if Officer Broomall starts asking around, I don't want him knocking on my door." I let that sink in before finishing.

"Yeah, I can't be getting caught for this" was the general fear expressed by the guys.

"And look," I continued with my final thought, "If someone keeps pressing you to admit, tell them: 'I'm not saying I did, but if you're **that** curious about Nelly Broomall, why don't you go spend a night there yourself and see what happens? Just don't ask me to go along.' Let them form their own conclusions."

It was a plan. You always had to have a plan. And this plan worked. Larry towed the line and we didn't have to worry about the girls because they ran in other circles of kids we wouldn't have to answer to. The last plan of defense if the police came to your door would be deny, deny, deny.

Once in a while, even a few years later in senior high school when some of us rode the same school bus together, someone staring out the bus window while passing the old house would bring it up saying, "Hey, you guys went in that old house, didn't you? What did you find?" And we'd always deny it, laughing and pointing to anyone on the bus and say, "No, I heard it was *you* who went in there," but everyone knew, *we* were the honorary sons of Nelly Broomall.

I included this story for two reasons:

- It is a fun story of harmless youthful adventure in the mid-1960s that, like the previous chapter, I really enjoyed writing, as opposed to other writings in this book that were more chore than joy.

- In another year, I stopped believing in the God of my youth, or at best, that the God of the Bible was not involved in the lives of mankind anymore. Therefore, he would not condemn us or reward us but let our puny lives terminate with non-existence, as if we never were. Yet, because of my experience in the Broomall house, and other life intuitions, I was reluctant to admit there was no life after death. I felt presence in that house. This contradiction was a bit of a conundrum I chose to ignore so I could believe what I wanted to believe.

Postscript:

I later got to know several of the Haverford police and never encountered or heard of an Officer Broomall. He may have served another municipality or moved. Nelly Broomall's kin are the family that sold off tracts of land to eventually include part of Broomall Township. I was able to trace the name Nellie Broomall of Manoa, PA, to a 1915 baptismal record at Epworth United Methodist. She was an adult and already married at the time of her baptism, became a member of the same church in February 1916. I could not find a cause of death in any records. The record may have been in The Philadelphia Bulletin, which folded 35 years ago.

About seven years after our adventure into Nelly Broomall's house the property was sold to Haverford Township and completely renovated into a community center or library. I haven't seen it for at least 20 years. Joe said it still functions in that capacity or something close to it. The trees and hedges are all gone; the yard is a parking lot. But the house still stood at that time (2000), but gleaming white, completely gutted and renovated, like it was resurrected. Last time I saw it, I could hardly recognize anything familiar.

CHAPTER 6

1968 Summer of Love

*Age 15 and restless. No names or places have been
changed in this story.*

Four years after the devil's triumph at Hunters Run, I found myself in
camp once more—Camp Firefly in Spring Mount, PA. I had innocently
agreed to take a job at summer camp with my friend Rob Madonna because
I needed money and I didn't want to spend another boring summer around
home. I had no idea what I had just signed up for, but once my parents and I
signed on the dotted line, I was committed for 8+ weeks. All we really knew
of our agreement is that it paid $225 for duration (that is, a TOTAL for all
eight weeks, not per week), provided room and board, and free use of all
camp facilities. Rob and I had no idea where Firefly was located, the hours
of work involved, or anything about the place other than it was a camp for
diabetics and we would be working in the kitchen. What I cared most was
the job provided my ticket out of Dodge when my wings were yearning to
fly, but before any of our crowd had a driver's license to work those wings.
Though I was clueless at the time, it would turn out to be the best summer of
my youth. But that certainly isn't the way it started out.

My parents fell over themselves signing me up and packing me off before I could change my mind. They had already been called a few times to fish me out of the Police Station this last year, so this was their sigh of relief to have me confined in a camp and working. Mom and dad were probably thinking more along the lines of *Stalag* Firefly.

On a Wednesday afternoon in early June, Mr. Salamasian dropped off two green 15-year-olds at the Camp Superintendent's office toting a duffle worth of gear and an aquarium containing my pet mouse. Mr. Hildebrandt was his name (The Super, not the mouse). Mr. Salamasian supplied the camp with all their food staples and was the one responsible for getting us the kitchen job. Upon arrival, elderly Mr. Hildebrandt informed us of our duties. The first four weeks we were assigned kitchen duty, the last four weeks as a 'Guide', better known as a counselor-in-training (CIT). Once a week we get a day off but could only go home once every two weeks if we arranged transportation. That was fine with me; I had told my parents in a defiant tone not to bother visiting and to just pick me up in August. It was further explained to us that the first four weeks were an all girls' camp and the last four a boys' camp; this is why we were in the kitchen the first four weeks of girl's' camp. His orientation spiel was boring me; I was itching to check out the lay of the land, see where the fun was. I signed up for fun and adventure, not work.

Camp was empty. We were informed that only medical, maintenance, and kitchen help were on premises at the time. Camp Staff would dribble in on Friday and Saturday, campers on Sunday afternoon. We had to get the kitchen up to spec before they arrived. Mr. Hildebrandt pointed us to a run-down little bungalow along the Perkiomen Creek, explaining we would share quarters with Chef Joe. "Cool, let's go dump off our gear and meet Chef Joe."

The bungalow consisted of two rooms, a bedroom, and a kitchen-living space, which Joe had already declared by the way his stuff was thrown around. There was also an entrance foyer not much bigger than a walk-in closet, so we left our stuff in the foyer for the time being and headed to the camp kitchen to meet Joe for something to eat. Chef Joe never acknowledged us when we walked in. This wrinkled grouch, hunched in his mid-70s, had a skinny black frame with nappy white hair. He wore a white T-shirt with white pants and apron. His walk was more of a bent shuffle, hardly lifting his feet but getting around quickly nonetheless. Joe acted too busy and barely glanced at us when we attempted introductions. He smoked while he cooked, cursed under his breath when he wasn't smoking, and had a permanent scowl of disgust for youth. Joe was off our list for new friends.

Across the kitchen, a large, homely, bleached white woman in her mid-40s with short stringy hair waddled over to intercept us from Joe. She introduced herself as Helen, Camp Dietician and our boss in the kitchen. Without any ice-breaking pleasantries like 'where are you boys from?' or 'how old are you?', she spun off a long list of our duties. I never heard anything she said after the shock of the hours blew me backwards. "You **will** be in this kitchen not a minute after 6:00 *a.m.* for breakfast prep, then serve, and cleanup 'til 10. Be back here for lunch from 11 'til 2, then dinner at 3:30 'til the last pot, pan and dish is clean, that will be 7: 30 *if* you're lucky." She seemed to relish the shocked look on our faces. Helen, I could plainly see, was a man-hater just as content to dislike young adolescent boys who thought they were men.

I added the hours up on my fingers but ran out of fingers! "You gotta be shittin' us, Helen," I blurted out. If she didn't have time for introductions, I could skip the prerequisite manners. "That's what? Like 11 hours a day! Do you know what they're paying us?!"

Helen shook her head and started walking away saying, "I can see this arrangement (us) is *not* going to work."

I turned toward Joe, cursing behind us and proclaimed, "No wonder the guy curses a blue streak; we'll all be like him in a few days!"

And with that Helen laughed, which was good, because as it turned out, Helen was all work and no play, no husband, no boyfriend (ever), no kids, no hobbies, no passions,

NO LIFE, *and* I was right; she is a man-hater, but at least she had a sense of humor. The four of us would need that to make it through the next four weeks. We made her laugh quite a bit that summer; that was our redeeming quality in her view of us.

When I asked Helen if we could get something to eat, Joe piped in, "You eats when I eats, and I'll tell your sorry #@^** ass *when* I eats"! I had to laugh at the guy. Helen cast her eyebrows as if to say, 'That's the way he is, take it or leave it.' I had to laugh at the two of them, what a pair. At least cursing and wit seemed on the table so we could vent our frustrations as we pleased.

"Man! You two are the original sunshine twins, aren't you?" I quipped. Helen smiled wryly then put us right to work, while Rob and I started plotting how to get out of that camp.

We had decided right then not to 'take it' but 'leave it'. That evening we were standing at the end of the rural entrance lane checking traffic flow for chances of hitching a ride home tonight. Trouble was we had no idea which way was home. We knew our location was an hour from home but it might as well have been another state. The two of us felt deserted, hoodwinked, disgusted, and, worse of all, homesick. No cars came by this rural lane; we'd have to call our folks to come get us. I told Rob he'd have to call his folks to come get us because I mouthed-off to my parents before leaving. He tried, they laughed, it was up to me. His parents had already called my parents by the time I called.

"*Oh-h-h*, so now you *need* us Richard?" was mom's reply. I tried to convince dad this place was violating child labor laws, but he didn't care if I was working for the Communist Party. 'You made a commitment, comrade, and now you have to stand by it' was about the size of their argument before I hung up hopeless.

"We're stuck, Rob." My heart sank to my stomach, then my light bulb went on. "Well, looks like we'll just have to get fired instead; that should be easy enough," I concluded, feeling Rob out. He didn't respond. I hated the idea of going home with my tail between my legs.

To make things worse, that evening when we got back to the bungalow, Joe had moved two cots into the foyer. THAT was our living quarters. With the cots opened up; there was just enough room to squeeze in between them to get by. It was the worse night of my life at that time. Chef Joe snored like a horse.

The next morning, Joe cursed us to attention around 5:00 a.m. as he shuffled out between our cots. We tried to go back to sleep while Joe smoked and hacked up phlegm on the front porch, cursing everyone from us to Congress as he listened to the morning news on his transistor radio. I never knew 5:00 a.m. really existed until then. Now was a good time to try getting fired so once Joe headed off to the kitchen we went back to sleep. Rob walked in first when we moseyed into the kitchen 40 minutes late. Helen smacked him flat on the back with a big wooden spoon while I dodged her attack, laughing at Rob's wide-eyed reaction. "This woman's a nutcase!" Rob said while sheltering his head and running beyond her reach. We tried to reason with Helen that since camp wasn't in session yet, we could start later. She looked at us in amazement saying, "Who put *you* in charge? You do what I say, kiddoes, three strikes and you're out and this is strike one! Do you understand?"

"Sure, will you sign a contract to that effect?" was my reply. And this is how we would get along with Helen, a constant adversarial banter.

Eventually, she treated us like sons she would never have; she certainly smacked us around like we were. Our antics were the only sunshine in her meager existence. Plus, we kept her plugged into to the camp grapevine. Camp Firefly was her afternoon soap opera and we were her ticket to front row seats each day. When talking camp gossip, she just lit up and pried us for more. Our comic relief put a smile on her face, but on several occasions we actually had her so angry she chased us, waddling around the prep table with a meat cleaver like a Three Stooges episode while we laughed in hysterics. Joe would be telling her not to worry about the #*%# bodies, he'd bury us in the woods for her, cackling like the criminally insane, leading us to believe we wouldn't be his first. Him, we weren't too sure of, so kept a distance. Helen loved the fact that we hated the 6 a.m. morning start more than anything, so she would tease our bleary faces each morning arrival with some comment, "Did you boys have sweet dreams last night?" To which one of us would reply something like, "Yeah Helen, I had a hot dream about your thigh blubber hanging over your rolled down stockings," and then tried to kiss her but she started swinging. She enjoyed our sarcastic wit and was always up to the challenge to counter our remarks. She smiled and laughed more as the days went on. We were her sole entertainment for those four weeks and let us get away with anything after the first week. She hung on our every word of the budding romance happenings among the cliques and soap operas around camp. Gossip was traded like currency for leniency in the kitchen. In no time, we had the kitchen routine down to seven- or eight-hour days. As long as we got the work done, she let us run our own hours.

The Cabin

The next day, Friday, was a big turning point. It started out normal; Joe waking us up with his hacking, spitting, and cursing routine. But today, by dinner time there were a dozen girls between 15 and 18 to feed. Our hormones a-stirring, we asked Helen what gives. "The counselors and guides for the girls' session are starting to arrive, you dimwits. The first four weeks are a *girls'* camp, or didn't anyone tell you that."

All of a sudden it dawned on Rob and I. *We were the only two guys under 18 in an all-girls camp.* With my arm around Helen's bulky shoulder, and daydreaming beyond my pile of dirty pots to the young ladies chirping away in the mess hall, I said, "Helen, my love, I just may have to forsake you for another this summer," to which I received four days of sore ribs. The realization was setting in; our ship had finally come in and the crew was all young ladies.

By Saturday night, all of the female staff had arrived. Earlier that day Rob and I had met Gordy, our maintenance man—if, at 19, he could be called a man. He was the only other guy under 60 in camp, a local guy who lived off

78

campus. This was the lowdown from his previous year working here: You only get to come to this camp if you are severely diabetic. Many of these kids take insulin shots three times a day, their bodies so numb from needles that they have to rotate injection points. All of the counselors and guides are previous campers. Half of the campers come on free grants, the other half from rich families that can afford it. They come from anywhere in the mid-Atlantic states and know that whatever they do here will not get back home. Gordy said we'd cry when the summer is over. Still not getting it, he explained to us we would never meet a *friendlier* group of girls. Very few of the Senior Counselors (SC) were over 19 due to the lousy pay, most were college kids. Counselors in Training (CITs) and Junior Counselors were 15–17 in age. Old Mr. Hildebrandt rarely left his office, the medical staff didn't care what you did as long as you didn't land in their infirmary; there was basically no supervision over us other than Helen and that was only in the kitchen.

That Saturday dinner was a full staff gathering of old friendships forged at Camp Firefly over many summers. Helen made us eat in the kitchen to keep us away from the young ladies. But after dinner, there was an official introduction of staff. For this we had to go out in the dining hall and stand before the assembled diners until our turn came. I was looking down the line at the girls, trying to remember which names matched which pretty face as they introduced themselves, where they were from, how long they had been coming to camp Firefly, when I realized most faces in the hall were not looking at the other inductees; they were staring at Rob and I. By the time the emcee had gotten to the two of us, I felt like I had been auctioned at a meat market! These girls were checking us out! I was working my coolest slouch, while Rob tried to keep the pimpliest side of his face away from the crowd.

We flew through the dishes before everyone left the dining hall and went out to meet anyone. We quickly made friends and wound up lamenting our dilemma of bunking with Old Joe. There was another creepy-looking bungalow in the woods, closer to the creek and further away from any other buildings, it looked abandoned when Rob and I checked it out. Part of the porch was falling in, but it overlooked the wide Perkiomen Creek. One of the girls suggested that if we could get permission from Mr. H., they'd all come down to clean and paint the interior, and decorate it for us.

And so it became 'The Cabin'. Not only did they paint it, they donated posters, bead curtains, and all kinds of late-1960s accoutrements to turn it into party central. Also, it was bigger than Joe's shack, having two bedrooms, a small kitchen (in disrepair), and large family room with a mildly warped floor. The old green Cabin became the central hangout for everyone 15 to18 for the rest of the summer. The door was never locked, everyone was welcome, and we would often come 'home' to half a dozen girls lounging around, some in our beds listening to records. Hey, it's 1968, after the Summer of Love. San Francisco had nothing on us; we had our own 'instant' commune, all girls…we couldn't have dreamt it up any better!

Mr. H couldn't deny us the cabin since we told him Joe was no example for us to bunk with. We often speculated Joe had an arrest record he never put on his resume or that management ignored. Nor could Mr. H give us any grief about girls in our Cabin, being no one but girls to hang out with. It would have been impossible to quarantine us from our new friends anyway. He only had two simple rules concerning our cabin.

1. Lights off and everyone out by half an hour after dark. So we burned candles after 10 and stretched his curfew.

2. No loud noise or music after lights out.

In just 48 hours, our world went from pitiful to 'no one back home will believe us'. At 15, we had our own house, all our friends were young ladies, no parents, practically no supervision, and a whole summer ahead of us. I went home once all summer, six weeks later for one day. Who'd want to leave this?

Shocking Circumstances

Camp Firefly was established to serve the medical needs and diet of severe diabetics in a summer camp program. Rob and I knew nothing about the disease, but boy would we learn quickly. The campers arrived that Sunday afternoon. On a bleary-eyed Monday morning at 7 a.m., Helen decides to give us a crash course on serving diabetic children, whom we would be serving in an hour. Helen assumed we were ex-campers who knew all about diabetes. Bad assumption.

Each child had a 3"x 5" index card to hand us at the beginning of the food serving line. Rob, myself, Helen, Joe, and sometimes a fifth server would stand on one side of the serving counter, while a line of campers stopped at each of our appointed stations on the other side of the counter. Each card has the kid's name, how many grams of fat, how many half patties of butter, packets of sugar, units of starch, bread, milk, and so on we are allowed to serve them. Some kids had a second card with special instructions.

"Seems dumb to me, Helen, why not let them eat what they want?" I asked clueless, halfway through our pre-serving training.

"Because they will go into shock, you morons, just do it as I told you!" and she dismissed us to our duties, thinking I was just joking as usual with my 'eat what they want' comment.

This was the first time I ever heard the term 'shock' for diabetes; it sounded kind of serious though and we probably should have asked, but that was the end of our schooling for now. Everything she said about fats, starches, proteins, and sugars went way over our heads.

"Did you understand any of that crap?" I queried Rob,

"Nah, I'm just gonna look at their card and ask them what they get," he said, convinced nothing was wrong with eating what you want. After all, Rob is Italian through and through. Mange!

"Me too," I agreed.

Breakfast began and in no time the line got frantic. I was the first one campers handed their diet cards to, being assigned to distribute butter, toast, jelly, juice and milk. Next, I would hand the card to Rob to dish out his oatmeal slop, and down the line to other servers with Helen at the other end serving eggs and meat with Joe. Items were divided into halves or wholes, like a ½ patty of butter = 2 grams of fat, or half a glass of juice = 2 units of sugar. Their cards told us how many fat, sugar, and starch units they were permitted. After a while, I just asked the kid if she liked butter and gave her a few patties and did the same with the other stuff. Their eyes lit up like I was giving them candy, which I was, but I'd learn that later. Rob was as bad as me; he couldn't even match up the kids' name to the card after a while.

"Are you Beth? No? Whataya wanna eat; oatmeal, cereal, or eggs?" and shuffle the kid on down the line.

Helen was at the other end of the serving line unable to hear us botching things up; she had her own concerns on this first breakfast. After everyone was served, Helen asked if everything went okay and if we have any questions. "Nope, no problem, Doll-face, we feed the flock and they disperse unto the hills from whence they came."

"Get to the dishes and quit insulting Billy Graham," and so we were dismissed.

That day we overheard a few counselors saying some of their kids were pretty wired, but they attributed this to first-day regimen in camp activities. When it came time to serve dinner, it seemed like the kids had passed it among themselves that the Candyman was in town, handing out whatever they wanted. They were asking for double desserts and we were aiming to please their hearty little appetites, God bless 'em. I did wonder why some kids stuck some items in their pockets or under their trays. About halfway through serving, Helen saw a double dessert jello being hidden under a camper's tray and came over to smack us upside the head, then she pulled us aside to read us the riot act. "You two idiots will get us ALL fired handing out food like that!" She was visibly upset and we knew better than to joke about it like we normally would. We figured she was just over reacting as we had discovered she usually does. However, at this point we definitely had abandoned our "get fired" scheme of three days earlier, so we did our best to please her.

About 1 a.m. that morning, Rob and I were rudely shaken out of our beds by an out-of-breath Helen in her bath robe. With her were some medical staff and a counselor wielding a flashlight over our faces. There was a commotion above our sleep-deprived bodies as they looked for lamp switches.

"Get dressed and follow me!" Helen demanded. Apparently, from the night dress she was wearing, Helen had been jolted from her slumbers also. Something big was happening and they needed men to help, I figured; Rich and Rob to the rescue! She marched us up to the light-flooded, white infirmary rooms where all of the cots were full, some zombies were sitting on the benches. And then it started.

"Get a good look at what you caused!" Helen said vehemently. "This is what happens when you give them what they want instead of reading off their cards!" She was visibly very shaken over the situation, probably fearing for her job at this point. There were half a dozen girls under 12 on the beds, all of them in various states of diabetic shock. A young nurse condescendingly lifted eyelid after eyelid to show us eyes staring blank from diabetic shock. It was weirding out Rob and I.

"Will they be okay?" Rob asked quite scared.

"Yes, they will be okay as soon as their medicines take affect but had we not checked on them they would have needed a hospital or even died by morning!" (Some exaggeration on Helen's part here, but death by insulin shock is a reality with severe diabetics). Okay, we were getting the picture now. Diabetes is a serious disease and these kids were some of the worst cases in the east. The kids that were sitting on the benches were lesser cases being observed. All of the kids in the infirmary were under 12 years old; this is because the older kids (campers are up to 14 years old) understand the seriousness of their illness and choose to control their diet rather than suffer the consequences. The younger kids took advantage of us to satisfy an urge for sweets, which, by routine, had always been rationed to them. For the kids' part, they figured the food servers should know the routine; if we were offering it, then it must be okay.

Doctor Vic then sent us with a med staffer on a tour of the last bunk houses not yet checked. I figured we'd be fired in the morning once this got to the Camp Superintendent. I knew this Camp Firefly was just too good to be real; just fate's way of teasing me—set a gourmet feast before me then yank it away before I took the first bite. Typical! Rob and I had blown the best opportunity to ever come our way. IDIOTS! Helen was right. Our hearts sank with each new shock victim that had to be helped to the infirmary.

There is a horrible sinking feeling that overcomes me when caught doing something over the top by anyone else's standard of 'the top'. It's a realization I may not be a normal member of the human race if I can't figure this out. In the moment it hits me, I just want to disappear or run; apologizing helps but can't turn the clock back. It seems there is no redemption for the deed. The assembled medical staff looks at you thinking, "Thanks for forcing us into an all-nighter, boys." They may not hate us, but certainly despise our stupidity. Their glares are piercing. I wasn't even sure they viewed it as a mistake, perhaps thinking we did it as a joke. In part, they were right. Rob and I were competing to ignore the diet cards. At times like this, shame overwhelmed me and I question if I'm not mildly dysfunctional to do something so stupid. Going from bunk to bunk with the med staff, it hit me in the stomach and I wanted to throw up, especially since they were girls and seemed so fragile. I shivered nervously in the night air, hating what I did.

As it turns out, a midnight patrol is routinely performed every night by the med staff and counselors, not just because of our screw-up, but we didn't know that at the time. They have to pull *every* child's eyelid to check for signs of insulin shock. Since we caused the *epidemic* (as Rob put it) on this particular night, we were required to watch patients until they started to come back around, then notify the nurse. It was a long night in the infirmary of watching, escorting recovered girls back to their bunks, apologizing, rechecking, before we were allowed to go back to our cabin before daylight broke. We felt worthless about the whole thing. Like Rob said, any of them could be his little sister. Well, let's get changed, prep breakfast and wait for the firing.

I still to this day blame Helen for the lickity-split poor training she gave us concerning a diabetic's dietary sensitivity. Like I said, she probably assumed we were previous diabetic campers returning as kitchen help and understood the seriousness of diabetes. Either way, breakfast came and went, lunch came and went, dinner too and we didn't get fired. I don't think Mr. H was ever informed of the debacle. I believe Helen asked the med staff to put it in the record, but keep it quiet, fearing for her own job. After all, she was Camp Dietitian and ultimately responsible for our training in these matters.

Bottom line is that we didn't get fired for this one. I would, however, throughout the next eight weeks, twice be put on one-week probations by Mr. H. for other episodes of lame braining. But we never got fired. Getting suckers to work for $225 a summer must have been harder than I realized. I'll explain one of the probation stories a little later in this chapter.

Over the next eight weeks, I would go on these medical night rounds many times out of curiosity, but also as part of my job duties during the boy's camp session. These diabetic children were so used to their parents doing nightly eye checks that they rarely woke up when a flashlight glared into their eyes. Once this knowledge was realized, many a joke was played on some of the diabetic counselors and CITs. Waking up next to a dead squirrel in your bed or missing undergarments always made for laughs or war. Well, you go to camp, you learn new things.

Swim Sessions

There are swim sessions and there are *swim sessions*. I am going talk about the *swim sessions*. Anyone offended by skinny-dipping, please skip this section and move on to the next. For those of you who have been there, done that… SHAME ON YOUR NAKED HINEY'S! Remember, this was 1968, the sexual revolution was gaining momentum, even at Camp Firefly. The following is Rated PG 15.

The camp pool was normally available to the staff for evening recreational swimming until 9:00 p.m. and then locked. On the first Tuesday night of the first camp session (our 6th day here) the staff girls throw the Traditional Moonlight Invitational Swim. They have Gordy pull the pool light fuses before leaving that evening and leave the pool unlocked. Some of the girls were excitedly talking about it after dinner that evening and asked Rob and I if we had been invited yet. We answered in the negative so Debbie insisted we **had** to come.

"Be there no earlier than 9:45, more like 10:00."

The other girls enthusiastically agreed, no questioning. But they never mentioned to us that the moonlight would not be lunar…we had no idea. Of course, we'd be there! I loved to swim, 10:00 sharp it is.

Come the appointed time, Rob and I are naively strolling down to the pool wondering if the swim has been cancelled. There were no lights on, neither was there any of the laughing and carrying on you would expect at a teen swim—everything seemed too quiet. Looking closer from a distance, I could make out heads in the rippling water. It was dark but easy enough to make out a profile on the diving board. She was lightly bouncing up and down on the board when I notice some extraordinary bouncing going on. I froze in my tracks and held Rob back. "Humina-humina-humina, . . . Rob!, that girl that just went off the board was naked!" I whispered loudly in amazement while pushing Rob behind the nearby maintenance shed.

Rob wore glasses and didn't see what I saw, but he could see I was seriously frozen against the shed wall. I was hoping no one had spotted us yet so we had time to decide what to do. Rob squinted around the corner trying to confirm my first observation but said everyone was in the water.

"Don't let them see you Rob, oh my gosh…she was naked I'm telling ya! Parts of her were still going down when she was jumpin' up!" I struggled around him to get another look. My mind was racing out loud to assess the situation.

"I mean, I can see *them* having a skinny-dipping party but they invited us too!" I pondered out loud. "Rob, do you think they knew they'd be skinny-dipping when they invited us? <aybe they planned a regular swim and it turned into this. Right? Right? That would make sense," I reasoned, agreeing with myself. "Or do you think it might be a trick to get us back for the dead squirrel in Lorraine's bed?" I franticly tried to think through why these girls (mostly older than us) would invite us to an all-girl dippity-doo party. Something fishy was in the air. I smelled a trap, but had no idea how inviting us in with young naked wimins was a trap. Then again, Ulysses men couldn't resist the Sirens.

Something had to be up; this was too amazing to be true. If I go in that pool I know God will drown me in the first minute; my life just doesn't get lucky breaks like this. Yeah…but I'd have a minute.

"Let's sneak around the other shed to get closer," Rob suggested excitedly, "Once we're sure they're all naked, *then* we'll decide what to do." "I'm telling ya, they're *all* naked, Rob!! That's why the lights are off!"

It was a good stall tactic anyhow. Just before scrambling to the next shed Rob stopped short and turned towards me.

"I just figured it out!" he announced, "That's why they told us *not* to come down 'til 10:00 while everyone else got here before us. That's it! That way they'd all be in the water and we'd have to stand there naked while they're looking up at us before we jump in! Oh man! We ARE invited!" he beamed.

"Nah, we could jump in, then take our bathing suits off," I countered.

"Not if they say no bathing suits beyond the gate, or in the pool, something like that," he returned, shattering my reasoning.

"I'm sure they have it figured out in their favor or they wouldn't have invited us. I bet they have their flashlights stashed under towels." I was getting nervous as a June bride. "Whadayathink we should do?" I was stalling.

"Let's check 'em out closer," said Rob. So we jumped the gap to the next shed.

"We see you between the shed, guys, so you might as well come down," the words pierced all our macho integrity like a sword. We were caught AND humiliated.

"Whatawedo, whatawedo?" Rob asked in a panic. "Do you think they really saw us?" he asked in desperate hope.

"Don't be an idiot, of course they saw us! I don't *know* what to do. We're gonna have to go out there to save face." I was scared and exhilarated at the same time. This was just too wild. "I don't know if I'm ready for this, Rob." **"We'll be down in a second!"** Rob blurted out before I could stop him. I cringed.

"What did you yell that out for, you jackass! Now they *know* were chicken," I snapped.

"Sorry ass wipe, but I think they figured that out when they saw us slinkin' around these sheds," he shot back, "and who says we're chicken?"

"All right. Man, I feel dumb now with swim trunks on. Let's go, and don't say anything stupid," I pleaded. "Let me do the talking." "Why not?" reasoned Rob out loud, "We already **look** stupid, and **you're** the one that pushed me behind the shed or I'd be in that pool with naked girls right now; I still can't believe this is happening." So out stepped the two biggest dorks in the county.

It was the longest 100 feet I ever had to walk. The girls were giggling and splashing at us by the time we reached the fence along the pool.

"Why are the lights out?" Rob asked the girls (so much for not saying anything stupid), pretending we didn't know they were skinny-dipping.

"Why were you guys hiding?" quizzed Deb teasingly from the edge of the pool, ignoring Rob's question. There was more giggling.

Then Rob said something that won him the 'I Can't Believe You had the Nerve to Say That' award for 1968. "Why don't you come over to the fence to talk? We can't tell who all are there."

RIGHT ON, ROB! The challenge had been presented for them to show first. If they refused to get out of the water to talk, then we knew it was a trap and I would defend our honor with, 'That's why WE were hiding behind the shed', and we would have been back on even ground again. Gotta save face.

After some giggling and whispering (dares among themselves, I believe), three wonderfully crafted angels boldly stepped out of the pool glistening in the available light. Deb, Pat, and Ellen, well stocked from the factory, were standing there dripping wet just six feet from our popping eyeballs. The girls still in the water let out a unified squeal of glee for meeting the challenge front and center. Actually, Pat was covering herself partway, Ellen was hiding behind Deb, but Deb was right out there grinning from ear to ear. I was getting a sneaking suspicion this was not the first time these girls had pulled this off. From what I was mentally photographing in the summer darkness with my speedy little peepers, though 16, Deb looked fully developed—and I was not. Oh man, this may be very embarrassing.

Then Deb threw the ball back in our court. "So, are you coming in?" she sassed as the three turned to jump back in the water. This was the moment of truth; they had met Rob's challenge front and center and now fairly placed the ball back in our court. There was no more stalling, but I still smelled a trap. It was drop 'em and join 'em, or run. I ran, sort of.

"Well, there's a little problem Deb, we…" but I was interrupted.

"Oh, we know how to take care of little problems, Rich!" she countered to my temporary speechlessness. All the girls laughing gave me the needed time to recoup.

"There is nothing in this world we'd rather be doing, but what if we get caught tonight?" Before she could reply, I came back with: "The rest of the staff may look the other way if **you girls** get caught, but after last night's 'Shock Treatment Episode' we would get fired for sure." I said this while nervously checking towards the infirmary to emphasize genuine concern. Then Rob chimed in with an excellent supporting follow-up: "Yeah."
Word of our sweet expertise in the serving line was now common knowledge and it was the perfect alibi. Yes! The con man honed his craft at just the right moment. We were saved. We could bow out gracefully now with our honor intact.

"Yeah, I guess you *would* get fired and we don't want to lose you guys," Deb agreed. "That was shocking when we saw what went on last night" came another voice from the dark water to lighten things up more. "Did they really keep you guys up all night?"

After some more small talk about the previous night's emergency, we escaped victorious. "When's the next swim?" Rob inquired.

"Oh, you'll know when. See ya then," said Deb.

"Yeah, *more* of ya!" a small voice added, followed by more unified giggling and splashing.

"So why didn't you want to go swimming with them?" Rob questioned as we strolled back to The Cabin, completely confused why I had just squandered one of the Genie's three wishes.

"Look, I don't know about you Rob, but I think they were gonna goof on us. Maybe hide our swim trunks while one of them is up the hill locking us out of The Cabin. Then out come the flashlights. Till I know them better, there is no way I'm skinny-dipping with these crazy girls. Did you see how developed they were?"

"Oh, yeah. I was thinking of that myself. MAN, did you get a good look at..." and off we babbled into the late of night about the wonders of the female form and dreamt of running free through the candy store of youth. There would be more opportunities.

There is one other skinny-dipping event that I can write about. It concerns a fine example of camp revenge more than it is about naked swimming. It also proved my point of setting a trap for us on that first invitation to skinny-dip.

Some of the girls were jealous of Deb for reasons I won't get into. Rob and I were Deb's best friends at camp because the three of us were peas in a pod when it came to setting up a practical joke or going for the fun factor. Deb had alienated herself from some of the other girls by helping us 'get over' on them with several practical jokes. On this particular occasion, Debbie was the victim of some well-engineered pay back crafted by Big Barb and Margie.

Margie was a real strange one; the prettiest girl in camp and completely liberated. She had a long unblemished face framed by very long auburn hair and lazy blue eyes that always looked like they just came out of a chlorinated pool, probably because she was the pool instructor. She was 17, from a New England moneyed family. I could never really tell when she was getting over on us because she was peculiar by nature; she spoke of politics, philosophy, and things we could care less about. She was the first women's liber I met, before I understood what women's liberation was about. Fortunately for Rob and I, the practical jokes that the girls played on each other often involve Rob and I seeing them in compromised situations.

There was a Scout camp a few miles away that was on a session break and had an open Saturday night without campers that summer. Camp Firefly, also on a session break, received permission for staff to hike there and spend an overnighter at their camp, sleeping in scout tents already set up. Upon seeing this camp had a bigger pool than ours, and further away from main buildings, we expected a late-night skinny-dip to materialize. We were not disappointed.

Around 10 p.m., Big Barb came to our tent and said there would be clothing optional swimming in a few minutes with lights off. Deb was tenting with Rob and I, so the three of us told Barb we would be there shortly. When we arrived at the pool, there were several counselor ladies in the water talking casually in the night. Someone came over to stall Rob and I while Deb dove in. As soon as she hit the water the others sprung out. They had bottoms on and quickly wrapped themselves in conveniently placed towels. Barb started jumping up and down with glee in anticipation of what was about to happen. Deb was the only one in the pool when the water became beautifully illuminated in the blue glow of pool lights. I had no warning of any of this; Barb knew if she told us we would probably have warned Deb. Plus, Rob and I had never burned Barb and I'm sure she didn't want to be on the receiving end of our fertile imaginations. I'm still surprised they didn't include Rob and I in their trap; or perhaps they did and one of our allies defected to stall us. We certainly had it coming, but Deb was the main target tonight.

Not only the pool lights, but large hand lamps (Barb & Margie) and flashlights were shining on poor Debbie. There was nowhere for her to hide. Now a handful of guys from the Scout staff were brought into the exhibition to step up the humiliation factor. This would be Barb's crowning moment of her summer. Rob and I were already familiar with Deb el buffo, but strangers were another story and it made the devious plan work. Even Rob and I had to laugh.

At first Deb tried to swim around the deep end doing the breast stroke or hiding under the diving board, but that couldn't last. Next, she tried standing in the five-foot section covering herself while trying to face the least populated end of the pool, but those high beams (the hand lamps that is) were too probing. This went on a few minutes while word got out, now the pool was rimmed half way around by staff from both camps. Deb was a pretty redhead with blue eyes and a nice figure, which we are all sure Barb was jealous over.

Deb later told us the laughter was the most hurtful part. The best she could muster back was nervous laughter and 'oh brother' comments to herself or anyone in general; she never lost her cool. The event was getting too large, too loud, and too bright. She knew she needed to get out quick before senior staff (adults) arrived to look into the commotion.

Rob and I were helpless to come to her aide; it just had to ride out its own course. At this point she was wondering if Rob and I had set her up too, so she couldn't really ask us to help. The crowd was howling. We felt bad for our friend, but we were definitely getting a kick out of such a well laid scam.

Finally defeated, Deb asked, "OK, Barb, this has gone on long enough, you've had your fun, what do I have to do to get my clothes back?" The laughter hit a pitch while Barb pranced along the edge of the pool holding Debs long T-shirt over the water. Deb would try to reach for it; only to have the shirt lifted higher. The hyenas were in a feeding frenzy.

"All right, Deb, here's the deal," gloated Barb. "I'll stand at the steps and you have to walk out the shallow end and get your clothes from me. Walk up the steps and you can have your clothes," Barb promised. Deb had no choice but to go for it. All the vultures crowded down to the shallow end steps where Barb had her Polaroid ready. The hooting and whistling accelerated as she went from the 5' to 4' to 3', and finally up the steps, covering just her briar patch with both hands in a shivering delicate stand. She was lit up like a statue from all the probing flashlights. When she went to reach for her clothes, Barb stepped back cackling, dangling the carrot. Deb was not surprised.

Instead of chasing after her clothes, Deb turned away from Barb and stepped right up to the glaring flashlights of the guys all gathered together. She knew there was no sympathy to come from the female contingent present. While shielding her *eyes* from the glaring lights with one hand and the other still protecting; she went on the offensive. In a chastising tone, as if to say enough is enough, she challenged the guys.

"Okay, little boys, now you've seen a real woman up close—and from the way you're acting, it must be the first time." The crowd grew quieter. "Now, is there a gentleman among you who would be kind enough to lend a lady a towel?" She held out one arm, palm up, expecting a response. Towels were immediately flowing towards her. She calmly wrapped herself and courageously regained a little dignity. Well, enough to silence the crowd until she was gone; then the joking and recaps were abundant again.

She was pretty good about the whole thing, but vowed blood against Barb. That night, back in the tent, Deb had time to dwell on a plan against Barb, with our encouragement. She was actually laughing at how it all must have looked. But she feared there just wasn't enough time left in the summer to match Barb on this one…and she knew it…and that's what bothered her most.

There are many lessons to be learned here, the obvious being: Never be first in the water when skinny-dipping! Second, what goes around comes around. But there is one other point more important I need to make here. Once a 15-year-old boy gets naked women swimming around his head, he'll never think the same. He will always be trying to get back into the water. His point of view concerning young ladies has just been prematurely altered. So these seemingly innocent stories are another life-changing perspective to throw into the confusion of my youth.

Throughout the century, teenagers at summer camp have been the most fertile proving ground for the practical joker. Being a practical joker from day one, I was in the best place, surrounded by the best pool of victims. Of course, if you play this game, you have to be prepared to pay the game too. In this next story I get my due—or make that, I get my doo.

Not So Sweet Revenge

As I mentioned earlier, after the girls' session ended, the boys' camp carried out the last four weeks. Rob and I became Guides, while three girls took our place in the kitchen. More male counselors arrived as some of our sweet female companions went home, balancing things out more to the girls liking.

About eight of our lady friends stayed on for this last four-week session. Rob's girlfriend Pat stayed on in the kitchen along with Deb and Midge. Helen complained to us that it just wasn't the same; she missed our antics and asked the girls about our latest practical jokes and romances with daily anticipation while sharing with the girls some of our practical joking in the kitchen from our last four weeks. I'll tell a few of those stories later.

Ownership of our Green Cabin was handed over to the ladies, while Rob and I were assigned bunkhouses with campers to supervise. The bunk I was assigned had 12 campers, seven to eight years old; it was the youngest bunk and I got stuck with it. Three of the 12 were bed-wetters—EVERYNIGHT bed-wetters. Apparently, severely diabetic children have trouble holding their water throughout the night. Being seven years old in a creepy bunkhouse far from home, with dark toilets at one end of the bunk, and having to use a flashlight to use the toilets at night, these three chose to wet the bed instead. So I came up with a *'piss in a bottle by your bed'* program to save me from changing sheets and hosing mattresses every morning. One day I got a few empty red catsup squeeze bottles from the kitchen. I told them that if they used them during the night and didn't wet their beds, they had my permission to squirt the bottles at any unsuspecting camper passing by our bunkhouse in the morning on the way to mess hall. As you can imagine, the program was very successful but never won me any awards. Every other kid in our bunk now had a squeeze bottle. Quickly, everyone from the other bunks learned to stay clear of our bunkhouse in the mornings while on their way to breakfast muster.

Next to our shower stall was a bunk bed. If you sat up in the top bunk, you could look right in on whoever was taking a shower. I thought it would be funny to give someone a golden shower unawares. Our head counselor Dave was the selected victim. For too often delegating the dirty work to me, I decided to pull some dirty work on him. While Dave would take his evening shower, I would grab a catsup bottles or two, spy until he had his eyes closed to soap up his face and hair, then add my golden sprinkling to his rinse cycle.

Usually it was done while the little kids were asleep or away from the bunk when I could sneak in a few girls to witness the prank.

Word got around and soon, too many people knew about it, but not Dave. I let Paul (the junior counselor from our bunk) in on it and he thought it was well-deserved. Dave was 19, Paul was 16. Dave was always ordering us around, treating us as if we were his lackeys and doing as little as possible himself. One afternoon Dave stepped out of his shower and sniffed around, "Smells like someone pissed their bed. Paul and Rich, check for wet beds and pull the mattress," he ordered. We were laughing so hard under our breath; there was no need to check, he just didn't rinse off good enough! This is what happens when you put teenagers in charge.

Eventually, with Piss-Head his new nickname, he got the scoop. However, I was never informed I had been ratted out. So one morning after breakfast, I returned to our bunkhouse and the door is locked from the inside; which was not too unusual. When this happened, we would go around to the first window and call in through the screen to see who was in there to let us in. Just as I went to shade my eyes and press my face against the screen so my day vision could penetrate the darkness in the bunkhouse, someone slammed me full in the face with a can of hot urine. My mouth was open and ready to call out right when they slimed me; they couldn't have timed it any better. As I stood there blinded and spitting, shocked at being snuck so well, in came round 2. Someone pulled the screen window off and a larger cocktail of urine mixed with putrefying crap nearly knocked me over. The stench was as strong as ammonia; all I could do was hold my breath and plead, "Shower! Shower!" But Dave and his accomplice weren't letting me anywhere near the shower.

"You might try the pool but I *don't* think you'll be too welcome, Shit-Head!" triumphed Dave. And that is exactly what I was, literally. Had it coming, just didn't see it coming.

I couldn't hold my breath any longer and until I wiped my eyes, I couldn't open them to see where I was going; and then my eyes stung too much to keep open. So I stood there bent over and dripping, a blind invalid of my own device, trying to think of what to do next when I hear,

"Give me the other one! Hurry up!"

They weren't done yet! I started running for all I was worth and discovered it was the only way to catch a decent breath as the stench blew behind me while running. I didn't know where I was running but it gave me time to think. The Perkiomen Creek came into view and it became my baptism back into humanity. Hallelujah! I dove in and surfaced, looking back to a gathering host of rubber-neckers and howlers.

I came out of the creek to a general consensus of those gathered, "Well, you can't say you didn't have it coming, Rich", and "You shoulda' seen the look on your face!" Dave was there with a well-deserved smirk on his face.

"Well, I gotta hand it to you, Dave. THAT was a good one" I admitted. "Peace?" I asked.

"Peace," Dave acknowledged, knowing that he who laughs last, laugh best.

And that was the end of the tricks between Dave and I until the last day of camp when tips got divided. I was excluded from Dave's generosity.

(Bridge) Jumping into hot water

How is it that something I think is such a good idea is so obviously wrong to everyone else? I could never see past the adventure quotient; that was my problem.

Each week we had one day off from camp duties. However, Dave, our irresponsible, lazy, head counselor with seven-year-olds in his charge, came up with a better plan. Our bunk supervision started at the top with Dave, head counselor at the ripe old age of 19 still in college. Next under him was Paul, 16, our junior counselor, then me as a Guide, three months from my 16th birthday. Guides were supposed to be counselors-in-training but Dave gave me full responsibilities for the kids. Each Cabin of 12–14 campers was supervised by this triumvirate so the children always had more than one supervisor with them. This redundancy of supervision is for reasons obvious to anyone with experience watching over more than three children at a time. Unfortunately, none of those reasons registered on our common-sense radar to three guys who never had kids. Our priority was goof-off time. So Dave decided to set up his Cabin differently. He took the kids by himself for one full day, then Paul would have them for a solo day, then ditto for me. This way we each only had to work every third day, or two days a week. It was great for the days off, but brutal the days on.

So, one day I found myself solely in charge of 12 seven-year-old severely diabetic boys. Kids wandered off; I'd have 12 before breakfast, then 10 after. I'd tell the kids to wait outside the mess hall while I went to find the missing two. When I come back, there's two bawling kids that were always getting picked on by the others. Children will also improvise instructions. When I had to leave them at the archery range (just be glad there wasn't a rifle range at this camp), I returned to a half dozen arrows sticking out of the ground about 30 feet from the pool. They wanted to see if they could reach the water.

"Hey guys, try not to get me in trouble here! Was anyone at the pool when you tried this?" I asked looking over my shoulder while scurrying to remove the evidence.

"Nah! Just those dumb kitchens girls. They left," said Murray the mischievous one.

Whew! At least the girls won't rat me out. But my luck will run out. Always does.

You can imagine the challenges of a responsible adult trying to organize and control 12 kids with a daily schedule of events. Now imagine replacing that adult with yours truly at 15. Parents, remember all of this before sending your kids off to camp.

Just outside camp, an active train trestle crossed over the Perkiomen Creek. There was one spot on the crossing, just three rail ties wide, where one could safely jump into the creek. From this spot on, the trestle it was a 30-foot plunge to the creek for a great rush. If you jumped left of those three ties, the water was too shallow and you risked breaking a leg. Too far right and you landed on a concrete support pier and broken everything. There was a metal inspection ladder on the downstream side of this concrete pier that gave the jumper a way back up to the tracks from the water. I learned all this by jumping with the local kids from Spring Mount on my day off. If the train rounded the bend while we were caught on the trestle, we all knew the drill. Jump before the engineer could see anyone, then ask the last jumper if he was spotted. If the engineer spotted jumpers, he was obligated to radio it in. I was told the Railroad Patrol comes out to issue fines to anyone they catch, but I never saw any policing of any sort on my days there. Even if the engineer didn't spot us, we had to jump anyhow. If you stood out as far as you could on the railroad ties when a train passed, you'd only have a foot clearance from the train; that would be 10 times scarier than jumping.

The best jumping days were at high water after a rain. If the water was normal level, you had to know how to 'bottom out'. At low water levels, it was too shallow to jump. When jumping from 30 feet, you have to enter the water like an arrow with feet together and arms at your sides. If guys' legs are apart when they hit the water that fast, you will feel like you got punched in the stomach. Girls who jump without closing their legs will be leaving puddles around for the next few days. To land with arms outstretched means a nasty smack and red arms.

'Bottoming out' is a technique the jumper employs so as not to hit the creek bottom too hard. It has to be timed just right, within a split second. At entry, you have to come out of the arrow position ASAP underwater and spread your arms and legs out to slow down enough so when you hit the creek bottom it is a gentle landing. A five-foot kid landing in 8 feet of water has to get this right if they wish to jump at normal water levels. It is a good idea to learn the maneuver at higher water levels first. If you don't get this deceleration method down right, you will hit the bottom too fast for your legs to stop the momentum. That means your rear end will slam the bottom and possibly knock the wind out of you if not worse. This happens to most jumpers eventually and it really is quite frightening to have the wind knocked out of you while underwater. The body's first impulse upon having the wind knocked out is too immediately suck for air; do that underwater and you've got big problems. Not only do you have to get your wits about you to remember to surface, but once you get to the surface you also have to swim against the current to get to the pier ladder, all this while sucking to get your breath back.

The last hazard of Bridge Jumping is the current. Though high water is the best time to avoid 'bottoming out', it creates another problem—getting over to the pier ladder before the strong current takes you for a ride downstream. As soon as you hit the water, you had to swim like the dickens and grab that rope trailing from the ladder. The proven method was to spin a half turn in mid-air so you landed facing upstream and ready to swim. Also, in brown high water, there was the risk of landing on a submerged log or object floating below the surface. But when you're young and having fun you don't worry yourself with such trivial problems. According to the locals, kids *did* over the years drown and get injured Bridge jumping but I was young and invincible. Bridge jumping days were a time of total abandon when I was free to ply the last of my boyhood follies. After thinking about it, scratch that 'last of' part; I was still 'quarry jumping' when I had kids. Still a kid at heart, may that never change. Now, with all this bridge jumping safety instruction in mind, whatayasay we show the seven-year-old extreme diabetics a good time?

Murray the Mischievous was one of the toughs in our bunk who didn't whine and was very adventurous. He understood camp; that it was the friends and adventures you created between the structured events that made it fun. He looked up to me and wanted to hang out with me on my days off because he was bored with the writ of sing-a-longs, arts and crafts, etc. Murray knew I was going bridge jumping and would ask me what it was like. He hung on my every word and then decided that's what he wanted to do. Couldn't blame him; I thought bridge jumping should be on the daily camp agenda if they could get the railroads permission. So I said he could come along.

Well, that soon got around to his little click and by the next morning I'd be playing pied piper down the railroad tracks to three wound-up firecrackers. It was a blazing August morning and the temps were already passing 90° by 10 a.m. I told Paul I could take three campers off his hands for most of the day and that was extra fine with him. Before we left camp, I laid down the rules:

1. Once you're on the bridge, you're committed to jumping. If the train comes, you'll have no choice. The freight train came maybe once a day.

2. No whining to go back to camp. We go back to camp when I say so.

3. We're skipping lunch at camp; I'll pack your lunches and meds.

4. Don't get hurt and get ready for the best day of your little diabetic lives.

"You still want to go?" I asked my little comrades.

"Yeah, yeah, man… let's go!" came Murray's raspy little voice as he spoke for all three heads nodding excitedly.

"Franky, is this going to be okay with your head thing?" I enquired, leaving the decision up to him.

"Yeah, I'll be fine," he assured me. Franky had an added burden on top of his diabetes as did a few of the campers. Apparently, it is not uncommon for kids born with severe diabetes to also have other medical problems (or the other way around). His was called 'water on the brain' or something along those lines. The lining that protects our brains is a thin membrane that contains a padding of water. His membrane was much larger, giving him a large, out-of-proportion head from the eyes up. Stick an electrode out each side of his neck and he looked like a happy smiling blonde Frankenstein. Thus, the nickname Franky; I never knew his real name. The med staff instructed us not to let him participate in any head contact or knock down sports like soccer.

For those events he had to sit out, but Franky always insisted there was no problem and he could do anything the other kids did. He seemed fine to me.

"All right then, give me your diet cards; I've got to go weasel some lunch from the girls." The day was set. My only concern was the creek height, which was at normal level. But I figured since they were half my size the water would be as twice as deep for them. They wouldn't have to worry about hitting hard when they bottomed out.

It was a great day for bridge jumping. After I went off a few times, Murray listened carefully to my instructions and flew off with very little hesitation. He loved it and the enthusiasm infected the next jumper to stop delaying the inevitable. Franky, on the other hand, was too scared to stand on the edge of the rail ties for the pre-jump psych out (that was the best part of the jump). He didn't trust his balance so I held him by the back of his shorts to allow him to focus on the jump instead of falling off by losing his balance. Then it struck me that it may be that head thing of his causing the balance problem. He wanted to jump, but just didn't have the confidence the other two gained with each jump. I backed off my "you have to jump rule" due to his circumstance and my impatience. His buddies understood his situation without me explaining it.

A few locals came to join us for a while telling stories of the first time their brothers took them to the bridge for initiation day, about the same age as my crew. We were all lying around in the sun stretched out on those creosote pungent ties when we heard the low rumble in the distance. Train! Without any hesitation, the local kids lined up and catapulted into space within five seconds of each other. There is *maybe* a minute, from when you first hear the train to when it rounds out of the woods. In that minute, each jumper has to jump, then clear away from the deep hole for the next jumper. Murray and his buddy lined up and went off next as planned. Poor Franky's face was sheer terror defined.

"You're gonna have to jump Franky," I told him as a mere matter of fact.

"I know, but I can't!" he pleaded, tears starting to roll.

"You don't have a choice," I stated with unquestionable resolve while pulling him to the jump ties. "There are no options." The train was getting louder. Franky was on the verge of bawling and visibly trembling. I didn't like this at all. The others were looking up at me from the water just under the shadow of the trestle. From there they could stand in shallow water, trying to figure out what we were doing above. I wished I knew.

"Look, hears the deal…we'll jump together and I'll hold your hand, you'll be okay, just shut your eyes and trust me…don't forget to put your feet together." I had him standing to my left on the three jump ties by now, his right foot and my left foot sharing the same tie. His eyes were shut tight but he was terrified and pleading; we were running out of time.

"But what if I hurt my head!" he squealed, cashing in his last chip for mercy.

I knew this head thing would be a problem. Why did I let him come? Stupid! The train can't brake in time once we're spotted, the distance is too short; we had to jump and I knew it. There was no way out but down. I was holding his trembling right hand in my left.

"You'll be okay!" I yelled over the train whistle, which always sounds just before the bend. "Ready, on three," but I didn't count. This was still wrong. *He's* not gonna jump and I'll wind up jerking him after me causing him to tumble. And that head was not going to survive high impact if he lands wrong. Dammit! Now *I'm* as terrified of what may happen to him if we jump wrong. Out of time.

At a last moment of clarity, I jerked my left hand out of his right. In one sweeping motion I grabbed him by the back of his shorts with my left hand while with my right hand I grabbed him tight around his right arm at the armpit, jerking him into mid-air in front of me, using his momentum to pull my jump. I held him in this upright position for three-fourths of the drop, then let go, pushing him away in front of me, satisfied he would land on his feet. "Feet togetheeerrrrr !" was my final command before we hit the water.

Once I hit bottom I felt around for him. Franky was just above me. I pushed him up, then surfaced myself, pulling him over to the bottom of the ladder. Everyone was yelling over the screech and rumble of the train entering the trestle.

"That was a crazy jump, man!"

"You should've seen that from down here!"

"Did the train see you!?"

I don't know who said what, I was looking at Franky's face for some kind of reaction to tell me he was okay. His surprised look of disbelief gave way to a wide grin.

"I DID IT, I DID IT, I can't believe I did it!" he started.

'Actually Franky, you didn't do it,' I thought to myself, but you're here now and I won't take that away from you. Full of relief, I assured the little guy I wouldn't ask him to do it again. We all laughed and rubbed heads in congratulations.

Being somewhat concerned the excitement could send any of them into mild shock, I decided to quit while ahead, so we headed back to camp. The afternoon was about shot anyhow. This adventure would have to tide those boys over until next year. They were dancing around me on the way back. "That was the best thing ever, Rich, I hope you're our counselor next year." But their enthusiasm would put the kibosh to me ever returning to Camp Firefly.

It was inevitable that word would reach the med staff, then Mr. H., concerning our bridge jumping lark. Though it was my screw-up, Dave and Paul were also called into Dr. Hildebrandt's office with me; this had me puzzled. This was familiar ground in my early years; getting 'called in' to account for myself before parents, neighbors, nuns, Mother Superior, priest, teachers, principals, store owners, Fire Chief, Police; now I could add Camp Commandant to that list. Dr. H was a laidback, slow-moving, gentleman in his late 60s who never raised his voice. I was surprised when I saw how upset he was over something I thought should result in a verbal hand slapping. Anyhow, I settled into a stuffed office chair for the routine 'bad boy' spiel followed by some sort of punishment.

"Gentlemen, a serious matter has been brought to my attention by the medical staff concerning the three of you. Now tell me," he started out, still in control. "Who is responsible for overriding camp policy of at least two bunk masters always present with their assigned campers?" Dave raised his hand, to receive the generic 'I'm very disappointed…' spiel complete with furrowed brow behind reading glasses.

I was breathing a sigh of relief as Mr. H reprimanded Dave. Maybe I'm *not* in trouble and word hasn't gotten to Mr. H about the bridge jumping, looks like this is about Dave's bungling. However, after reprimanding an embarrassed Dave, the good doctor brought up the feared agenda.

"Now, which one of you took three of our campers jumping off that trestle?" he asked, pointing a trembling finger in the direction of the trestle for effect. So much for thinking I wasn't found out. He was done with Dave and this abrupt shift snapped me to attention.

"Uhh, that would be me, Dr. Hildebrandt," I said slightly embarrassed while raising my hand part way.

"You other two may leave now," he said, staring at me while waving Dave and Paul out of his office. I didn't like the sounds of that.

He got up and started pacing behind his desk, shaking his head, visibly upset. He paced uncomfortably long, searching for the words to get started. My mind was searching the maybes, maybe he knew more than just the bridge jumping episode. I could be in deeper than I know. Finally, he jumped in with, "*What* in the *world* were you thinking to take three severely diabetic young boys to jump off an active train bridge?" he asked putting great emphasis on the words **three, severely, diabetic, young** boys. Suddenly, that one question plainly painted the stupidity of what I had done, "And I'm sure you knew about Ronald Delp's brain condition!" he followed.

"Franky *wanted* to go, he wanted to stick with his buddies," was my first blundering reply.

"Franky? I'm talking about Ronald Del," then he stopped, figuring it out mid-sentence, "Do you mean to tell me you call him that name in front of his bunkmates?" he asked incredulously.

I knew 'no' was not a believable answer, so I lied with, "Sometimes, but his friends gave him that name."

"Young man, you are *supposed* to be an example to these…" but he stopped short, not wanting to get sidetracked from the more serious issue. I decided to keep my mouth shut unless I really had to answer. Besides, he obviously wanted to unload. Veins were visible at his temples while he kept sweeping his hand over his bald head as he paced to let off steam.

"Didn't you realize some one could have broken their neck and been killed doing that?" his pitch climbed an octave, "and sometimes **do** out there!" He gestured again in the direction of the bridge. I thought of the hair-brained jump with Franky to avoid the train. Lucky.

"What do you think would happen if one of those children got hurt?" he enquired, expecting no answer. "YOU could have single-handedly shut this camp down if someone was injured in such a manner as that!" he stammered, once again pointing solidly in the direction of the trestle for emphasis. "There would be an investigation. The association that supports this camp would want accountability. And how do I explain this now to the parents of these boys when they come to get their children in a few days!? I can't just brush it under the carpet! Your irresponsible actions affect all of us! This camp may not open next summer when I inform the association (Delaware Valley Diabetes Association) about this," he stated as he quieted down, considering that prospect.

I had landed old Dr. H in a world of poop. I felt bad; he was a nice guy that gave me enough rope to hang the two of us, him for sure. I just thought I'd get fired, which I pretty much figured on anyhow this summer. But for him to wrap up his career getting fired for some punk's day on the lark was too much for him to consider. This talk of the camp being shut down had me pretty worried. Getting yourself fired is one thing. Getting *everyone* fired would be a heavy burden.

For the next five minutes, still pacing around his office, Dr. H mentally spread out my stupidity and the consequences of "what if" scenarios, along with having to include the incident in his end of season report. It was as much about him blowing off the pressure he was under as it was about my mistake. I apologized as best I could and did my best contrite face to match the humiliation I felt. Part way through all this it dawned on me I wasn't getting fired or by now he would have told me to call my folks and pack my things.

In hindsight, I'm inclined to believe there may have been a child labor issue or something along those lines that impelled him not to risk a firing or investigation so close to the end of the camp season. The DVDA were certainly paying less than minimum wage; I had mentioned this fact loudly enough several times to Helen. As it turned out, probation and an apology to Franky in front of the bunk for nicknaming him Franky was my worse for wear. Dave was put on probation too and he blamed me for that. I was more careful with my decisions over the next 10 days until camp season ended.

Dr. Hildebrandt had it worse. He had to explain the bridge jumping incident to those parents and apologize for what I did. The parents asked to see where it happened. I stayed clear of that procession, hoping they wouldn't ask to meet with the CIT who endangered their child.

Could you imagine if Dr. H. didn't tell the parents? Junior is riding home with mom and dad: "So son, tell us what you liked best about your two weeks at camp?"

"Well, Dad, we were on this really high bridge our CIT Rich taught us to jump from…and then a train was coming…."

Needless to say; I was not invited back to work at Camp Firefly next summer.

Working with Helen & Joe

I'll step back now to the first four weeks at camp while working in the kitchen.

Going into the kitchen to work was a forced effort every day—joking with Helen or getting Joe all torqued up were our work diversions. Joe didn't bother with us much; he didn't like the "rich white boys". He told us a few stories in the beginning but his manner was so animated and speech unintelligible that, except for his cussing, only half the story was understood. Chef Joe had a deranged laugh, which creeped us out as he shuffled and jived, telling his stories. One day we told him he needed to have himself committed and shouldn't be around young children; and that was the end of Joe talking to us. He didn't get our irreverent teen humor at all.

Early one morning I pointed out to Joe that he was dropping cigarette ashes in the scrambled eggs.

"Where?" he asked, playing dumb.

"There," I said, pointing out the obvious line of expired Marlboro remains.

Joe looked close with great mock concern and very carefully carved the square of contaminated eggs out, flipped it on to a plate and said, "They yorn now!" he grinned toothless in my face, bobbin' his head up and down while laughing like a nut. My eggs had ashes in them for the next few days. Every once in a while after that, as we were washing our dishes and pots, he'd start shuffling and laughing then look over our way and say, "Hey boy! How's them eggs?" and go into his animated cackle, cough, and cuss that always made us chuckle and shake our heads. Joe was his own entertainment.

Back to Helen.

The woman was a 'portion control' freak. Being on a tight camp budget, she only cooked what was required for the campers and staff and never threw anything away. At the time, it never entered into our young irresponsible minds that she was trying to get 8+ weeks of food to last 8+ weeks. The pantry room was a supermarket of smells; all the dry goods were kept there under lock, same with the freezer closet. The freezer room wasn't as enticing because the only item of interest there for us was ice cream; the rest of the freezer was meat. Helen didn't trust us around her precious horde of wonderful smells so she would only send us in to pick the day's rations while under her watchful eye. Every food found in a common American kitchen was in there, only in bulk. The only trucks we ever unloaded while working there were the daily bread, egg, and milk deliveries. Everything else was, frozen, boxed, or canned, and delivered before the first day of camp.

Except for breakfast, kitchen help ate after everyone else was served, getting stuck with the chicken legs and leftover food skipped by campers because it didn't look as appetizing; sometimes all the mashed potatoes would be gone. We ate all we wanted for the most part, but often had a narrow selection of what was left over. So we felt totally justified when we bribed Gordy, the maintenance guy, with a week of unlimited ice cream if he ran out and got duplicate pantry keys made for us. He was back in an hour and Helen never missed the keys.

So started the slow erosion of Helen's precious pantry on week two. Like all well-intended plans of junior thieves, we started slow; a bag of Cheerios here, a block of cheese there. But once we let on to our girlfriends that we had the keys to unlimited sweets and food, the pressure got too intense, prompting late night food parties in our cabin. To snitch the food, we'd have to wait 'til dark, set up watchers between the kitchen and our cabin, then run armfuls of goodies through the darkness to the cabin. It was too easy.

The girls were baking cakes in our kitchen (only the oven worked); there were ice cream parties where institutional size buckets of ice cream disappeared under a dozen digging spoons within minutes. I remember setting down a gallon can of crushed pineapple among our friends, counting, "One, two, three, go." It was gone in two minutes. Soon food became a new currency, then there were birthdays to celebrate, then anything to celebrate. We didn't care; we were fat, dumb, and happy.

Towards the end of our four-week kitchen tenure the raids got bolder, but we finished our time without getting caught. Since we always did our snitching from the rear of stocked shelves and cases; Helen didn't notice. That is until she eventually reached for a can of Brand X from what should have been a stocked shelf, only to see air behind the item. From what Patty and Deb who replaced us in the kitchen explained, Helen must have had a panic attach. First she accused the girls who had to run away from Helen's rage; they were in the kitchen when the theft was found out. Ranting and raving like a woman possessed, she threw a few things, then broke into tears. Helen didn't handle pressure well. Next, they said she abruptly brought her head back up, stopped crying in an instant and demanded with clear resolve to her flying monkeys, "Bring me RICH and ROB. GO, find them and bring them HERE!" she commanded.

The girls carried out their mission, but there was no way either of us were about to go back to a raging Helen, avoiding her until dinner; we had to eat eventually. As soon as she saw us enter the mess hall, she called us in her screeching voice and signaled us over to the Superintendent's table where he and his family were already seated. We had to go over; Mr. Hildebrandt saw us. Helen was already there accusing us before the staff table. Her red face demanded to be heard as she swung her big gravy spoon in all directions, waddling in her soiled apron between us and Mr. H, who sat there bewildered. We didn't get any closer than 15 feet to his table while keeping a close eye on the spoon. Should the ole' spinster go into whacking mode, we were ready to run.

"I demand you garnish their wages to replace the stolen food!" she pressured Mr. H.

"We don't know what you're talking about," was our only reply before Mr. Hildebrandt put his hand up and said he wanted to see Helen in his office after dinner. That was about the last we heard of it. Helen had no proof we stole the food. Mr. Hildebrandt had to question whether this was Helen's way of covering up for not properly budgeting her food. Keeping the food stores under lock and key was her responsibility and she had failed. Either way, he never mentioned it to us and very likely told Helen not to go accusing others publicly and causing a mess hall commotion like that. Plus, there was only maybe two more weeks of camp left and not worth looking into any further; just order more food.

The only other event to arise from this matter was a small encounter I had with Helen a few days later at the pool, around dusk. Helen rarely used the pool because she was too embarrassed about her weight, having to where a moo-moo sort of bathing skirt. I didn't see her get in the water; she came up from behind and grabbed me by the hair, pulling me backwards and tried to hold me underwater. When I reached behind me and grabbed a wad of thigh in my hand, I knew it has Helen, so I pinched as hard as I could to wriggle free. I surfaced quite angry to her threatening me, "I'm not done with you yet, Buster...this isn't over." Pulling my hair put me in a foul mood with a foul reply.

"Helen, you can't convince anyone we took anything! Do I look like I ate all that food?" I said, presenting my skin and bones before her. "*You*, on the other hand..." as I waved my open palms towards her girth. She vowed to break me in half if she ever got her hands on me again; I didn't doubt her bad temper.

Oddly enough, she didn't seem to hold it against me for long. At the end of the season, the association which owns the camp treats all camp staff to a fine buffet at the Perkiomenville Hotel. Surprisingly, Helen chose to sit across from Rob and I. After throwing a few sincere Eddie Haskel lines at her about how lovely she looked in her dress, or sincere thanks for teaching me so much this summer, she softened up to the flattery. Recounting the summer's events, one of the girls at dinner did venture to ask Helen if the missing food was ever accounted for. She just smiled in a very charming way, and for the first time all summer she actually looked feminine. "I'll just say this; *next* summer, **no boys** on kitchen staff." And she wagged her finger knowingly at Rob and I while still grinning.

"But Helen, look at all the fun you'll miss," I stated innocently. Laughter filled the table again and all was well.

In retrospect, I don't think Helen ever disliked Rob or I; not on that first day and not even for snitching food. She would just over-react to the moment. In fact, we made her summer. In double fact, I *know* we made it an interesting summer for many people at Camp Firefly; certainly, for three little bridge jumpers. Several of the girls and staff told us that our joking, shenanigans, and romances were the life that little hill along the creek desperately needed. Now that it was all behind us and no one got hurt or fired, everything seemed to turn out fine. As we sat along the table that evening exchanging addresses with all our camp friends, "You guys better be coming back next year", or, "I'm not signing up next summer unless you guys are coming back" was the mantra among our friends. Then looking down the table at the resolve on Dr. Hildebrandt's face taking this in, and Helen's wry smile, I could see there was no way I'd be invited back. Well, it won't be the last place I wore out my welcome.

It's great to be liked. Being popular by doing the edgy things most people have the common sense to stay away from gave me shallow legitimacy for my actions; as long as I'm not caught or no one is getting hurt. Getting caught is a given. It's the getting hurt part that is always a gamble. Gamble, and you will lose. This summer, luck was surely with me. But that luck would run out.

CHAPTER 7

We Should Form a Union

Age 16-18 and more restless. Changed names have been italicized in their first presentation .

Spending that summer of 1968 as Joe Independent at Camp Firefly put me through some adolescent growth pangs. I had just been through the best summer of my short life and didn't want to come down from the high. Arriving back home, sleeping in my bedroom seemed very strange. The neighborhood looked smaller, my room looked smaller, my friends seemed boring, and worst of all, living again under the discipline of my parents' petty rules had me ready to explode. (Six years from now I will go through a similar awkward homecoming after returning from hitch-hiking around Europe most of a summer, hanging out with the bohemian element.) My world had expanded, now coming back made the place I grew up look insignificant in the grand scheme of things. *"Kicking around on a piece of ground in your home town, waiting for someone or something to show you the way,"* - Roger Waters lyric in 'Time'. For now, something had to give. I was starved for any adventure outlet to feed the independent free spirit, which just feasted all summer. Two events would present themselves in quick succession to meet that need.

The first was my introduction to marijuana. I never knew any dope smokers because they were few and far between at Haverford High School (HHS) in the fall of 1968. The few puffers kept it amongst themselves. No one I knew in the neighborhood or at school smoked. Bell bottoms and shoulder length hair were far from the norm yet at HHS. In nine months, all that will have changed. The Woodstock generation was just awakening and won't amass at Max Yasgur's farm until next summer.

Enter Jim *Wilson*, whom I knew from elementary school, now in my study hall. His parents had sent him to a reform school in England for a year and now he was back as a peace-nik. He remembered me as a neighborhood tough, so he felt safe asking where he could score some smoke. Jim was a 'Mad Comics' character personified with thick glasses, a studious demeanor, witty, cynical, and full of humorous anecdotes. I was clueless to his request or lingo. Coming from London, he couldn't believe that HHS and, specifically me, were not yet 'experienced'. He quipped, "Well, that has **got** to change or I'll have to get myself sent back for another stint at the Gulag," referring to his school in England where many of the kids were already 'turning on'. So over the next two weeks Jim answered all my questions and doubts about pot smoking, then sold me a few grams of hashish the next time he scored.

"Don't smoke it all at once and listen to this album with headphones," he advised as he handed me Cream's Disraeli Gears. "Satisfaction guaranteed," he promised with the certainty of a doctor prescribing a well-proven cure. And so, I was added to the emerging Woodstock generation.

Enter my old friend, Steve Sisca, the third part of our childhood trio from Chapter 1. Steve's mom had died of cancer a little over a year earlier, so Steve had fallen out of circulation while helping to take care of her at home before her passing. The rest of his time was spent working at his dad's store in South Philly where his dad could keep an eye on him. I ran into Steve trying to sell me bootleg cigarettes cheap, but I never liked cigarettes. He was getting cases of unstamped cigarette cartons from a contact he made at his dad's store, then selling them cheap to local hoods up at Manoa Lanes. He was on a cigarette delivery to some familiar names I had fought or known in the past, so I tagged along curious to see what these guys were up to. Actually, I was looking for someone with whom to try out the hash I just bought from Jim Wilson. Steve said these guys smoked anything and that he was up for trying it too.

These guys, the local misfits in their black leather jackets and Geoff caps, had recently started hanging out at a bowling alley known as Manoa Lanes, a central meeting point for several neighborhoods now that some kids were starting to drive. I singled out a few guys I knew pretty well, told them if they had a warm place to go (it was winter), I had a few grams to burn. "Yeah, *Scarfo's* parents are out all night and he has to watch his little brother, meet us at his house, just you and Sisca."

What can I say…that night was a blast. Me, pot, and my new friends were a perfect match. Let me be clear up front that even light drugs are nothing but a bigger problem waiting to happen. I don't do, condone, hang out with, or tolerate drugs for over 45 years now. Neither will I detail in this book pointless drug or drinking episodes; I would be boring both of us. However tonight, at this time in my life I did not know what door I had opened and everything was looking rosy. Surprisingly, we spent much of the night having wrestling matches in Scarfo's living room. This arose from some jovial bragging over who kicked whose butt a few years ago at some forgotten playground. Steve stayed out of the fray since he was never good with his hands or fighting in any form.

While wrestling *Ric Freilicht* that night, he became frustrated that he couldn't pin me after several attempts; nobody beats Ric. I told him to forget it; if we were boxing instead of wrestling, I wouldn't have a chance against him and that he could count on me if the need ever arose. With that I was officially initiated into Manoa Lanes, a growing gang of rejects from local neighborhoods. If Ric accepted me then everyone had to. No one wanted to mess with Ric.

Manoa Lanes, over the next year, grew into two distinct groups known as 'the Old Heads' and 'the Young Heads'. The old heads consisted of the 18 to 20 age group of township rejects, including a few returning Vietnam Vets with good drug connections, which they were reluctant to squander away to the younger guys. Getting busted was serious business until the mid-1970s and didn't relax to misdemeanor status (for small amounts) until the next decade.

The young heads consisted of about 12 guys aged 15 to 17. The gang was formed by its own momentum of like-minded kids being attracted to each other for a common union of power, intimidation, bravado, risk, daring, fun, independence, and adventure. The common bond was an unspoken understanding not to let anyone step on us, to stick up for each other, and whenever the opportunity presented itself, lash out against an unfair world putting us down. The other bond, of course, was drugs. Over the next few years, the bond of drugs would cave in on itself to destroy the first bond of brotherhood. Drugs (and ourselves) became our own worst enemy. Back then, drugs were a great divider and still are. Straight people didn't want to associate with dopers in case they got busted, or because they can't be trusted, or a lot of other good reasons. Dopers couldn't trust straight people because they might turn you in or tell the wrong people about you, but most of all because they hadn't 'opened their minds'. What a crock.

It was all a farce founded upon a lie from the very beginning, but at the time we thought it fitting that we should form a union of the strong and rejected. One of the unofficial prerequisites to being accepted into the Alleys is that you had either been in trouble with the police, thrown out of school, were a proven fighter, or deemed crazy enough from some previous occurrence to qualify the individual as a social reject. I met most of those criteria, but there were a few exceptions that didn't, like Steve Sisca. Steve was accepted because his cigarette scam kept everyone in smokes and he had a car, other than that he was squeaky clean. While his mom was alive, he was a reluctant momma's boy. With his mom's recent passing he was itching to make up for lost time. Steve had stood on the sidelines too long watching JoePec and I as we graduated from one neighborhood calamity to another. Steve wasn't permitted to hang around with us, but wanted to in the worst way. He was disgusted with being the shiny-shoed, 'keep your church clothes on all day Sunday' kid his mom tried to promote. Steve Sisca was ready to step out—way out. Steve thought trouble was good for trouble's sake and the reputation it got you. He lacked the concept of thinking an idea through so as not to get caught. As long as I was his handler, he was okay. When I stepped aside, he was a runaway train.

At this same time, my lifelong best friend Joe Peca was struggling with long-term illness that took him out of the picture a few years. Steve and I became brothers at the heart. He was also one of the first Young Heads to get his license and a car. Cars opened our jurisdiction beyond Haverford Township. He who had wheels had control. Not only did Steve have wheels, he always had money. In place of wheels, I had a strategic mind. Our resources were a good combination that I put to work at once to meet a need—drugs at a profit.

My first connection was with two other kids in high school who were starting to deal quantity but were not dependable. At this time 'quantity' was an ounce of hash or half a pound of pot. But still, you could turn it for a profit and smoke free all month. Being naturally cheap, dealing was the only way to smoke for free. Steve and I had money, wheels and a large base to sell to; what we needed desperately was a trusted dependable source. Pulling together quantity deals at HHS was difficult and sporadic. The devil was just sitting there waiting for this moment. Enter the devil himself. This time his name was Steve also; never gave a last name, just Steve "why would you need to know my last name", from Philadelphia.

At the beginning of senior high (which was 10th grade), the school sent home a form for your parents to sign and return. I opened and recognized it as the master signature form from which all future permission signatures will be compared against; you know, for sports permission, field trip permission, *excuse my son for missing school* permission. Hot dang! I'll just fill that in myself with my own penmanship in mom's name, lick here, drop off there, and BINGO! I'm clear to cut school for the next three years as long as I don't wear it out! I didn't wear it out until 12th grade.

Sometime around fall of 11th grade, I met Philly Steve, not to be confused with Steve Sisca. It was a beautiful autumn day so *Beau Gerhardt* and I used one of my self-allotted cut-school days to shop for clothes and hang out around the head shops at 20th and Samson Street in Philadelphia. There were a bunch of counter culture shops on that block known as Samson Village. One head shop, The Apparatus, had a big poster in the front window depicting all sorts of cannabis products bountifully spread out in a cornucopia. Beau and I were gawking at the poster and wishing out loud when this Steve walks up behind us to ask if we'd be interested in buying some of those sweet dreams.

Steve looked the typical University of Pennsylvania hippy type from that era with his blond unkempt frizzy hair and wire rim glasses on a thin Garfunkel face.

"Sure, but we don't have much money left, we just blew it on clothes," I explained.

"Too bad," he lamented, "I have some very fine Viet I'm sure you'd be pleased with. How much ($) do you have left?" he inquired curiously.

Beau and I conferred. "Only 10 bucks," we let on, not including our dinner money, subway, and bus fare home.

He looked around hesitantly then came back with, "OK, I usually don't do dimes but it's a slow day, so follow me." We followed our pied piper without speaking, curious as to how fine this Viet smoke would be.

Our new friend took us a few blocks to a center city townhouse on Locust Street he rented with other students. Once inside, he flipped us a doober to share. After a few hits, Beau and I were laughing and dumping out all our cash and coins on his cluttered coffee table. "Make that an ounce, Steve," we drooled, "you're right, we never had weed this good, we can panhandle to get subway fare and skip eating." He weighed out a precise 28 gram lid on a triple beam lab balance; that was unheard of for the deals I had ever been involved. No one we knew ever weighed out in front of the buyer; this guy could be trusted, a real professional. "What's the bigger scale for?" I asked pointing to a balance I had never seen before.

"Bigger deals," he stated obviously.

"How big," I asked.

"As big as your pocket can handle my friends."

"Wow! How about hash?" we both blurted out, stating our preferred smoke.

"Good deals on quarter pound breaks of Leb," Steve offered nonchalantly. "Acid and mescaline is available for a couple weeks right now, speed anytime." After talking price, delivery, passing phone numbers, code words, and best times to call, we were all hooked up. "I'll be in touch; you can be sure of that," I promised. I rode the subway home with visions of kilos dancing in my head. A chance meeting, a boy seeing a quick route to easy money, and free smoke, absolutely no consideration about getting caught, or respect for the laws—this is how one drifts away.

With Sisca's money and my new connection, we had the Alleys rolling in non-stop dope for the next school year, which created another problem. We were non-stop high, every day, all day, before school, during school, after school, every night, for the next two years. When you sell pot, it is customary to share with the buyer a gratis sample joint so they know what they're buying. 'Stoned' became a permanent state of mind. Straight days were non-existent. I took my SATs for college while on acid because I believed it made me brilliant, but couldn't keep the pencil from bending, so quit the exam because the utensil kept melting and falling out of my hand.

No one ever thinks when they get high that first time that they'd be high *all* the time or they never would have tried it. Like most of life's problems, you let one foot in the door and before you know it the problem is running the household. On school days, we mostly just smoked pot, but on weekends, concerts, parties, we'd do harder drugs. If the authorities (health education class, teachers, government, police) lied to us about pot being addictive, what else were they lying about. "Try it all" became our philosophy. We would be our own guinea pigs. Pot became the gateway to other drugs.

Along with bigger deals came other problems; like collecting money. Also, there were non-Manoa Lane kids getting busted and ratting me out to their parents or police, resulting in my need to have them 'disciplined' for ratting me out. The police stopped me once for an illegal random body search while walking home. Frustrated at finding nothing but matches (it was at the *end* of the night), they warned me it was only a matter of time before they nailed me. There was a certain Detective *Slueth* (not his real name) who really had it in for a few of us and wasn't shy about it. We countered by taunting him whenever we could get away with it.

Around this time (age – late 16), I had traded in my fighting ways for a fringed jacket. Dope had mellowed me out and I left the fighting to the other guys as much as I could. Everyone else was bulking up and filling out while I was stuck at a skinny 135 pounds. Had I not joined Manoa Lanes, it would have been too easy for old enemies to get their revenge on my scrawny frame. Ric Freilicht (nicknamed Washel) became my strong arm for collecting delinquent accounts. He relished this roll for a cut of the money or free dope. Those who owed me sometimes got their head pounded just for paying late. The COD method tightened up very fast once word got around Wash (pronounced as one word, *W-ash*) was my collection agency. We'd be driving down the street and I'd mention to Wash that the guy we just passed riding his bicycle owes me $20 ($100 in 2020 dollars). We'd go back around the block to come up behind the guy traveling the same direction. Just as the car came along side doing 25 mph, Ric would shove the car door open into the guy, sending him into space to land in some driveway bushes. This was commonly known in our circle as a 'door job'. While we were laughing it up, Wash went over to stand over the cowering heap and say, "*Thirty* bucks at Bonnetts' homeroom tomorrow morning or more bike riding lessons." The extra 10 bucks were Ric's' fee.

Some insight into the person of Ric Freilicht will give you a good idea of the mentality of our socially defective gang. A few decades ago, I started seeing 'NO FEAR' bumper stickers on the cars of teens. I'd always think of Ric, Mikey *McNicol*, or Steve *Underhill* when I saw those stickers. If we were cruising town 'back in the day', and came up on some stranger dumb enough to hang that sticker on their car, or to test us in any way, I know exactly how Ric would respond to it; he would see it as a direct challenge. Once the challenge was presented, he'd turn to me and grin, "Now you *know* what has to be done here, don't you Rich?"

"Oh yeah, but wait for the next red light, Wash."

Wash would then walk up to the driver for no reason other than the joy of fighting, open the door, pull the guy out, and ask him if would like a lesson on fear. Ric was one of the few guys I ever knew who *was* fearless. "No Fear" stickers didn't exist back then, but I had seen Ric do this very thing because someone gave him the wrong look at a stop light. For me, watching him in action was always a curiosity to behold from a sociological point of view. Of course, we thrived on putting him in those moments. He was one of a kind. The following story is a good example of Ric surprises we were sometimes thrown into.

Some jock was throwing a keg party at a girl's house from school. Some girls we liked and wanted to get to know better were going to be there. Steve or Timmy actually got invited to the party by one of the girls. Ric, Scarfo, and I invited ourselves along. The conversation before we arrived was along the lines of, "No trouble, no fights tonight, we're here to meet girls." Since Ric had brought his girlfriend along, and she knew the girls, we figured he would behave.

We were let in with a bit of skepticism but no major problem. With what seemed like a quarter of the HHS football team there, we stuck out like sore thumbs, but were used to it. After an hour or so, it seemed all was going to be mellow tonight when without any notice other than "watch this and get ready", Wash went over to the keg and called for everyone's attention.

"Oh no," we thought in a 'not again' sort of way. I knew enough from previous experience to get off the sofa and into position, so did my friends. *Position* is a good place to push someone into a window or over furniture once the inevitable fight breaks out. When you're outnumbered, *any tactic* is fair.

Ric starts, "I'm getting the uncomfortable vibe that some of you jocks are thinking you're better than me and my friends here," he said in a cocky way while staring at the football players. "Now I didn't come here to start trouble, but you're not making me feel very welcome, so if any of you think you can kick MY ass…" He hesitates while looking over the room, "You need to let me know right now so I can get that cleared up." No one said a word. While saying this, Wash has a big grin on his face like he is having more fun than anyone in the room. Not content with that, and now visibly disappointed at no challengers, Wash then proceeded to strut around the room staring down one or two of the team players until they look away. They knew Washel, they knew they had maybe a second to look away or he would be on them like lightning. Wash truly loved to fight. Some of these guys out-weighed Ric, but I never saw that stop him. I never saw him lose a fight either. Most guys only fight if they have to. Ric HAD too, and to his genuine disappointment had trouble finding opponents in Havertown. After making his way to the other side of the room, he announced, "Thank you, I just needed to get that out of the way," he beamed with his brilliant signature clam faced smile. "Now that we are all in agreement that I am the greatest*, you may now enjoy to all the *free* beer you want, enjoy the party and don't forget to thank the host." Up until then the jocks had been charging $ at the keg.

I won't go into any more detail about the fights he got us or himself into, but we all learned from Wash that it wasn't just winning a fight that mattered but the genuine projection of loving to fight that so intimidated would-be opponents and brought him respect. Unfortunately, fighting was the only field where Ric excelled. Fortunately, I did not have this killer instinct, but was glad Ric did. To us, he was a riot waiting to happen, we edged him on whenever things got slow.

* * 'I am the greatest' is a Mohammed Ali line (his hero) Ric loved and often used.

In the beginning, before we had money, when our new-found union first started chumming around, our scams were small. "Garaging" was a favorite sport of ours that provided many thrills, chases and, cop dodging. Let me explain how Garaging worked. First of all, at 16 you're too young to buy beer so you have to get someone to "run" for you. ("Run" is a term used for getting someone legal age to buy beer for you.) This wasn't always reliable and you still had to have the needed money to buy the beer. Garaging was our way around this dilemma even though it involved a bigger risk such as minor burglary. For me, stealing the beer was more fun than drinking the beer. It was ventures like this that drew me to hanging out at the Alleys.

Garaging 101

Saturday afternoons from April to September was prime time to walk or cruise our suburban neighborhoods in teams looking for our quarry. On Saturdays, the men of these suburban homes were deeply immersed in their routines of lawn maintenance, washing the family car, or working with power tools in the garage. The important thing was that the *garage door was open* for most of the day while they plied their domestic talents. Often these open garages contained the booty of beer, stored there by its rightful owner where it would stay cool or where it was held as a staging area before making the final leap to the refrigerator. A refrigerator in the garage was counted as beer sighted; every garage refrigerator has beer in it, who doesn't know that! If the garage was open but not facing the street, one of us would walk up the driveway acting like they were looking for the Smith residence and scope out the garage.

The idea was to reconnoiter open garages that had visible cases of beer or a refrigerator showing, write down the address then come back after dark to creep into the unlocked garage, and snitch the beer. This was before the paranoia of security swept through the suburbs, creating the home security protection systems we know today. Most people didn't lock their garages back then, neither were electric garage doors a common item; only the wealthy had electric garage doors in 1969. Holiday weekends such as Memorial Day, July 4th, and Labor Day were particularly fruitful times when folks were planning a party and stocked up on beverages.

Ideally, the later you go Garaging the more likely the owners will be in bed; even more ideal if they were out for the night, particularly Saturday nights. Since Garaging wouldn't start until after 9:30 p.m., we wouldn't start putting down a few warm ones until close to midnight, which is late for a mid-teen to start putting on a buzz. So usually, a night of Garaging also meant a sleep out.

A sleep out is a matter of one guy telling his folks he'll be sleeping over Steve's, while Steve says he's sleeping over Rich's, etc. In truth no one is sleeping over anyone's house but instead all meet at a park or large wooded lot to ditch a sleeping bag and camp there. On one particular July night, six of us had chosen a park just a few doors down from Scarfo's house, which had a small stream to cool the liberated brews.

Now Garaging is a skill learned by example and not approached without training. On your first night Garaging, you are always a 'runner' and not yet trusted to do the actual garage entry. The runner is the guy to whom the goods are handed off to after the initial snitch. Usually the hand-off is over a cyclone fence or other barrier to discourage any pursuer from following his stolen beer once handed off. The guy who handed off the cargo is supposed to keep the pursuer running after him instead of the beer. Beer handed off would then be run to some predetermined bushes to stash the cargo until he is sure there is no pursuit. Next, if no car is available, as often was the case in the early years, he would employ a shopping cart into service, hiding the cargo under cardboard boxes or whatever ingenuity should provide as conveyance to transport our cargo along well-lit streets to the wooded park. You were never home safe until the cases of beer were safely back at the park. Cops would stop us for something as suspicious as a kid pushing a shopping cart at midnight. So, if a police car so much as saw us, the load was abandoned and feet took off. To assure success, some six-packs or cases were stashed here and there along the route home to the park for retrieval later or the next day. Once at the park, it was a camp fire and beer till dawn unless the refreshment induced grander ideas to pursue throughout the night.

On a typical encounter, getting the beer out of the garage was a race between the moment the rightful owner heard his garage door open and the new owners liberated the bottled hostages. This is why the hand-off to the runner was so important. One, the runner was always strategically placed on the other side of a fence or other chase impediment such as a series of backyard mazes so as to lose or thwart the pursuer. Two, a pursuer who was often out of shape and puffing would give up the chase when he saw his beer just receive a fresh set of young legs. The predetermined stash point also allowed the runner to stash the load around a bend and run freely without the burden if the homeowner decided to follow his Schlitz Premium. The pursuer wouldn't know where the ale was stashed during the chase since we were cutting through and around a bunch of adjoining backyards in the dark. The offended would rather go call the cops. Then it was a race between the patrolling cops and our knowledge of backyard shortcuts in our respective neighborhoods. For us, there was nothing like an adrenaline pumping chase of hide and seek with the police to make us feel alive.

Actually, the chase was the darling of our heist and if we hit, say, two garages without a chase, we would be a bit disappointed and emboldened at the last garage so as to guarantee a chase. So, with Garaging now explained, let me tell you a story about a comical night.

As just mentioned, on this particular night in July we already had enough beer from two successful hits. Not content with warm beer, we were now trying for cold ones in a garage harboring a vintage old refrigerator. Refrigerator hits were always held for last since we would rather drink cold ones. Though their brewski was cold, a refrigerator rarely held the quantity as, say, warm emerald Rolling Rock cases stacked along the wall. Refrigerators, unfortunately, often only yielded a six pack or two.

Washel and I were the Garagers tonight; Peeps was the first runner. I volunteered to work the garage door (doorman), which meant Wash would slide under the door to check the fridge. You only had to get the garage door open enough to slide your body under; a full opening risked too many squeaking springs and noticeable noise familiar to the homeowner. The doorman stayed at the door to watch for cars or heave the door up for the Garagers' quick escape should bedroom lights go on. We always had to be ready to bolt outta there.

Wash slipped under with his flashlight and disappeared. Usually the next thing I would hear is the jingling of bottles, or a case would come sliding out from under the door like a shuffleboard cock, but tonight nothing came sliding out. Getting down on my hands and knees, I peered into the dark garage, no sign of Wash's flashlight at all.

"PSSST! Wash, what's up!" I whispered loudly. No reply.

Just as I lay down to slither under the door and investigate, the door goes flying up all the way with the accompanying squeaks and deep house rumbles associate with opening garage doors. There stood Washel over me with a mouth full of cookies, laughing at the stunned look on my face, spitting out crumbs with his assessment.

"I think they're out for the night" he stated assuredly. "There's chicken in the kitchen fridge if you want some," he said in comic dryness like he lived there. A door inside the garage opened to the kitchen; there, a low light was on from where Wash had just emerged.

"You sure there's no one home?" I asked pointing to the car in the driveway.

"No, but I'm sure we'll find out in about two more seconds!" he laughed.

"Oh man. Wash!" I chuckled, incredulous at his boldness. Then we both hushed to listen if anyone was stirring in the house. Sometimes you could hear beds creaking or someone alarmed talking in the bedroom above the garage. Nothing.

"Are there any cold ones in the fridge?" I asked, making my way towards the garage refrigerator.

"Yeah, and a case next to the fridge."

"I'll load up on singles from the fridge; you take the case," I instructed.

I had just shut the fridge door after sticking a bottle in every pocket, loading my beltline with more bottles, and loading as many as my arms could hold when a heavyset guy in a T-shirt stood in the kitchen door and turned on the garage light to see Washel standing under the garage door with the case of beer, waiting for me. Lucky for me, once he spotted Wash, the guy never looked to his left where I was frozen. He immediately took pursuit after the ghost of Ric who disappeared behind a chuckling, "Time to go!" Had the guy looked left and taken two steps, he would've had me cornered.

In an instant, the garage was quiet as though nothing had happened. I waited two long seconds, then took off. Washel had run out the garage and cut a quick **left** into the guy's backyard. At the back of his yard was a four-foot cyclone fence screened by a row of five-foot bushes. Behind these bushes waited Peeps for the hand-off. All Peeps ever saw of that case was it smashing on the ground 10 feet behind him after Wash shot-put the thing from a full run with the warning, "Here it comes!" The beer never had a chance. Immediately after the beer crashed, Wash came hurtling over the fence yelling at Peeps for not catching the load. With the two blaming each other for the smashed beer on their side of the fence, the owner of said beer started cursing out the thieves from the other side:

"I'm calling the cops!" came the familiar refrain.

Peeps looked at Wash. "That's the owner, I take it."

"You want me to introduce him?" Wash joked.

"Real smooth job, Wash."

Once over the fence, this particular backyard bordered the back of Manoa Shopping Center where a wide strip of grass separated the fence and parking lot. Wash and Peeps were rooting through the smashed case for survivors when the police, on routine night patrol of the shopping center, saw them and ordered them to freeze. Obediently, they both jumped the fence again, one yard down from where Wash had first jumped. When the owner of the smashed beer saw them in his neighbors' yard, he took up fresh pursuit through the backyards in a row.

In the meantime, I had run out the garage turning **right** for about four houses before bearing right again to cut through a backyard to Manoa Shopping Center. As I'm cutting through the backyard, Wash and Peeps zoom right by me laughing with no time for explanations. Looking right, this guy in his T-shirt has his eyeballs glued on me now; so I turn back from whence I came toward the street, not knowing the cops are now involved and will have backup on the street any minute.

With an armful of shaken beer and my loaded pockets heading to my knees, I had no choice but to jettison. So with the burgled homeowner puffing in hot pursuit, I loped down the middle of the street lobbing shaken Schaeffer's one by one on a high arc behind me until I was able to get my pants back into running position. Bottles landed with the popping vengeance of aggravated fermentation set free. They were chasers for my chaser! Though not hitting him directly, a few exploding bottles must have sprayed him with beer and broken glass enough that he gave up what chase he had left.

He stood there in the road cursing me as I slowed down to a backwards trot watching him. Headlights turned down the street on me and in an instant the twirly lights of Haverford's finest were flashing as the Cruiser accelerated in my direction. I cut back to the backyards, playing hide and seek with several cops for the next half an hour while working my way back to the park where beer, friends, laughs, and stories awaited. Fearing the police might see the flicker of a fire in the park, the decision was made to forego any fire tonight.

The evening's escapades shifted with the dawning of a new day. Because we couldn't risk a campfire, the mosquitoes ate us up pretty bad the rest of the night. In our inebriated state, we fell asleep nowhere near our sleeping bags and awoke at first light, miserable and all bit up. Dozens of mosquito bites covered our clammy beer-stinking bodies. When beer is free and warm, it often gets shaken and popped at a buddy. We had to clean up before going home. That meant Pool Hopping.

Pool Hopping 101

Now Pool Hopping is another fine suburban sport that requires a little explaining before I can conclude this story. Pool Hopping is merely the act of using a stranger's pool without permission for as long as possible before getting run-off, then hopping off to another pool on another street. The term *Hopping* came from the fact that we usually just hopped in for a five-minute swim, then hopped back out before getting caught. Prime time to Pool Hop was late at night or while it was certain the homeowner was away. Stealth was the key factor determining how much time one had to enjoy the pool. The idea was to quietly sneak in to a backyard, slip into the water without splashing, and just cool off while sipping on a beer. If it was a particularly nice pool, we would always leave quietly so the owner wouldn't notice. The idea was to return again and again. There were only so many pools in our neighborhood and we had our favorite pools.

As mentioned, we awoke miserable and bug eaten after a few hours' sleep. Just a short walk from the park lived an older wealthy couple with grown kids who had a preferred pool which Ric, Tom, and Scarfo often frequented since it was in their neighborhood; so it was the logical choice. I forget if it was the only pool to be hopped that morning, it was certainly the last.

Approaching our chosen country club this morning, the dares started to fly. It was around 6 a.m. on a Sunday morning and we were still a bit juiced from a night of consumption. Since the best remedy for a hangover was to chase it away with a few more beers, we were in vintage form to accept the most absurd dares presented.

"I dare you to go naked on this hop," someone presented.

"No problem, I'll streak this hop." Wash grinned back in defiance to the challenge, "But you all have to give me your share of the remaining beer," he bargained.

"Hell, I'll do it for less than that," we agreed in unison.

"All right then. Each guy has to skinny-dip to *keep* his share of the beer," said Wash, upping the ante to get everyone involved.

"Done," we all agreed and started to laugh at the prospect. Bob Conaboy who joined us late the previous night was the only one to back out.

We quietly made our way to the pool area, stripped down to our birthday suits and slipped into water, grinning the whole time. Some guys threw their hop reeking clothes in the water to soak, I had the presence of mind to hang my clothes over the fence in one bundle easy to grab.

Silently, we each picked our spot in the pool to kick back and finish off a bottle as if we owned the joint. Bob Conaboy stretched out on a chaise lounge like he was assigned kiddy patrol to watch over us. Within a few minutes, a palatable calm required us to do something to make the dare more risky, so a new deal was offered up by Wash; he was just too eager to win the remaining beer.

"I'll dive off the diving board for the rest of the beer," he whispered, realizing the bid was too low for the prize as soon as the words left his mouth.

"No way!" we all shook our heads as we thought for a moment of a better challenge.

"How 'bout this," I beamed. "We *all* have to do a cannonball off the board." I laughed, knowing the occupants of the house would surely wake up when they heard the commotion in their pool. "Then when the owner comes out, the LAST guy out of the pool wins all the beer," I said, sure the challenge was too good to turn down. We all had visions of the guy running around the edge of his pool, cursing five naked teens who would be laughing at each other waiting to see who would chicken out first and who would stay last for the prize. It was too good to pass up.

"Yeah, that's good, that's real good!" everyone agreed.

Some of us went off the diving board and a few off the side. There were cannon balls, jack knifes, belly flops—anything that made a loud splash. The diving board was loudly bouncing on its mount with each artistic leap. We were laughing in anticipation of what would happen next. I noticed movement at a second-floor window.

"Well they're out of bed now," I warned.

Thick suspense hung in the air for the next few seconds as nothing happened.

"What gives? You think they're calling the cops first?" wondered Scarf.

"Get out then," said Wash hoping to increase the odds of his winning.

"You first, buddy," I retorted, swimming closer to where my clothes hung for a quick exit. I had no intention of winning this one. Wash, on the other hand, we all knew, would not get out unless he was the last guy, even if the Pope asked him.

There was a sliding glass door with drapes drawn shut facing the pool; the five of us had our eye on those drapes…waiting…waiting. A single hand came from behind the drapes, unlocked the door and slowly slid it open about 18 inches. There was a second delay and then all hell let loose when two German Shepherds came barking out of the house on command like we stole their breakfast.

"When did they get dogs!" screamed Scarfo.

Now *we* were on the menu as the brutes planned on exacting his pound of flesh from the slowest hiney offered. Ten eyes popped out of shock and

131

curses flew as the canines worked in tandem to corral anyone who tried to get out of the water. The dog's master was in his glory, psyching the dogs with, "Get 'em! Go get 'em!" The team was barking mad.

Someone was attempting to give instructions to distract the dogs while a few of us could get out, but I saw my opportunity when the dog at my end jumped in, nearly on top of us. In a second, I was out of the water. In two giant steps, I was diving through the hedges over the fence while grabbing my clothes in one acrobatic motion. I landed on my back but didn't feel a thing, nor did I notice the scrapes in my birthday suit. Job one was to get away from those jaws. So I ran for all I was worth down Eagle Road in broad daylight; naked as a jay-bird until I thought I was far enough away to franticly struggle with jeans over wet skin.

As I repeatedly fell over in my haste to run and shimmy pants on; I looked back at the house just a few hundred feet away. Some guys had run out the driveway gate, heading in the opposite direction from me; a few naked bodies came flying through the same hedges I had parted. One dog had flown out the gate and turned in my direction for the guys who just cleared the hedges. I took off again as they approached. Just across the street and parallel to me, Washel was running full bore, barely staying out the Shepherd's bite. I glanced over to see Fido nipping at Rics bouncing buns. The poor guy was doing his darndest to keep his hams out of those snapping jaws by arching his back as he ran. It is one of the most comical snapshots captured in my mind to this day, chuckling as I write.

To be sure the dog wouldn't change course and come after me instead, I cut into backyards and hopped a few fences. The other comedy worth mentioning is that I was one of two guys able to grab my clothes before getting out of there. The other guys had to circle back naked to the park to fetch sleeping bags to wrap around themselves and sneak into their own homes that way. Wash said he snatched his sleeping bag on a full run and was able to fend off the dog with it while he backed up to the park fence and hopped over it to safety, losing the bag to the dog. He then had the honorable humiliation of trotting home another eight blocks or so in his birthday suit on a Sunday morning.

Of course, the story wouldn't be complete unless the cops caught us. The owner of the pool had called the police and described us well enough and had a few sets of clothes for the police (never carried ID or wallet on Garaging events). A patrol car picked up Bob Conaboy walking home. Thinking he was in the clear, he didn't see them coming. Also, when the police pulled up they addressed him by name (the cops knew most of us), and presented some left behind clothes, so there was no use in running. Bob, having the physique of a junkie with aids, knew running wasn't his strong point but could think fast on his feet. He was brought in for questioning at the police station and acknowledged our names once the cops told *him* our names from the pool owner's description and the clothes left behind. They also asked him a lot of questions about a garage break-in at the Sunny Hill section of town last night. Bob thought it best to throw them the bone of our names over the pool episode, but denied all knowledge of any garage theft. It was a good tactic; none of us would fault him. If the cops were slightly on the ball, they would have rounded us all up and had the owner of the beer come pick out Ric and I as the thieves. But the cops knew we would just deny it and it was too small cookies to bring to court.

Contentedly thinking they had us on property invasion for the pool trespassing or something else hardly worth pressing, the police never pursued the garage incident. Fortunately for us, we had not destroyed any property, broken into the pool or house, nor did they have any witnesses of our nudity beyond the pool (for a public nudity charge). The police could harass us on trespassing charges, but the pool owner must have decided against filing charges for fear of any retribution. I imagine seeing the look on our faces when he let the dogs out was enough satisfaction for him, so nothing happened with the police. But we didn't know all this at the time and spent another nervous few days wondering if the phone or doorbell would ring with an officer describing another embarrassing charge to our folks. Chases, dares, and risk are an adrenaline junkie's life blood. This was the addiction that glued us so tight to each other in those early days. How far could we push the envelope of daring before we had to pay the price?

Garaging later became the larder for more than beer. As time went on, it became a dependable source for tires on our cars, or whatever else we could find of value to use or sell. Wash entering that kitchen also demonstrated how easy it was to walk into someone's home. So that is how thieves start out, they always start small—the Hecklers house, some beer, a few cookies from a kitchen. This is how stealing cars gets started too; you start out small by "borrowing" a car from someone too intimidated to turn you into the police.

Stealing the occasional car was always an adventure; we threw an unusual twist into it though. Usually, the theft was from someone we knew and could intimidate, like some kid from school. Then we'd tell him that if he didn't report it to the cops, he'd get his car back in one piece when it ran out of gas. The victim always complied after futile pleading and frustration. Usually, the next day in school, we'd even tell the panicked kid where it ran out of gas. Sometimes we'd *borrow* each other's parents' car for the joke of it. It had to be your parents' car though; the joke was to see if the guys' folks would catch him 'losing the car'. Try explaining to mom and dad you don't know where the family car is, but not to call the police. You're sure it will turn up in a day or two; that was hilarious to us.

My initiation occurred with my mother's VW Bug soon after I started driving. We were always driving each other's car anyway. On this occasion up at the Alley's, Steve went to run a short errand in my mom's VW and didn't come back. They all loved that VW Bug and had talked Steve into hijacking it. When it happened, I didn't know if they got in trouble with the car or if it was my turn to get goofed on. So you go home, wondering if you should tell your mom you don't know where the car is or wait a day or two in the hopes she doesn't notice it missing before it finally turns up. Or don't go home at all until it turns up; it's easier to explain an all-nighter to my folks than losing the car. In my case it happened on a weekend in winter when my mom didn't miss the car. Steve told me Sunday morning the Bug was parked on Walnut Hill Lane behind my street…almost out of gas. 'Borrowing' the car was only half the fun. Listening to the story the guy had to tell his folks was the other half. You had to laugh with them, I loved those clowns.

Well, as you can imagine, hanging at the Alleys was nonstop adventure. A week couldn't pass without some sort of calamity. That's what kept me there throughout those valuable developmental years. I can say with all honesty that I could count on one hand the nights I stayed home in that two-and-a-half-year period.

The drugs got progressively worse until most of us realized it was a way of life no one was walking away from. Physical addictions were not a problem yet but, like I said, it was a way of life. As time progressed, a few guys would start carrying guns. My common sense told me it was just a matter of time before one of us got killed. More than a few times I woke up the next morning thinking, "Amazing no one got killed last night," then shrug it off. Imagine if the homeowner in that garage greeted us with a gun. The invincibility of youth had been much too kind to our little gang. That was about to change in another year.

Eventually, by age 18 my common sense started to wonder: where is all this going to take me? I wondered if I would have been a different person if had spent my teen years straight. Finally, my mom caught me growing two-foot starter plants (pot) in my bedroom. Now she was wiser to the drugs and this answered a lot of her questions why strangers came and went from my bedroom all the time. None of us even wanted to *try* to quit drugs, we enjoyed them too much, and *everything* revolved around them. Drugs fed the era of social revolution that was turning the previous norms upside down; drugs were becoming common place, sexual freedoms were breaking all boundaries, rampant political corruption was being exposed, government couldn't be trusted, civil unrest was in the news every day, politicians were getting shot, religion was being challenged on all fronts, being replaced by rock bands and their Pied Piper lyrics we set our watches to. Then the National Guard shot 17 students at Kent State University, killing four; that really blew my mind. There were no absolute truths left to hang your hat on. The motto of the 1970s was, "If it feels good, do it" and "Try it, you'll like it." Timothy Leary, a Berkley professor, was teaching kids to "Turn on, tune in, and drop out".

The old morality flipped 180° in a matter of five years. Our generation was giving birth to Moral Relativity, the new religion in town. What is moral is only relative to your point of view. And if your morals don't meet someone else's morals, that's okay because we are individually our own judge and jury.

All of this had created a generation gap that pitted us against them, the WWII generation, today properly acknowledged as "The Great Generation". When **The Who** came out with the lyrics *Hope I Die Before I Get Old* in their song *My Generation*, we sang it like a new national anthem. Among this society in flux, our little gang was creating our own ride. In our minds, this rent in the social fabric of our day justified our gang. There wasn't too much we were feeling guilty about. Society was learning to question all the rules. I had been questioning all the rules since the first grade.

By 18, I had too many close calls getting busted for drugs; I knew that candle was burning low too. I once had a state policeman search my car and *miss* a half pound of pot visibly jammed in a VW door pouch only because he was so intent in looking under the seats. Back then if you were caught with anything larger than an ounce, you were considered a dealer and dealt with seriously. On another close call, Detective Sleuth came to my house to serve me a court summons while we were dividing up a kilo and partying; I thought he was Steve so I opened the door when he rang the bell—good thing I didn't just yell "come in" as I normally would. If that detective had listened at the door to our conversation or had *looked* past me into the next room or if he had used his nose and gone for a search warrant, we all would have been right where the police were trying so hard to put us. We could never get over the fact that he handed me a summons and just left. I thought he was there to bust me when I opened my door. I was so stone shocked at thinking I was being arrested that I just stood there in the doorway staring at him as he read me the summons. I thought he was reading a search warrant and everyone in the next room froze. He tried to hand me the summons, but I was too stunned to reach for it. He jammed the papers in my shirt pocket, poked his finger in my chest and said, "You'd better be there (in court), pal!" then walked away. We scattered like flies thinking he saw what we were up to and would be back, but nothing happened. Opportunity lost.

Soon after that episode, Joe Peca and I got caught red-handed smoking dope by a Marple policeman. I just continued denying possession before the cop. I had tossed the evidence and then accused the cop of setting us up when he retrieved the tossed evidence.

If you're wondering how we kept the drug use from our parents, we didn't succeed very well. Nearly all of parents caught us red-handed doing, possessing, or growing. Mrs. Gerhardt caught us regularly and threatened to call our parents and the cops. So did Mrs. Freilicht. It was usually comical when Mrs. Freilicht caught us because she would yell at us in rapid fire German while we stood there saying "Yah, Yah," and shaking our heads in agreement. She spoke little English. Her husband (Washel's dad) was in the Nazi SS and emigrated here after WWII on some special visa deal after exchanging valuable war information. He died shortly after coming to the USA. His picture in full SS uniform hung on the living room wall and always drew our attention when hanging out at his house.

One Saturday morning while getting high under the watchful eyes of the SS picture in Ric's living room, his mom came home early from work unexpectedly, or we lost track of time (more likely). She came through the front door and went into a rage swinging her big pocketbook to destroy our homemade water pipe sitting on her nice coffee table. Wash intercepted the pipe and ran into the dining room while *still* trying to get a hit off the lit pipe, protecting the recently filled bowl of herb. He had placed his back to his mother while she beat on him and yelled in German. This blew our mind (Kevin and I) so we tried to sneak out the front door. Mutt (mother in German) dragged us back inside and lectured us in thick, accented German, smacking us lightly now and then for emphasis. We'd promise to go to confession with our sin to speak to a priest (she was a strict Catholic) just to get out of there, trying not to laugh at Wash who was grinning and toking on the water pipe behind her as she railed at us. It was like being in a cartoon.

Back to the local police; by now the cops knew us all and hated the reputation our gang gave their jurisdiction; it was constant war with them. They weren't shy to lay into us physically either. Wash loved to pick fights with one rookie cop in particular. This resulted in his being handcuffed and arrested. I realized I was never cut out to be Joe Citizen around the time I found myself standing by and rooting for my friend as he wrestled an officer on the ground. When the police backup sirens got too close, we scattered. Ric couldn't bring himself to run from a fight even when it meant arrest, so he'd be the screen for us to get away.

One time, with Lori (now my wife) standing next to me, a Marple Newtown officer laid into me so fast I was on my back before I knew what hit me. Seeing I was about to get a follow-up barrage from the enraged cop, I yelled to Lori, "Make sure you remember who started this police abuse when I get him into court." It was the first thing to come into my head to stop him. Those two magic words "police brutality" back then reigned in a lot of rogue policeman. Even with the magic words, they still held me an hour for questioning at the police station before letting me go. Again, I just denied everything, threw the dice, and challenged them to produce a witness. I was guilty as sin but knew how their own procedures constrained them and worked the system in my favor. I finally demanded to be released or I'd sue for abuse and harassment. That's how cocky and sure of ourselves we were back then. They had to let me go. Did we *ever* get prosecuted? Sure, we had our days in court. That will come later.

There was no truth, just *their* laws vs. *our* laws; Moral Relativity.

Our Second Commandment: Thou shall not get caught.

The Third Commandment kicked in when the second failed: Thou shall deny all guilt.

The Fourth Commandment kicked in when the first three failed: Thou shall get a good lawyer to do a better job at the Third Commandment.

The Fifth Commandment: Thou shall not worry about what God thinks, he has left the building.

So what is the First Commandment you ask? In our words it was:

"Get, before you get got" and we all had that memorized. It translated to, Get over on them (society), before they get a chance to get over on you. This was solely based on the idea that everyone was against us.

Briefly, why would someone still so young (16–18) be so jaded about his view of society? Well you've been reading the stories. Dad, nuns, teachers, etc., all the authorities in my life have convinced me I'm no good. I can't stay out of trouble as hard as I may try, can't get good grades in school, or excel in anything society respects. If a kid doesn't fit in with the good crowd, where will he naturally turn? It's not rocket psychology; go where you are accepted, especially if it's a lot more fun to hang there.

One thing was sure, at this rate I recognized I wasn't going to live to a ripe old age. Neither were any of the other guys from the Manoa Lanes. If you read between these lines you can see there is much I can't write about and have no will to record, you should be getting the idea by now. As you can see, the only thing we tried to avoid was getting caught. Once we turned 18, the stakes got a lot higher. Previously, it was just a matter of having your folks come sign for you at the police station and taking you home. Now 18, if we got caught for the kind of things we were doing, people could press charges, take us to court, send us away… I should have gotten out right then.

Moving on now; when most people back then think of being in a street gang, they conjure up images of West Side Story with knives, chains, and a gun or two—the quintessential gangland fight. No gang membership would be complete without one. So here we go…this one was a doozey…and had the fingerprints of Steve and I all over it.

CHAPTER 8

The Worst Night of My Life

Senior year of High School, 1971
Italicized names have been changed in their
first appearing.

I had just turned 17 when my parents gave up trying to discipline me. My dad was 61, semi-retired, and done raising his hand against me. He just got too weary of it all concerning me. Gone were the groundings, curfews, and car restrictions. Mom was the only one to see my good side and hold out any hope in my direction, though she let me go my own way too by now. My brother and sister had married (not each other), which allowed my parents to start traveling. Dad's main concern was that I didn't get drafted for the Vietnam War next year. Mom hoped a nice girl would straighten me out. She was always praying for her children and trusted God to watch over us. She'll never know how much those prayers were needed, particularly on this night.

Picking one night to call the worst in my life would not be entirely accurate. However, this story would definitely make it into the top three. The reason it stands out above any others? Four days of dreaded anticipation leading up to this night. The other incidents that could qualify as runners-up for worst night happened spontaneously without time to think about what lay ahead. These four days allowed me too much time to think, fear, dread, and speculate an outcome I knew to be inevitably terrible.

Until I actually experienced it, I thought uncontrollable knocking knees were something that only happened in cartoons. The fact is that when you are *really* frightened, your knees will knock and wobble till they can't hold you up anymore. You have not known fear until your legs won't hold you up. You can also faint from fear; that's because your brain shuts down before your knees had time to knock. *Terror*, on the other hand, is not the same, terror is to face death (real or perceived) only to realize you are totally unprepared to die…and you can't stop the clock; that instant of panic is terror. Terror is only realized just before you die, or *think* you are about to die. I have experienced terror once, when I was a kid and blacked out. The last thought in my head before fainting was, 'Oh no, I'm going to die.' The term 'Terrorist' in the media has been much overused for sensationalism, those folks are actually *fearist,* that is until they are actually holding a gun to your head, *then* they are terrorist. Hey – *fearist,* new word! It is impossible to exist in a state of constant terror as properly defined; you would lose your mind from the constant terror. Those we call terrorists today have people in a state of constant, varying degree of fear. I have seen the look of terror in young men's faces. It happened in this story.

———————————

Sue *McGarvey* and Kathy *Fallon* worked behind the counter at the local bakery on the corner across from Manoa Lanes. Steve and I used to stop in to satisfy our munchies on cold nights. They let us get out of the cold on winter nights at the donut shop because they liked us and felt safe from weirdoes while we were there. Often, we would drive the girls home or hang out together after closing for the night. We soon became sweet on each other, nothing serious though; I think it was the donuts.

Friends would sometimes call the girls at the bakery shop looking for us. The bakery was on the corner of West Chester Pike and Eagle Road, a major intersection that gave the girls a good vantage to see who stopped at the traffic light, who was cruising with whom, that sort of thing. The shop was empty on weeknights and the girls had nothing better to do than check out who was cruising around. If you had trouble finding someone, it was always worth stopping into the bakery or calling to ask Sue and Kathy if so and so had cruised by.

One Tuesday night while hanging out at the bakery, Kathy answered the phone and started arguing with some guys, telling them not to come to the shop. As she was speaking on the phone, Sue explained to Steve and I that they were a couple of guys from Long Lane in Upper Darby who couldn't take "No" for an answer. Steve grabbed the phone and told the guy never to call this number again and hung up; the girls went pale. "Oh man, you shouldn't have said that, those guys are crazy like you guys but older!" The phone rang again, Kathy tried to get past Steve but Bruin (his nickname) picked up first while Sue listened on the other line.

"Who is this?" Steve demanded.

"You better hope you never have to find out" was the stoic reply on the other end.

"If you ever bother these girls again, we'll set your car on fire, got it?" Bruin barked into the receiver, and promptly hung up before any reply could be made.

Sue was still on the other phone listening to this guy's reply in silent fear. "I'll tell them, but don't come here," she said and hung up.

"You guys better get out of here," she warned us, "He said he's gonna round up a few of his boys and be here as soon as he can."

"How crazy are we talking here?" I interrupted, a bit concerned. "Do these guys carry knives or guns?" I thought we should know what we are dealing with.

"I don't know but I know they have a gang like you guys called Long Lane and you better not be around when they get here…not in the shop anyhow." Sue was worried about the place getting wrecked.

"Tell them to stop at the bowling alley," Steve instructed to put the girls at ease about the shop.

Tiny are the events and so easily started that snowball into catastrophe. A simple phone call at the wrong time was all it took in this instance. If those guys called when we weren't around and the girls dissed them, we never would have met. With the hornet's nest stirred up, Bruin and I went driving around trying to locate our guys, but it was around 9 on a weeknight and everyone had divided up by now—except for an unsuspecting Tom Harvey and Bill Scarfo; they were just walking into the bowling alley that night when a carload of guys from Long Lane walked into the Manoa Lanes looking for "Bonnett and Sisca". The girls had given them our names out of fear they would tear up the donut shop; they knew the girls sided with us and wanted nothing to do with them now.

At first, the Lane gang mistook Tom and Bill for Steve and I, so they walked up and started pushing them around before realizing these were the wrong guys. Tom and Bill saw these guys were cruising for a fight and warned them not to come messing around if they only had five guys with them.

"Don't be coming around here threatening us unless you want to get seriously hurt" was the challenge Tom presented to the Lane. "You've got no idea what you're up against." Truth is: if they had any idea, they would have dropped the matter right then.

After roughing up Tom and Bill a bit, they left looking for Steve and I. Immediately after The Lane guys walked out the door, half a dozen of the old heads walked in and asked who the toughs were out in the parking lot. Scarfo gave them the lowdown. Blood boiled and the old heads charged into the parking lot and proceeded to beat the tar out of the outnumbered Lane gang. The offenders were sent packing with their tails between their legs and a warning not to return. *That* should have been the end of the matter. But no, we were only getting started.

A gang is not defeated until every member has thrown in the towel. As long as one member is still willing to fight or won't acknowledge defeat, the gang is still at war. The revenge factor will always keep the war in seasonal ebbs and flows. The only way to really nip it in the bud is to overwhelmingly crush your opponent so they wish they never heard your name. The same goes with civil wars, national wars, no difference. In the 1990s Iraq War, the US military called it "shock and awe".

Well, unfortunately, Long Lane had more members who wanted to even up the score. Bruin received a call from Kathy saying *all* the Lane guys would be at the Manoa Shopping Center parking lot around 10:00 Saturday night for a *real* fight. This is when we found out why Kath gave them our names—because they threatened to trash the donut shop. We couldn't blame the little sweeties, not after all those free donuts. The girls were now in constant fear of a brick through the shop window and we were not about to hang at the donut shop alone to protect them. Steve and I were still clueless about the previous night's fight and couldn't imagine anyone stupid enough to challenge Manoa Lanes over such a little thing as two girls in bakery uniforms. But hey, this wouldn't be the first time that armies marched on account of a few women.

Wednesday after dinner, Steve came to my house a little concerned that this thing was starting to escalate; it seemed to have its own momentum which we had no control over. There was no choice but to inform the rest of our guys, so up to the alleys we drove. On any given evening between 7 and 8 o'clock, groups from both the old heads and young heads would start to gather in front of the spacious parking lot at Manoa Lanes (bowling alleys) to hang out. It was the general meeting place and the source of our name, 'The Lanes' or 'The Alleys'. People would say, "Those guys are from the Alleys" and you knew they meant guys that hung at Manoa Lanes. Apparently, since the Upper Darby Long Lane gang was too far from us, they hadn't heard of our little fiefdom nor us of theirs. They derived their name from a major thoroughfare in Upper Darby, Long Lane, not a bowling lane.

This evening as we approached Manoa Lanes we could see things were a bit busier than usual. It was common to see three cars and maybe 10 guys milling about waiting for a party or idea to cultivate some direction for the evening escapades. It was rare that all of us had one place to go unless it was to go swimming up at Earls Lake or somewhere that could accommodate all of us. For the most part, we divided up into fours or fives as circumstance presented itself. On this particular evening, Steve and I were greeted en masse from 20 of our guys with a slew of questions from every direction. The old heads were gloating over last night's victory romp while Tom and Scarfo got in our face about nearly taking a beating on our account. We listened to their accounts, then told them how it all started from the bakery, not ready to drop the bomb about Saturday night yet. Up until now, Steve and I didn't really know much about these Lane guys, such as how many they were, if they were all older than us. Neither had we figured on bringing the old heads in on this fight but it looked like they were already in.

Bruin and I were reading each other as close friends do while the buzz surrounding us continued. Both of us thought the same; that this thing is getting out of hand now that the old heads were in on it. Well, might as well tell them. "They'll be back with all their guys Saturday night," Steve blurted out in a bit of a challenging tone. That was throwing fuel into an already smoldering fire. The buzz now peaked with questions we had no answers to.

"How many?"

"What terms?"

"Do these guys carry guns?"

All we knew is the time and place—10 p.m. and here. We also figured our opponents would be scouting us out between now and Saturday night; hope they were watching the present frenzy. One thing we learned though is the guys who got beat up last night were older than our young heads. So that put all coordination for this fight in the hands of our old heads who were chomping at the bit. Guys started popping trunks and showcasing their preferred tools of destruction—pipes, bats, crowbars—and the accompanying stories of how well that tool had served them in the past. Steve and I were taking all this in…the train had definitely left the station. My plan was to discreetly move to the caboose, but I knew instinctively that even there I wouldn't be safe.

"All right, let's break up," announced one of the old heads with authority, "We don't want them driving by and scouting our strength. Let 'em think there's only a dozen of us," he warned as he scanned the distance. Then he added an imperative I knew was no idle talk and ran a chill down my spine. "We need to put ALL of these guys in the hospital or this will drag on for months of retaliation. This ain't no mercy fight, once and done. All in agreement?" It was unanimous as we broke the huddle.

Scarf, Harve, Wash, and I loaded into Steve's big Ford Galaxy to go cruising with eyes peeled for scouts. The conversations that night and the next few were electric with scenarios of certain victory and who could be counted on to do what. Past stories of how 'Biff' had laid out 'Spike' with a fire extinguisher since it was the only thing accessible in his trunk were retold, followed by boasting, "That was nothing compared to what he'll do to these guys." For Washel, this was the Christmas present he always wanted and was finally going to get. "These are the only weapons I need," he beamed admiring his raised fists. He was so pumped he was picking fights with anyone he saw. "Rich, your job will be to keep count for me and tell me how great I am with each sucker I drop," he gloated with certainty. I wish I could get off that easy; but in these affairs everyone has to make their mark so each has his own bragging rights. It's a proving ground.

In my case, I'll try to match up with someone my size and release my wild side, letting adrenaline and rage work its stuff. It really is amazing how absolutely horrible we are all capable of being when we let go. Afterwards, if the person you fought was a real jerk who had it coming, there is an elated euphoria of satisfaction that you just made the world a better place. If the fight is just some macho challenge without a wrong being addressed, you'll later think it was dumb and maybe have some regret. In the past, I tried to keep my fights in the first scenario, but as I stated earlier, now at 145 pounds I wasn't getting in many fights anymore, just backup when necessary since hanging at the Alleys.

News came Thursday night that Underhill (Steve-o) and his friend would have their guns Saturday night in case things get out of hand. That meant he would watch the fight as a roamer in case Long Lane pulled a gun. The Underhill team would shoot the guy in self-defense if any Lane guy flashed a gun. Steve-o loved his gun; he didn't like to get dirty fighting. One time when Peeps Peterman chided Steve-o for probably never even firing his gun, Steve-o, for the fun of it, shot a few rounds at Peeps' feet "to make him dance" just like in those hokey Westerns. The shots were two feet on either side of Peeps, but that was enough to never question his gun or sanity again. On another occasion, a few of us were walking through the shopping center parking lot towards Murphy's 5 and 10 department store when Steve-o came gleefully running past us to his car.

"What's going on Steve-o?" we asked.

"Some guy with a gun is holding up Murphys (dept store)!" he said excitedly, "I think I'm legal to shoot the guy if he aims his gun near me during a citizens arrest! Right?" he asked, anticipating our legal confirmation as he hurriedly got his pistol out of the glove box and started running back, fearing the guy would get away.

Of all the loose cannons at Manoa Lanes, his was the loosest. Even *we* were afraid to hang around the guy. But on this Saturday night we'd have him standing "referee" in case Long Lane showed a gun. Everyone understood having Steve-o stand in as judge and jury is not a path toward wisdom, but none of us were about to try and talk him out of it and have to 'dance'.

Bruin and I were getting pretty freaked at this point. The anticipation got worse each day. Sleeping was nearly impossible; as soon as I'd shut my eyes, I would start to imagine how this thing could play out and it was never good. We had come to the conclusion that in a worst-case scenario, some-one was going to get killed. A best-case scenario was that we were the ones killed and didn't have to deal with the aftermath. The only bright spot was that the rumble wouldn't last long, 10 minutes maybe, but it wasn't much of a bright spot.

Rumbles don't last long because a man at full steam in a fight will fall down spent with fatigue after 10 minutes—if he can even last that long. Anyone who has strapped on boxing gloves for three rounds will realize what I'm talking about. Unless you're well-conditioned, you won't even be able to hold your arms up after 10 minutes. All of us knew this from experience, so the chosen method of attack was to make every swing of the crowbar or club count. A gang fight is a ten-minute all-out blitz to lay out as many of them with the least economy of effort. We also had to figure on the police being there in 15 minutes max. You don't want to have to run from the cops when you're already winded.

What really kept me up nights was one needling fact that no one else seemed to care about: the names Bonnett and Sisca were the only names known to Long Lane. Actually, this was a fact most everyone at the Alleys liked; their names were out of it and they knew we'd keep our mouths shut. On the other side, if someone from The Lane is seriously hurt, they only have our two names to offer the police. Let me rephrase that; those Lane fools *will* wind up seriously hurt and will only have two names to offer police. Parents, certainly the police, will want an investigation. That investigation will start at my house and Steve's house. It's a given that we couldn't hand the police any Alley names when the time came. All of this is now inevitable and there ain't a damned thing I can do about it. Three days of this waiting and no drug in my stash could make it go away. For Steve and I, the rumble will only be the beginning of our problems. Saturday night hung on the horizon like Doom's Day.

While everyone was talking about how solidly we'd win this thing, for Steve and I there was no winning. While everyone else was focused on the main event, Steve and I were scheming on how to deal with the police the next day. By Friday night, word came that the old heads were bringing in reinforcements from a friendly smaller gang in Ardmore. Truth is that the word was getting around and all local nut cases wanted their pound of flesh. The draw was free bodies to pound without anyone having to worry about arrests. Any police retribution was going to fall on our gang and Long Lane. Everyone (except Steve and I) was hoping the police hadn't gotten wind of it yet. Three days is a long time to keep it from the cops when word is spreading like wildfire. We knew the Ardmore guys well enough; they were the typical incorrigibles who were shaving in 9th grade. Those that eventually graduated high school received AARP memberships the same year.

As it stood now; it appeared the old heads and their friends numbered around 25 guys. The young heads had another 10. We were very confident with those numbers and the caliber of the combatants.

Saturday Night

The time had come.

Around 9 p.m., our carload of doped up warriors pulled into the parking lot of the bowling alley. I never saw so many black leather jackets in one place. An old head intercepted us before we could get out of the car and gave us our instructions.

Here is how it would go down. Manoa Shopping Center is a long plaza split halfway with a 15-foot wide breezeway to allow foot access to the mid-plaza stores without having to walk all the way around the ends. There is front and rear parking for the plaza. The front of the shopping center faces West Chester Pike, a four-lane business route.

The young dudes were to put a few scouts in front of this breezeway; that would be Wash, Mikey, Scarf, Tom, Steve, and myself. We would signal the arrival of Long Lane to the rest of the young heads, who would hang at the other end of the breezeway, who in turn would signal the old heads scattered in the shadows at the rear parking lot loading zones at the back of the stores. Young heads were instructed to lead the first wave to give the impression we were few and young. The moment we had them engaged and they were confident our numbers were too small, the old heads will swoop in and overpower them like the cavalry coming to the rescue. It was as good a plan as any, as long as the old heads didn't string us out there too long before the swoop. That wasn't much of a concern.

Standing there, waiting for the Lane to arrive was intense. All the stores closed at 9 p.m.; half an hour later the parking lot was nearly empty. The girls had told us our opponents would be at the front of the plaza at 10. If Long Lane had a brain, they would have chosen the poorly lit rear parking lot instead of the brightly lit front lot where traffic along West Chester Pike stops at a major traffic intersection at Glendale Road. This is the main entrance to the shopping center. Some local traffic was about to get front row seats to a head bashing.

The February night was clear, cold and breezy. None of us had dressed for it; looking cool was more important than staying warm. The anxiety of the last four days was accentuated by the cold night air. I kept pacing, or tried to stop my knees from shaking by squatting down. Adrenaline kept my body stoked; my senses were stretched to their limit as I watched each car on West Chester Pike. "Come on, man, let's get this going," we were all saying as we paced in the shadow of fluorescent advertising.

"These guys better show!" Scarfo stated incredulously a few minutes after 10.

The thought had never struck me that we might get off so easy. Not a chance.

Then they appeared. "There they are!" someone blurted in excited relief. A procession of cars snaked its way from the Glendale traffic light into the parking lot facing West Chester Pike. There were: one, two, three, four, five, carloads; each car packed with bodies. Two were really nice cars all suped up. What moron would bring his nice car to a rumble?

A simple hand signal had our party of young dudes charging out of the alley at full speed just as the last car came to a halt in the parking lot. Half dozen of the first arrivals to get out of their vehicles had their backs to us, nonchalantly sorting through their trunks for weapons like they had all the time in the world; the rest were keeping warm in their cars, facing away from us, probably wondering where we were. Even the few at their car trunks saw us too late to react. They were the first target while the rest of us surrounded three more cars. Some of us started smashing headlights and grills, while others kept them trapped in their cars. Trying to rise from a car seat position to confront a crowbar wielding maniac is a guaranteed crowning. The standing man has advantage. The poor guys caught outside their cars took the brunt of the first wave, going down before they even got started. It was probably better they didn't stay conscious long enough to see their cars and friends destroyed.

The Laners in the surrounded cars saw their friends drop silent. Now showing fear, they started locking doors and screamed at their driver to GO so they could get out of the cars safely and mount an attack. So we proceeded to smash in every window, going for the driver's first so they couldn't drive away. One guy, in order to stop us from unlocking his door once his window was shattered, was dumb enough to hold his hand over the door lock. I know his hand had to be broken after getting crowbarred at full swing; he was out of the fight. To be inside a car and have glass flying at you from every direction by people coming in to get you is pretty terrifying. Those who come looking for a fight should not hide in glass houses…or cars. To my utter amazement, they had actually brought some of their girlfriends along, I would guess, to impress them. Now, instead of showing their bravery before the ladies, these girls were screaming while their cowering boyfriends struggled to keep the doors locked and start their engines, now that the windows were busted. They must have been hoping for the guys in the other two cars to get us off them so they could get in the fight. That wasn't going to happen, though they made a valiant attempt.

Simultaneously, the second group of carloads came piling out in an attempt to rescue the first three cars, which were now surrounded. To say they were enraged about their cars being smashed is an understatement. Right at that moment, the main wave of old heads rounded the corner at a full screaming run. That wave of black leathered screaming mayhem exploding out of the breezeway 100 feet away at full run towards us was a sight I can never forget. I was glad they weren't coming for me. There was no hint of hesitation on any of their faces as they came on like a stampede of determined barbarians wielding their pipes, chains, crow bars, and baseball bats. Most were also carrying knives if it came to that.

When the rescuing three carloads of Laners saw the old heads turn the corner, they froze in their tracks. It only took them an instant to do the math before franticly scurrying back to their cars for Plan B; hightail it outta there. Before they could get those shiny engines started, the old heads rained down on them like hail. I was standing next to Joe *McGeever* when he pulled one of the guys screaming out the passenger window and broke the guys' collarbone with one swoop of his bat. I was close enough to hear the bone snap. Joe left the guy corked halfway through the tight hole in the broken elastic safety glass. The guy pushed himself through the hole, then ran holding his arm, screaming for help to a car stopped at the Glendale Road red light; the driver and his wife were stunned from what they were witnessing. The kid tried to get in their locked car to get away from his pursuers even though no one was after him. The slumped kid moved down the line to try other cars stopped for the light, pleading for a ride out of there. It was eerie, the pitch of fear in his pleadings as it caught my attention for a moment. There was too much going on for me to watch what happened to him, but he set the pattern for the only way of escape and soon others were following his example.

I had mentioned terror earlier; the look on some of these guys' faces was pure terror. They knew they were about to be violated as they had never seen nor given, and death was a very real possibility. It was the fury on some of our guys' faces which had them in terror. Long Lane realized we had them at our mercy and that mercy was not in our granting. Already, three unconscious bodies were sprawled on bloody asphalt; some of our guys still wanted to outdo that and it showed in their faces. Some Laners were curled in a fetal ball on the ground, while three or four of our guys were kicking their heads and beating on them. It was a horrible free-for-all; Haverford Hospital would be busy tonight, and I knew Steve and I were going to be the ones to pay—tomorrow or the next day, it will catch up with us.

Not many words were being exchanged; it was screaming and pleading from their side, quick instructions to each other when needed from our side to stop them from escaping. The few girls were left alone but their shrieking and screaming filled the night air the loudest; begging us to stop. Steve-o was excitedly hopping from car to car asking us, "Any guns? Any guns?" I think he was a bit disappointed. That was the last I saw of him for the night. If Long Lane had brought a gun, they would have been fully justified to use it in self-defense. We just got lucky it didn't come to that tonight. There wasn't a Lane member that wasn't bloodied and badly beaten. They took a terrible pounding. Once the ambulatory had ran off down West Chester Pike, we turned back on the cars to take out any remaining rage.

One bloodied Laner lay in the back seat of his car by himself with the doors open. He had crawled there for useless protection, his eyes swollen shut already, his hands up in front of his bloody face repeating, "No more...you won...no more." In 10 minutes, it was all over. The last thing I remembered was a remarkable throw by Scarfo. He threw a sawn-off baseball bat with all his might to see if he could reach the last victim running away. I stood with him and watched that bat twirl end over end along a high arc. "I think you're gonna get him, Will!" I said in disbelief as the bat spun down on the moving target. It was like a long touchdown pass without the receiver knowing when to turn around. It came down right on his head and stumbled him to the pavement. As we ran off, I kept turning to see if he got up. He rose up on all fours looking back at us and just stayed that way as I hesitated before rounding the alley back to Bruin's car.

"That was a one in a million shot, Will!" I said.

"Yeah! The guy was probably wondering where it came from!" he laughed shaking his head in disbelief.

"Hey! Did you guys see that toss," we asked. But everyone had their own story to tell.

Getting out of Dodge was now our current concern. Cops would be swarming this place any moment now. On the way out, we drove by to survey the damage from West Chester Pike. There was only half a dozen of the original 25 guys that started out from Long Lane still near the cars. A few were still prostrate on the parking lot with friends stooped over them, some were lying in their cars, a few were in a daze surveying their shiny cars, re-approaching the scene they had run from. I didn't see an intact window, windshield, headlight, or grill. Some door panels and trunks were dented in, tires were flat, radiators were draining with crowbars hanging out of them. It looked like a junkyard. In a few moments, that shopping center was a sea of flashing police lights, then ambulances and tow trucks. But that had to be left to the imagination, we weren't hanging around to find out.

It was finally over. 'Nothing left to do tonight but kick back and party,' I was thinking with relief. Well, I thought wrong. I did not understand yet, but this is the worse night of my life.

Just When You Think You've Seen the Worst of It...

One of our favorite cruising areas was out Gradyville Road beyond Newtown Square to the roads around The Tyler Arboretum. There was still some rural farmland back then, a break from the endless suburbia we were raised in and hardly a shadow of what has been built up there since. A new State Park (Ridley Creek SP) was being developed on the property of a wealthy industrialist. The property was vacated for a few years before the state had money to develop a park. This was our chosen retreat tonight to lie low and out of sight. These grounds were our private hangout where no one ever bothered us. There were no homes around for quite a way, and no lighting whatsoever. The park service had recently put up temporary gates, even though the park was a year from opening. You could drive around these gates and have the place to yourselves late at night; build a campfire, party, and generally kick back without a worry… until tonight.

There used to be a derelict farmhouse off Old Forge Road where we would park. Tonight, we backed Steve's Galaxy into the old farm lane across from the house, turned off the engine, lit up, and popped a few cold ones as we recounted the night's events. None of us had a scratch from the fight except Tom. In his enthusiasm, he had tried to punch in a car window with his bare fist and learned safety glass doesn't give that easily. We laughed about that and were bragging about the hammering we bestowed upon those poor guys.

"Time for them to change their name to So-long Lane now that they're gonna be short on personnel!", and that sort of boasting.

"Did you see *Tamorelli* ? He swung his pipe at this guy and the pipe flew out of his hands! He was so ticked off about losing his pipe that he tackled the guy, who lost his shoe as he tried to get up, so *Tam* used the guy's own shoe to beat on him!" Wash said laughing while trying to tell it.

Everyone had a story to tell. I'm glad to say that other than breaking things, I don't remember laying a serious hand on anyone. Mostly I just went from downed victim to downed victim, whom already had a few guys on them taking care of business and thinking, 'Looks like everything is under control here.'

With the late-night temperature below freezing, we stayed in the car speculating what the police were doing at the moment. We didn't have to wonder anymore. One was shining his flashlight in Steve's driver window catching us red-handed rolling joints and drinking.

"Everyone step out of the car!" was the familiar command given as his bright light blinded us. "Oh s#*+" was our uniform response as everyone instinctively tossed all contraband out the opposite window, like it was going to disappear. I was in the passenger seat rolling joints. The only course of action was to roll down the window and toss everything to the wind, which took it as far as I could spit since lids don't sail too well. The point is to get anything illegal off your person so you can deny it was ever yours; no matter how obvious the truth is to the contrary.

"Out of the car I said! Out of the car NOW!" he commanded, frustrated at our tossing the evidence. As we got out, it was impossible to see more than one cop from the way he stood behind his bright light as trained. All we could make out was a uniformed figure behind a flashlight.

"OK, everyone over on this side!" he barked as his light landed on our hesitant figures considering whether to dash. Will, Mikey, and I reluctantly went to join Steve, Ric, and Tom on the driver's side.

"Hand over your driver license," he said to Steve. "Don't move!" he said to all of us after Steve handed over the license.

The officer now went to shine his light on the passenger side of our car where baggies and beer lay about the ground. "Stay here while I call this in," he commanded as he stepped away 15 feet to read the car license and presumably radio in for backup. His brief absence was far enough away to let us whisper amongst ourselves; a verdict was quickly decided.

"We gotta roll this pig before he calls in Steve's license!" Wash stated as the only logical way of getting out of this...and he was right. We all shook our heads in agreement knowing Mikey and Wash would gladly do the rolling since they were presently on probation and couldn't absorb another arrest. If they cold conk the officer before calling in Steve's driver's license or plate, we'd be in the clear to drive off scot-free. Wash would gladly thump him upside the head hard enough to make him forget our license number. Steve would grab his license back and swipe his notebook in the event he wrote the identification down. Some things you just have to do as a matter of simple arithmetic, basic street smarts, and quick thinking.

As far as we could tell, he was alone and hadn't called in for backup yet. Maybe he wanted to brag back at the police station about bringing us in. Well, that wasn't going to happen; not as long as wind blows, green grass grows, and we're desperate.

One thing for sure though, this cop *wasn't* following procedure as we were familiar with it. While sitting in the car, the six of us had not shown any hint of leaving before his intrusion. He could have laid low, called in the vehicle license, then simply waited 10 minutes for backup to arrive, and been on easy street to confront us. This guy is violating a cardinal rule of his training: always wait for backup when highly outnumbered; something is fishy. He didn't tell us "hands on the trunk" either; maybe we had a rookie cop? Meanwhile, we all noticed he wasn't on a radio, just shining his light on Steve's car license.

"Wait here," he said, then proceeded to briskly trot down a trail behind our car without coming anywhere near us again. I knew the trail; it led to a building that would assumedly be the park office.

This left us alone to discuss our options. "We shoulda' rolled him while we had the chance!" Mike lamented. "I can't violate my probation, neither can you, Wash!"

Problem was that the officer took off so abruptly we didn't have time to react. A gamut of opinions began flowing when I decided to run down the trail behind the cop to see if I could ID his Cruiser. That would narrow our options or eliminate them. If he was a state cop, we were cooked. But I was questioning myself if this was a township cop, park cop, rent-a-cop or what. Behind me, I could hear where the discussion was going.

"I think he's a rookie cop?"

"I don't see his Cruiser. Maybe he's parked at the new building?"

"We can't jump him once he calls in Steve's license number!"

"Why didn't he wait for backup?"

"I don't think he called it in, if he did; why didn't he just wait for support?"

"Something ain't right; it don't add up."

"I say we jump him anyhow."

"There are no *local* police out here. Staties (state police) patrol this area."

"He ain't no Statey, that's for sure."

I could not believe Mike and Ric still wanted to jump the guy knowing he was calling in Steve's license as we spoke. I ran 150 feet down the trail into total darkness and couldn't even see the gleam of his flashlight in the wintry woods; there was no sign of a Cruiser between me and the empty park building far off. Then it hit me! Maybe he's a Park Ranger! That's why he didn't call in backup and follow standard police procedure. Now it all made more sense, but it didn't change the fact he could be calling the state police right now with Steve's license number. I decided against letting the others in on my discovery; they would definitely want to roll him if they knew he was a ranger. If he calls in Steve's license to the state police, rolling him won't accomplish anything but more charges.

Running back to the car, I could clearly hear the guys arguing amongst themselves. "I don't know where he went; I couldn't find a Cruiser," I exhaled as I approached. "What have you guys decided," I asked even though I had heard enough on my way back to put it together. Three still wanted to follow through on the original agreement to jump the guy and retrieve Steve's driver's license, two were against. Steve was sunk either way because he would be the guy IDed from his license. Mike and Ric figured gang ethics prevented Steve from turning in their names to the state police if they jumped the guy and the cops came to arrest Steve later because of his license information. Mike and Ric were idiots and hadn't thought far enough to realize they would eventually be IDed by the jumped cop from pictures provided by Haverford police once Steve was picked up, even if Steve kept silent. The reason they were on probation in the first place is because they never thought the chess game through three or four moves down the board. The other three of us were adamant about not getting into deeper trouble over their stupidity. The hot heads against the strategizers, this was always the divide.

I was the tying vote against jumping the guy, but in a gang might carries more weight than democratic principles. This guy was going to get jumped; that much was settled. Our only hope now was the dwindling chances this ranger or whatever he was didn't call the state police.

"Look…just give me a few minutes to try to get some information from him before you jump him," I pleaded. It was my last chance for reason in an increasingly hopeless situation. While still arguing loudly, the flashlight popped on from 30 feet away where the trail leaves the wood's edge; he had been listening to our arguing over his fate and wasn't about to approach us any closer now than 20 feet away.

I could not believe how bad this night was going. Sometime tomorrow I would have the Haverford police at my house to investigate the gang fight; that much was sure. Just as my parents would be wondering why I was involved in this brutal gang fight, the state police will arrive and charge me with assaulting some sort of uniformed officer (as if beating up kids my own age wasn't bad enough, *we* decided to rough up a ranger or cop). Then, just so mom and pop would be sure I was never in my right mind, I would also be charged with drug possession. Before this night is over, Steve and I had to seriously think about running off to pick grapefruits in some southern state. Don't laugh, a year from now Steve, Will, and Ric will have run off to Florida to try and escape similar charges.

Slowly, we started to maneuver closer to the officer.

"Police will be here in five minutes!" he said to stop us. That told us all that he wasn't a cop. But that still didn't help us now if he already called in the license.

"Newtown Square doesn't have a police department, who did you call?" I asked, knowing only state cops patrol this area. Without answering, our new friend now saw the predicament in which he had himself; he didn't *have* five minutes and knew he wasn't dealing with a bunch of scared school boys. We had nonchalantly lit cigarettes and moved within 10 feet; he knew he couldn't outrun us if it came to that.

"Everyone back up! I have mace!" he threatened, pulling out his mace. "Backup is on its way, I already called it in! Now back off boys before you get in big trouble!" This guy was beaucoup scared and had no gun to pull out or he would have drawn it instead of mace. I was now convinced he was a state park ranger or rent-a-cop.

Was he telling the truth? And were we willing to gamble he *wasn't,* so as to jump him and get Steve's license back? When he flashed his light at the mace in his hand, I observed he didn't have a gun holster on his utility belt, but I didn't know if the other guys had seen it. In a few more seconds, Wash and Ric would be all over him.

"You're not carrying a gun? Cops carry guns," Steve asked out loud to inform the others what was becoming more obvious. Apparently, a few of us had seen the same thing. Now we all knew he wasn't a cop; this would embolden the wolves. Time was up.

"I already called this license plate in with my radio!" he bluffed nervously. He was too scared to be a cop. Mikey had been listening to the radio transmissions and simply stated to all present, "That radio isn't on police frequency." To us that was Mikey's way of signaling, 'Here we go,' waiting for Mike to make his move. With that said, some ran to cut off his escape, while Mike made his move.

"**Stop Right There!**" he yelled running backwards into Steve & I. "I'll let you guys go with a warning! I, I've decided to let you guys go with a warning," he said holding his hands out for Mike to stop in his tracks. Caught off-guard, all we could do was stand there speechless. Warning? Sure, we *love* warnings. We collect them like coupons. My heart pounded a long sigh of relief. Intimidation had prevented violence. He was one lucky guy, and so were we. We waited for his follow-up.

"Ju…just get in your car and go!" he sputtered in complete surrender, handing back Steve's registration at arm's length.

"So you're a Park Ranger?" I asked trying to wrap up our doubts. He acknowledged he was. "He never called it in," I assured our group. "Leave him go."

Wash swayed over to our "let him go" side upon hearing the word 'warning'. Mikey now felt isolated enough to go with the majority. He wrapped it up, "All right, walk back into the woods the way you came. If I see that light shine on this license plate you won't be able to run fast enough. Do anything like calling the cops and we'll send someone looking for you one of these nights. Go."

Before we left, Steve may have asked him to produce his notepad to tear out the license plate number if he wrote it down. There was a lot going on and said in those 15 minutes.

And with that, the man walked off having narrowly escaped the wrath of two desperate young men. The other guys picked up the beer and dope, but I hid my bag under leaves in the bushes. I could afford the financial sacrifice in case cops did stop us on the road out. Mikey returned the next day and retrieved my bag.

We drove home that night, thinking we were the hardest guys in two counties. Big deal. We were assholes, punks; just everyone was afraid to say it to our face. Except the police, they were about to voice their opinion loud and clear. Though cocky tonight, hanging in the back of my mind was the question of whether Mr. Ranger would call Steve's name in to the state police. He could have easily memorized, 'Sisca from Havertown', off the license with little effort. He wasn't much older than us and considering his pay grade, was probably glad just to walk away.

Picking up the pieces

Every day but Mondays, Steve's father left home early to look after his store in South Philly, unintentionally leaving the house to Steve and company. Hanging out at Steve's on Sunday morning for me was a weekly ritual, which started a several years ago when our parents still made us go to church; this was the place to cut church. This Sunday I wasn't in Bruin's house 10 minutes when a police Cruiser pulled up across the street. We both watched from the front window as they got out. It was Detective Sleuth and the police chief. Crud, here we go, offer nothing, play dumb, lie through your teeth, deny everything while both parties feel each other out for what each other knows.

The doorbell rings, Steve opens the door without saying a word. "Steven Sisca?" they inquired by writ.

"Yeah," Steve answered flatly.

"And you're Richard Bonnett of xxx Glendale Road?"

"Yeah," I acknowledged, standing just behind Steve. Procedure.

Looking up from a clipboard, the policeman smiled, "Well, seems you two have a list of charges against you, would you like to hear them?" This sort of intimidation didn't faze us in the least. Cops always huff and puff; it's the first clue they don't have much yet, but they usually don't smile like that.

"What's the problem," Steve asked.

"Are your parents at home?" the officer asked in frustration, seeing we were going to play the dumb and innocent line as long as we could.

"No."

"When *will* they be home?" they asked impatiently.

"Mom's dead, Dad works late." Up until now, one of the chiefs had been parlaying the perfunctory lead in; Detective Sleuth impatiently stepped in with, "Just open the damned door. You two have a lot of explaining to do." Until then we had parlayed through the screen door. Detective Sleuth had come close several times in his attempt to get something worthwhile to stick to anyone at Manoa Lanes, something always fell apart for him… and we'd rub it in. His job was on the hot seat to clean up the budding gang sore on the township's face. So far, he had blown every chance with nothing more than probations and fines. To make matters worse, someone had spray-painted in two-foot letters across the very visible wall of the bowling alley, 'SLEUTH

SUCKS!' Now he was eager to question us, figuring he had something big this time around and he CAN'T come up empty-handed. He had a lot of township pressure on him and would have to give it his best effort.

"Steve," I said signaling him away from the door where we could talk. Steve stepped just out of sight from Gestapo. "We better let them in, if we don't answer some questions now, they'll only take me up to my house next," I said, thinking maybe I could put off a police visit to my folks another day or even head it off now for good. "We can throw them out whenever we want if the questioning goes bad for us, since your dad ain't home." Steve agreed. Our curiosity was getting the best of us and we wanted to know how much they knew about our involvement.

They came in and sat on the sofa like they planned on being there a while. Steve and I stood by the front door as a signal for them not to get too comfortable.

"Were you two present at this fight last night?" Sleuth started in while laying out his notes on the coffee table and expecting us to say "no" and fall into his trap.

"What fight?" Steve deadpanned.

"Ah, come on! Don't play games with this! I have over a dozen witnesses you two are all over this thing!"

"Who are your witnesses?" I replied trying to determine what they knew of our part in the whole scheme and if they had any other names from Manoa Lanes yet.

"The guys you beat up last night! Look, your little welcoming committee put eight people in the hospital last night, three are still there. Their parents will be pressing charges for what happened based on what action township enforcement is going to take against you and your friends! All of these guys gave us *your* names for putting them in the hospital."

"Well, I'd say your witnesses are very mistaken," I countered. "First of all, I'm not Superman, I'm only 140 pounds. Do you see a scratch on either of us? Second, I never laid a hand on any of those guys and I'll swear that before them and any judge." I forcefully informed them. At least I was telling the truth so far.

"But you **were there** and saw what went on," Detective Brainiac smiled, thinking he was on his way to cornering us. It's all a cat and mouse game and I had played it before. Don't assume because they wear a badge, they have street smarts too. Strip away the uniform and they were just dads trying to figure which of their kids is lying; in the meantime, all parties are innocent. We always had the advantage because we knew the whole truth while they had to try to piece the truth together from only a few pieces of a puzzle; not that this event was hard to figure out. Either way, the truth is very elusive when you're trying to nail somebody with the law. In a street fight like this, police assume BOTH sides are probably lying. Always throw a few curves their way to convince them they don't have a worthy case to bring before a judge. Each time one of us got off scot-free for the most ridicules reason, we ALL learned a little more about how to deny, lie, and frustrate the police. I had previously batted 1,000 at this game and knew pretty well where he wanted me to go with his questions.

"Oh yeah, we were there," I said matter of factly, "Steve was posted in front of Penn Grocer and I was posted at the rear breezeway by Murphy's. We were spotters in case you guys (the police) showed up." Check Mate. They knew both of those positions would have logically been deployed and both locations took us out of view of the fight. The detective turned dryly to the chief as if to say, 'See what I mean? We're not going to get anything from these two.' I followed up with, "As soon as I saw the first sign of your flashing lights; I ran to warn them but all I saw was a bunch of busted up cars, everyone was already gone. What took you guys so long to show up, anyhow?" Oh man, that dig had the Police Chief's neck veins busting his collar. It may have been a bit premature to start pouring salt in the wound. We really needed to find out more of what they knew, but it told him loud and clear, I knew he had nothing and better go do some more detective work if he thinks ole Dickie Boy was about to cave in and start pouring out names to save my keister.

"Who's *them*, who else was there?" he said flatly on cue, knowing he was wasting his time. This questioning was so predictable.

"No names," I said with a smirk as Steve shook his head in agreement while looking at his feet. "I'd rather face whatever lame charges you guys come up with than hand out names and wind up in a hospital bed next to those other saps. But I can describe them if that would help you?" I said feigning sincerity. They (as well as Steve) looked at me puzzled, apprehensive of my follow-up, "Everyone was wearing a black...leather...jacket" I punctuated with a finger in the air, as if each of the last three words revealed the answer to their mystery. Steve let out a laugh of relief, which acknowledged nothing given. "So what are the charges?" I quickly continued to get back on subject.

Reading off his clipboard, "So far, pay all medical bills and vehicle damage," he said almost embarrassed, "but we haven't spoken to all the parents yet." "Those don't sound like charges to me, officer." I felt a token of respect at this point would piss 'em off even more. "But you might want to remind those parents when you meet with them next, AND their darling little children that **we** didn't drive to Upper Darby looking for trouble, **they** came to Havertown. It seems to me that *you* should be charging *them* for coming up here with intent to disturb the peace or something like that, instead of coming after us." I was getting a little indignant now and Steve picked up the scent.

"Yeah, why don't you fine *them* and arrest the whole bunch for coming up here and causing trouble. We weren't looking for any trouble; they brought it on themselves! Tell them to drop any charges they're thinking about or this thing is not over!" He couldn't have put it better. Unwittingly, that statement touched off a nerve in those two we hadn't considered yet.

"No!" they said getting up as if they had just realized the cat peed on the couch. "No more fights, we don't want any more of this stuff going on in this township." It was as if a beam of light had just shown down from heaven and illuminated an 11th commandment there in the middle of the room. 'Thou shall not continue such shenanigans and chance it landing in the News of

166

Delaware County'. They had cleaned this thing up to keep it out of the local rag. The whole event was on the down-low so far. This was golden for us.

I seized the sterling opportunity now to wrap this up neat and tidy. "Well, I'll agree with you guys on that much; Steve and I are not looking for any more trouble, but we can't speak for or persuade 30 other guys, especially some of the older hotheads up there (the Alleys). They'll be livid when they find out those losers, or their parents, are pressing for compensation over something Long Lane brought on themselves. So I think it's up to *you* guys to convince those parents from Long Lane that Haverford Township won't prosecute their bad little boys if they drop all charges they might be thinking about. After that I don't see any reason why the whole thing wouldn't just go away as if it never happened". Ahh…at shining moments like that I wondered if I shouldn't become a criminal lawyer. The coppers didn't look happy, but saw the logic in it all. They were barking up the wrong tree and knew it before knocking on our door. Our pointing it out was humiliating to them.

Now Sleuth had the choice of taking our suggestion and putting this touchy township embarrassment to bed, which also meant dropping any chance he had of nailing our gang for any charges unless he was also going to charge the Long Lane boys on the same. It also meant reversing the conversations they already had with parents at the hospital last night, or continue coming after us on questionable charges and risking a 'Manoa Lanes vs. Long Lane, Part II'. It was a no-brainer. His frustration was apparent at losing again.

"Yeah and you can tell those losers in the hospital to go ^ °#* themselves from all of us," Steve threw in because he wanted to be able to tell our guys he said it with me as his witness. That was Steve and he couldn't help it. I personally thought it was unduly rude. We were all just starting to get along so well.

"My dad will be home Wednesday night if you want to tell us anything else," Steve threw at them as they shuffled down the steps back to their Cruiser.

As they headed down the driveway, I turned to Steve to double-check, "Your dad still works Wednesday nights, right?"

"Oh yeah" Steve assured.

"Good one," I said and turned to go back in the house.

"Now I just hope that park cop never called in your license," I said, feeling lucky. Things were turning our way.

The state police never did call or show up at Steve's, so apparently the park incident was never called in. The guy must have been too freaked out to memorize Bruin's name and address, which was simple enough to do. Personally, here's my take on it: When the ranger went down the trail behind our car, he quickly turned off his light, stepped off the trail, and listened to us while assessing our predicament. His radio was probably a one-way police scanner. In the dark he couldn't write down Steve's information without turning on his flashlight and giving away his location to us as he was spying our intentions. I probably went right past him when I ran down the trail to see if he had a Cruiser parked at the lot near the end of the trail. Had he memorized any of Steve's information and the police came to our house the next day, it would have been our word against his, he never picked up any evidence and we never assaulted him. He was most likely the first night ranger hired at Ridley Creek State Park. Within a few weeks, we confirmed the park had now hired full-time rangers to protect their newly constructed assets. That was the end of night visits to soon-to-be-opened Ridley Creek State Park.

Back to the rumble, our rehearsed excuse as sentinels for the fight was one of my last-minute ideas that materialized from a moment of cannabis-induced brainstorming before Steve dropped me off that night; then it all seemed so simple. At worse, by saying we were sentries meant admitting to abetting some sort of minor misconduct, which we could always argue; we were trying to avoid a fight by warning the Lane guys to leave once we spotted them.

As far as our being the only Manoa Lane members Long Lane knew, they only knew our names, not what we looked like. None of them could identify Steve and I in a line-up if it came to that. It couldn't have worked out any better. The key was to be calm under pressure and ignore the badges. Once that first whopper is out of your mouth, it all just flows like poetry. After dancing a few victory laps around Steve's living room, we headed out to find our friends and party. We also had to inform all involved how we came up with an alibi that kept us in the clear and relieved any old heads of any concern that we might hand over names. 'Man,' I thought to myself, '**if there is no great score keeper in the sky, law-abiding citizens are the biggest saps on earth.' And I didn't believe anyone was keeping score.**

So with three victories behind me: the fight, intimidating an officer of some sort into letting us go, then spanking the local police detective, why was it the worse night in my life? Well, first of all, it was now morning and all nervous speculating on how the fight would go, if guns would come out, if someone would get killed was over. Remember, Steve and I started this fight; it would be on our conscience for the rest of our lives if someone got killed. Even though I didn't believe any God was keeping records, I didn't want to chance having someone's death hanging over my head. I thought this would be the event that got me sent off to county jail. As it turned out, there were broken bones, concussions, and too many stitches to count, and that was as best it could have turned out. Second, getting busted for dope (if we didn't intimidate that park policeman to let us go) in 1970 was still a serious offense, especially when the local cops had my number and would not be lenient. Three, intimidating police is not on my high priority list for weekend entertainment; it is always nerve-wracking. And lastly, you don't want to break dear old mom's heart no matter how rotten your own is. I figured the police would come to my house after the rumble and expose something I never wanted mom to know about. I didn't care what dad thought; he already thought I was a loser. The chances of coming up three for three is pert-near to using up all of my luck. *If there was anything I was learning about (my) life, it was that* **sin will take me farther than I was ever intending to go, and cost me more than I was ever willing to pay.**

Steve and I negotiated the final peace with Haverford's finest over the next week, mostly over the phone, and a drop in at the police station by Steve. They did a good job of keeping the whole deal quiet while getting all charges dropped, if there ever really were any charges. The worst of it from our end was paying the deductible on one of the totaled cars. One of the parents were unreasonably adamant about having the family car (which was taken by *their* son to a gang fight) paid for by the people who rightfully destroyed it, not the responsible driver. I believe Steve paid the whole tab of $250, but never admitted to it or asked me for any money. Steve's generosity was his finest quality. Too bad he didn't live long enough to share it with a wife and family; he loved kids. We weren't all bad.

CHAPTER 9

Justice – Just-isn't

*Italicized names in their first appearing means they have
been changed. Age 17 – 18, 1971–72*

I had learned firsthand a long time ago that if you literally play with fire (Chapter 1), you'll get burned. Just as Joe Peca and I threw matches at each other's leaf piles waiting to see how many matches it would take to torch the other guy's shopping cart, I was throwing matches at my own life, wondering how long I had before I got burned. My leaf pile was smoldering.

One of the ironies of life at Manoa Lanes was that trouble often eluded us when we expected it, but zapped us when we didn't see it coming. A good example is the gang fight. I expected all kinds of law trouble to come from that night, but little happened. In this following story, after a seemingly routine night with the guys, I'd be standing before a judge. Go figure.

By now some of us had turned 18 and any criminal action would land us in adult court instead of juvenile court. No more being released under parental guardianship. None of us really considered the rules changed in a matter of one day, our 18th birthday. Since the police were aiming to clean up Dodge, leniency wasn't expected from them. Even so, our age change didn't sink in.

* NOTE: You need to pay close attention to names and events in next three paragraphs in order to understand the rest of the chapter. The rest flows easily.

On this particular night, I had gone to Westgate Field with my friends to do a little business with the Westgate Boys. Westgate Field is a recreational park with playing fields, tennis courts, playground, etc., for the community of Westgate Hills. The Westgate Boys were a loose band of basketball-loving jocks developing a taste for drugs. We all got along well, no rivalries. I was trying to get rid of some mescaline; the Westgate guys had some cocaine, so we traded. Coke was just arriving on the scene so we had to try it out; this night was the maiden voyage for most of us. The Westgate Boys played mescaline basketball in the dark, while our guys were talking to another small group from Lawrence Park and just idling away the time laughing at the basketball game. Lawrence Park was a small gang from Marple Newtown whom we also got along with well.

For reasons unknown, most of our guys went out with girls from Marple Newtown. Steve, Harve, Scarf, Timmy, Tommy, and I were all dating Marple girls. *Ronnie Woodbine* was the only Marple girl present tonight. She decided to stay with Scarfo when her ride—the Lawrence Park guys—left around 11ish. That seemed normal since Scarf and Ronnie had dated recently and were perhaps flirting with the idea of getting back together. Anyhow, no one was paying attention to what they were up to. I knew they had gone for a walk because we were waiting for their return so we could leave. In the meantime, Joe *Gergen* had shown up from Manoa Corner, another smaller gang that didn't look for trouble. Joe was all spaced out on acid and looking for someone to drop (acid) with him, or at least stay up all night with him since LSD is an dusk to dawn' event. Our minds were already pre-occupied. Joe got real belligerent when none of us wanted to drop with him so he left in a huff; he wasn't the most stable guy, even when straight.

Half an hour later, around midnight, Scarfo came back and joined us, I saw Mikey talking with Ronnie as the rest of us decided to split up to go home. Mike yelled to us not to leave yet; he needed a ride home. He and Ronnie disappeared for 15 minutes. When he came back to us, he informed Wash that Ronnie needed to talk to him, then added, "Hurry up before she changes her mind." Washel ran off towards her yelling behind him to wait 15 minutes because he needed a ride home. This was the only hint we had that Ronnie was handing out candy behind the bushes. The only comment he made about Ronnie on the way home was something to the effect of "that girl is hard to figure out". No discussion arose from it. Mikey went home with the Scarf, Wash went home with Steve and I, and that was the end of another routine night hanging out with the guys. What I just explained to you is the full extent of what I remember happening that night.

The next day, Joe Gergen came up to Manoa Lanes saying he spent the whole night driving around with Ronnie and brought her home around sun-up. Looks like Joe conveniently found someone to stay up 'tripping' with him all night. Ronnie was probably talked into dropping acid with him, then was afraid to face her waiting parents while tripping so stayed out until morning when the effects wore off. Conversing with mom and dad while tripping *can* pose a challenge. Ronnie was 16 so her mother was waiting up for her (we were 17 and 18). Joe informed us that Ronnie told her mother she had been raped in order to avoid being punished for being out until dawn. Dumb move. However, if she was tripping at the time, this excuse may have seemed like clairvoyant brilliance.

At this point, Wash, Scarf, and Mike started joking about imagining Ronnie tripping while trying to explain to her mother she was raped when she wasn't. Joe silenced the joking when he stated, "I'm pretty sure she named you guys to her mother." The three named erupted, "Hey man, she spent the night with you, Joe. If anyone is getting named for rape, it *better* be you!"

Gergen didn't like the way his planted message was received, so he left. Before getting in his car to leave Wash warned him, "You better straighten that girl out and tell her not to be spreading false accusations against us."

As Joe drove off, Mike turned around incredulous, "Gergen was probably bangin' her all night. How else could you spend all night with that diz?" Everyone was growing indignant over what Joe had just tried to pull off.

"He's probably the one who convinced her to yell rape on you guys," I said stirring the pot. "That way Joe would be in the clear in case he got her pregnant." Everyone agreed on that scenario.

"I better straighten that boy out in school tomorrow," Wash said, to put everyone back in good spirits. Wash and Joe were in their last year of high school.

I had hit the nail on the head. When Gergen was confronted by Wash the next day with the scenario I suspected, Joe looked guilty as sin. Wash physically threatened him but didn't want to fight in school, so Joe got a warning to straighten it out or face the consequences. Joe wasn't one to back down easily; he must have gone to the Corner Boys where he hung out to see if he had backup; this would strain the relationship between our two gangs over the next few months. Our gang was larger, but many of our guys were close with their clique. Neither side really wanted a fight so the Corner Boys pressured Joe to back off. But Joe was already in too deep, he couldn't change the mind of Ronnie's mother. Unbeknown to us, she was ready to take this thing to court to restore her daughter's reputation. Dumb move. At least this one wasn't my problem. I wasn't involved; let those guys figure it out. I deleted it from my concerns.

A few days pass and I'm just about to go out for the evening. I'm running late, it's about 8 o'clock when the doorbell rings. I figure it was Steve ringing up for me; I get to the door the same time as my mom, open the door and there stands Detective Sleuth looking just too chipper. 'What does *this* guy want?' I'm thinking, 'It has to be about selling dope; apart from that, we haven't been caught in anything worthy of Detective Sleuth getting involved.' One thing was sure, him coming to your house was never good.

He ignored me and politely introduced himself to my mother and asked if he could have some of her time. My mom saw him to a seat and asked what this visit was about.

"I'd like to ask your son a few questions, Mrs. Bonnett."

"Go get your father," mom commanded, knowing he'd want to hear whatever was about to transpire. My mind was racing backwards to recent events, trying to figure out what Sleuth had on me; nothing was coming to mind. Even still, I was feeling trapped.

I was totally unprepared for this questioning, not having any idea of how to weave my defense of an unknown. These few seconds of answering the door, introductions, and fetching Dad are the precious moments a scheming mind needs to come up with an alibi of any sort. I was blank. I didn't have a subject to craft an alibi around.

"Dad, could you come up here to talk to some detective?" I asked nervously. The first thing to run through any father's head if a detective is standing in their living room is: which child is hurt? Or has there been a bad car accident as he rushes to the living room? But not my dad; he disgustedly trudged slowly up the steps, looking at me blank without any of those parental fears; he knew it was about me.

With everyone introduced and seated, the questioning began. I was sitting between my folks who sat on separate living room chairs while the Detective opened his briefcase, spreading out papers on our big coffee table across from us. Sleuth wore thick glasses, which made his eyes difficult to read unless he looked directly at you; then his eyes were golf balls. His suit hung baggy like a Barney Miller TV detective of the era. He wasn't the sharpest knife in the drawer and had a short Irish temper.

He started with questions about my friendships with various individuals up at Manoa Lanes. The conversation was very general without any illumination of why he was here. It was obvious to me that he was painting a picture for the benefit of my parents to understand the company I kept by dropping bombs like, "You ARE aware that Mr. Frielicht is on probation for assaulting an officer?" He exuded rare confidence and was a bit unnerving playing cat and mouse—only he was the cat this time. His rare confidence worried me that he already had me no matter what I said. The questioning was laid out to trap me as much as possible. The game was on again. Walk the minefield, don't step on any mines.

"Were you with any of these boys this past Saturday night: Michael McNicol, William Scarfo, Ric Frielicht, Steven Sisca?"

"Saturday night?" I was stalling, "Let me think, yeah, a few of them for a little while, we come and go."

"Which ones?" he asked. Four mines laid, step on as few as possible until you know why he is here. What did we do Saturday night?

"Sisca," I replied, like I knew I had chosen correctly from a multiple-choice test.

"Anyone else?" he enquired with a smirk.

"Depends on what time." I injected for another line of defense. "Throughout the night I saw a lot of people." Now he would have to get a little more specific at least. My parents looked at me in surprise at how cocky I was getting with a law officer. Juggling my parents AND the Sleuth might be beyond my abilities.

"Between 10 o'clock and midnight" he calmly replied, patient with his trap.

"Yeah, I saw a few of them on and off, I said doing my best to be vague. "Can't say I remember what time it was though."

"So you were at Westgate Hills Recreational Park with them," he asked shaking his head affirmatively.

Damn! It's about the cocaine, but what could he know about that? I never heard that anyone got stopped that night. "Yeah for little while," I admitted.

"Between 10 and midnight?" he wanted to confirm.

"Yeah, somewhere in that time."

"Who else was at the park with you? I want names." He clicked his pen to start writing down names.

"Just a few of the guys you mentioned already," I said.

"Name them," he challenged me. It was like having to turn around and walk through the minefield you thought you just cleared. I started to panic.

"Mom, Dad, I don't have to answer any of these questions unless he's charging me with something," I blurted out in last-ditch plea before I had to start naming names.

"Answer the man!" my dad said sternly, taking the side of the law. Sleuth offered a nod of appreciation toward my dad for respecting his position.

"Scarf and Sisca," I relented.

"What about Freilicht and McNicol?"

"I don't remember them being there," I lied. If I had to set off a mine, don't set off the big ones.

"No?" he enquired once more, pleased I was caught in his trap. Then under his breath, but loud enough to hear as he scribbled more notes, he added, "You're just digging yourself deeper."

"Were there any drugs being passed around or sold at the park that night?" he asked expecting my 'No'. My parents leaned up and looked at me with that, 'Just what in the world is going on with you' look.

"No."

"I didn't think so," he smiled wryly back.

I was too freaked to look at my parents for their reaction.

"All right then, were there any girls there while you were present?" he changed direction.

"Probably, but it was dark and I didn't recognize anyone other than the guys I came with.""Oh good! Then who were the other guys you came with."

"Just Scarf and Sisca, like I already said."

"Is that who you left with?" he stretched the trap again, while shifting to other papers in front of him.

"Yeah." (I had left with Steve and Washel; I was trying to distance myself from answering any questions about Wash/)

With that last lie, he hurriedly flipped through pages of handwritten notes and found the one he was looking for and excitedly made more notes. It never struck me that he may have already been to some of my friends' homes and all those notes he was flipping through were their woven lies of self-preservation. I was still unsure as to why he was here; still suspecting the cocaine deal. It seemed to me he was asking questions from all over the place, but didn't stay in one place long enough to give me the clue I was desperate for. Until he did, I knew I was burying myself or my friends with my answers, and that was exactly what Detective Sleuth wanted. After 10 more minutes of questioning, he finally asked the one that told me why he was here. And when he asked, I knew I was sunk, and I was bringing the ship with me.

"Did you see Ronnie Woodbine at the park that night and did you speak with her?" With that question I wondered if she had ratted us out about the cocaine or something.

"She may have been there, but I never talked to her," I replied. He seemed delighted with that answer too and hurriedly flipped to other hand-written pages to scribble in the margins. Everything I said seemed to make him happy. This is in complete contrast with past questionings in which he always got frustrated with our answers and lost his temper getting nowhere. I was frightened at this point; trembling and sweating in my chair.

"At any time did you see Ric Frielicht lay his leg over Ronnie Woodbine's face?" he asked a bit embarrassed for my parents. I thought, 'What in the world does he mean by that?' So I said:

"What in the world do you mean by that?"

"Did you see Ric Frielicht forcing oral sex upon Ronnie Woodbine?"

"NO, no way," I said finally understanding the first approach to the question. Then the light bulb went off and I realized all this was about Ronnie crying rape.

"Did you hear her call *your* name for help?" he questioned as though she had already told him she did. He must have already been to her house for questioning before coming to my house.

"No. I saw her go for a walk with Scarf and then talking calmly after they returned; in no way was she in any trouble." I figured this would protect Will and was the truth.

"So now you're sure you can place her there with Will Scarfo; just a minute ago you said you didn't know if she was at the park." He happily pointed out how he had just tripped me up.

"All right, she was there," I conceded. "But there was nothing like what you're insinuating going on." Eventually he trapped me into saying Ric was with us too.

My dad had been sitting quietly to this point, but now saw the direction this whole thing was going, jumped in to see just how involved I was in the accusations. He wanted the bottom line question answered without all the suspense…and so did I.

"Mr. Sleuth, could I ask you if my son is being named as an accomplice in any way about this?""At this point, Mr. Bonnett, your son is only named as a witness, but you should speak with him about the company he keeps," he replied.

I should interject here that Ronnie Woodbine was school friends with my then girlfriend Lori whom I later marry. It also became apparent now that Ronnie probably named me as a witness in the hopes I would support her claims since I was dating her friend. My allegiance was too *my* friends, not Ronnie, so her assumption was another dumb move.

The questioning continued for another half an hour with more sexual embarrassing interrogation in front of my parents involving Ronnie's claims about her ordeal. I need not elaborate other than she charged she was raped by two and assaulted by the other.

Never did Detective Sleuth show any sign of being on the defensive. I knew I was in big trouble. I had the feeling the present ordeal was only the scratch on the surface, that this was going to blow up bad and not go away soon. No matter the consequences, the truth could not be told tonight. Matter of fact; the truth would be so butchered over the next few months that even our merry band couldn't keep track of what was true and what we made up.

After a long hour of extensive questions about Ric and Scarfo, he moved on to Mikey McNicol's involvement on said night. I decided to keep Mikey out of it completely and say I never saw him that night since he was the hardest head amongst us to reason with should I have too.

"Tell me everything you saw go on between Mr. McNicol and Miss Woodbine." My father's support for Mr. Sleuth allowed the detective to take big liberties in asking broad sweeping questions that he knew I normally wouldn't touch, but with dad there I had to give reasonable replies…except for this question just asked.

"I never saw Mikey at the Park that night, so I'm sorry I can't help you there." Somewhere into the questioning, once I saw I wasn't the target of this investigation but a witness, I decided to act like I really wanted to cooperate but just hadn't witnessed what Ronnie claimed. I was throwing around so much bullshinski so fast that even a court stenographer couldn't have kept up with it.

"Are you saying he wasn't there that night?!"

"No. I'm saying I didn't *see* him there that night." The detective shifted in his seat, sitting up a little as if this shuffling would help him better craft the wording of his next question. "So you were there for two hours and never saw Mr. McNicol the whole night? Is that what you're telling me?" he grinned, waiting for my answer to bury me.

"Sorry, but I didn't see him there," I lied in my best Eddie Haskel innocence.

Well, this was the moment our frustrated detective had been waiting two years.

"OK, I am done with my questions," he abruptly announced with evident satisfaction. "Now here's what I want you to do," he gloated with confidence. "Take this sheet of paper and write down your timeline and statement of what you saw, did, and who you were with from 10:00 to 12:30 just as you told me since I got here. It WILL be used in court," he emphasized.

"Hey man, you can't seriously expect me to remember everything I said in the last hour."

"Well, sure I do," he said with a 'gotcha' deadpan stare on his face. "If it's all true, you should have no problem recollecting what you told me onto that paper," he said with obvious sarcasm while pointing with his pen at the sheet trembling in my hand. "Here's another piece of paper if you run out of room," he added, struggling his bulk up off the sofa again to hand me a clipboard with another blank sheet. Tonight, the guy could have given lessons to Colombo.

Up until now I had done my best to stay cool, but my nerves were starting to bail out on me. All the mental pressure of lying to protect myself, my friends, my parents caved in when I realized I had to put it in writing. This would be the statement I'd have to stand by in court. I couldn't reconstruct the night's events or remember the order of lies I just spewed. I was sure whatever I put in this statement would bury at least two of my pals, myself, and maybe more. If I could write a vague statement, then call Will, Mike, and Ric ASAP after Sleuth leaves and alert them to what is in my statement before Sleuth gets to their hou....

Only a few times in your life does blood flush your head in an instant of panic when you realize you have just made a crisis-inducing irrevocable mistake. It's a horrible feeling impossible to describe. Some people call them panic attacks. It came on like a locomotive when I remembered what my mom said to me earlier when I came downstairs after listening to 'Let It Bleed' at parent-raving volume. Whenever I was in my room, I locked the door; whenever I listened to music it was loud, so whenever someone called on the phone, my folks wouldn't bother to let me know unless the caller left a message. Rarely was it important enough for one of the guys to leave a message; usually, they didn't leave messages so I had to ask if anyone called. Tonight, someone had called and left messages, messages I should have called back.

"Ric and Will called you and said to call back right away," was the message I should have paid attention too. Now it hit me like a brick; Detective Sleuth had already been to their homes and they tried calling me to tell me what to say. Oiy, yuy, yuy. THIS is why Sleuth wore that canary-eating grin all night. He already had the scene constructed by Ronnie, Gergen, and my friends. He was getting a big kick out of how the six of us were butchering each other's testimony.

I sat between my folks and tried to write on the clipboard, but my knees were knocking and my hands were visibly shaking. All I could write down was: **around 10:00 – arrived at Westgate Park with Steve Sisca**. Anything I wrote after that would cook someone's goose if not my own. I had to excuse myself to the dining room table "where I can write at the table" in order to try and snap out of it. What I needed was a stiff drink to settle down. I remember trying to stop my knees from knocking by holding them with my hands, but they were now on auto-rattle, which I couldn't control—like uncontrolled shivering when you come out of really cold water. I can only recall a few times in my life when I was out of control and shaking. It was never a good circumstance.

I just plowed through it and handed back a page of half crossed out scribble that even contradicted the horse crap I shoveled out earlier. Let the cards fall where they may; I can't do much about it now. I heard the detective explaining to my parents the charges against my three friends as I wrote. Scarf and McNicol were charged with rape, and Freilicht with sexual assault of some sort. I didn't want to leave him with my parents for a minute longer than necessary so I wrote as fast as I could. The last thing I wanted is for him to bring up drug dealings or other events that never made it home.

I stood across from Det. Sleuth as he reviewed my statement. He'd huff and chuckle like he was reading the comics. It was that bad. He threw mine on a stack of six or seven other pages and looked up at me smiling. I recognized Steve Sisca's handwriting on top of the stack.

"This is gonna be one fine day in court for your little troop young man," he concluded with me, then addressed my parents. "This was my last stop tonight," he said holding up the stack of statements, "I've been to his four buddies' homes and all four stories contradict each other and *none* of them agree with Ronnie Woodbine's account, which Gergen's story backs up 100 per cent." Addressing me now, he continued, "You and Sisca I visited last to see how the witnesses for your three buddies would stack up." He shook his head woefully as he got to the words 'stack up'. "McNicol named *you* as his prime witness and you say he wasn't there that night!" he laughed, "and if you and Sisca were together all night as you say, it's amazing how opposite your two stories are, just amazing." I can still see him standing there shaking the stack of statements, grinning through those thick glasses. So much for Mr. Sleuth being a second-rate detective. I was sick.

"If your son goes to court with this pack of lies to protect his friends, the law can't help him," he assured my folks, trying one last effort to get me to finger my friends.

With that warning, my dad told me to go sit back down and write the truth. We argued back and forth about me rewriting another statement, but I was done writing. My head was ready to explode, my temper was at its end, my mind was total confusion. I just wanted to get out of there before I snapped;. Sleuth was waiting to see the victor in this father-son debate before him about re-writing my statement.

"NO!" I said with rage apparent enough to convince both we were done for tonight. "I'm *done* writing and I'm *done* answering questions!" Anger was my only way of dealing with my nerves.

Det. Sleuth got the message and left, content with the contradict-ing statements he had already mustered, leaving me with my parents who attempted to start grilling me about my friends and what really went on that night. But I had had enough and just grabbed my coat and walked out, ignoring their questions. I couldn't deal with them right now; I had to find the guys and see how much damage we caused ourselves. The Alleys were only a 10-minute walk from my house and I needed to burn off my shakes so up the street I started running. I was hardly a few houses away when Steve's car came screeching to a halt next to me and the door flew open. They had been circling the block waiting for Det. Sleuth to leave; they had even considered knocking up for me and pulling a rescue. I could have seen that; what a lame-brain crew. Steve and Wash were in the car. They had stopped up for the Scarf who couldn't leave because his dad's lawyer was asking him questions over the phone. No one knew where Mikey was. The last time a girl turned on him, he kidnapped her for three days until she escaped and the cops arrested him. That's another story that won't get told. One thing for sure, Mikey's story would stand the best chance of going to court since he'd threaten to pound all of us if we didn't back up *his* version. Mikey was the unelected leader of Manoa Lanes by fact of unpredictability. He was the only person Wash had hesitated to challenge yet. You might win a fight against him, but he might drive by and run you over on your way home that same night.

You can imagine the conversation in the car that night:

Rich: "How long was your statement?"

Steve: "I don't remember half of what I wrote and I don't even have a copy to study! Man, I flunked that exam royally."

Wash: "Who did you say you were with that night?"

Steve: "I think I said I never saw Gergen but in my statement I might have said I did, who knows. Who knows what I said about you, Wash?"

Rich: "Exactly! I couldn't remember all the crap I said. I was freaking out; I didn't even know why Sleuth was there for the first half hour!"

Wash: "You and Bruin (Steve) had it worse. He wasn't even at my house half an hour before I over-rode Mutt (German for mother) and told him to leave."

Rich: "Let's stick with what we wrote and not what we said. What we said isn't on record unless McNabb wrote all that crap down as fast as I could say it. I don't think he did, but he was writing down a lot."

Steve: "Yeah, every time I said something, he compared it to another sheet of paper and wrote something."

Rich: "I wrote that I never saw NcNicol that night so I won't have to deal with Mikey."

Steve: "So did I!" Steve agreed laughing as if that was a given for survival. "I'd rather lie in court before dealing with that temper."

Wash: "Ah Man, that blows my testimony! I said you two were with me and Mike all night," Wash lamented. Then shifting gears, he added with encouragement, "Sleuth said I'll be assigned a lawyer since my old lady can't afford one, I'll see what this lawyer says to do."

Rich: "Those 'Rent-A-Dent' lawyers are all flunkies, Wash; that's why they're assigned by the court, so they lose." **Steve:** "Yeah, you better start waxing your bung hole if you think a court-appointed flunkee is gonna keep you out of county." Even in the face of disaster, there was always room for joking.

On one thing we all agreed, "We're in a world of stank."

And we were. All of us would have to get together and come up with the same story before the court date. But that wasn't going to happen, the agreeing that is, the court date was imminent.

So, what really went on that night?

When the five of us got together, the quasi-truth came out. Ronnie had asked the Lawrence Park guys to leave without her so that Will could give her a ride home. But she was quizzing Will about Mikey, as if she wanted to go out with Mike. Will took this as a tactic to get him (Will) jealous. She then *willingly* 'entwined' herself to Will, who afterwards sarcastically asked her after if she was still interested in Mikey. Ronnie was now angry with Will and said "Yes", possibly to get back at him. So Will sent Mikey over to her and she *willingly* entwined herself to him. Why Mikey told Ric to check her out, I don't know, but Ric said she offered to 'accommodate' him in a different manner. Eric doesn't have a car to offer her a ride home; everyone had already left, so she was left at the park without a ride home. We assume Gergen came back to find her abandoned and angry sometime after midnight. Whatever developed between those two is speculation, but we know they stayed out all night. As far as Steve and I could figure out, it all sounded like the truth. The only area of doubt was whether Ric's favor was voluntary or not. We were close enough to hear her call for help if she had yelled for us. Without hearing any plea for help, Steve and I saw the situation as consenting sex.

Over the next few months, harmony broke down at the Alleys. Ric, Will, and Mike were feeding their three separate lawyers a line that protected themselves as best as possible. The three lawyers did not coordinate their efforts together for various reasons. One reason being neither of the first two wanted to work with Eric's court-appointed lawyer. Second being the only bright spot in this bungle: Scarf's dad hired a top lawyer who specialized in teen rape and didn't want to fight the case carrying the other two lawyers. He worked out of a Pittsburg law firm where his dad was referred to him through business connections.

Steve and I were named as main witnesses, though neither of us really saw or heard much that night. The two of us were caught between the proverbial rock and a hard place. Here are a few examples of the boomerang effect resulting from whatever our final testimony would be.

Example: Ric, Will, and Mikey all named Steve and I as firsthand witnesses to their version of their stories because they knew we would stick up for them. For any single individual exclusive of the other two, this would work out fine. The problem was all three of them were claiming Steve and I as witnesses to events we never mention or completely contradict in our written personal statements. Contradicting our statements in court would certainly get thrown in our face as unreliable witnesses or perjury?

On the other hand, Gergen wasn't in the predicament we were in; he only had to back up Ronnie's story from when he picked her up after we left. If the testimony of Steve and I got dismissed as unreliable, then Gergen becomes the only reliable witness. Scarfo's lawyer had Will point this out to us in order to back Will's account.

Steve and I concluded Will's lawyer was the only one on the ball so we leaned toward supporting his version of the events. However, we couldn't admit that to Mikey and Ric; they would expel us from Manoa Lanes if we didn't support their case. To the reader, that may seem a reasonable price to pay; but to us, the last two years of our lives have revolved around the thrill of Alley culture; it gets in your blood. Everyone became more desperate to enforce their version as the court date approached.

None of the lawyers ever asked to meet with Steve and I; maybe that would be witness tampering. All three accused were assuring their respective lawyer we would support their testimony. However, Will was the only one to convince Steve & I his lawyer was absolutely sure of winning in court because he dealt only with rape cases.

In order for Mikey to have his way in court, he started threatening Steve and I to support his version. When we informed Ric of Mikey's threatening, he informed us to follow his (Ric's) story and he would take care of Mikey. This mini episode came to a head one day at the Alleys when Ric confronted Mikey with most of the Alley guys present and proceeded to kick Mike's ass, dethroning him as self-appointed leader of our divided band of merry idiots. After that, Ric assumed we would go with his version, since Mikey was no longer in a position to intimidate us. New cliques formed within our gang, supporting one guy or another. It was the beginning of the end for Manoa Lanes; our union was crumbling. Det. Sleuth was winning his personal war with our gang through an internal battle, which he was completely unaware of. Because of Gergen, there was a lot of tension between Manoa Lanes and the Corner Boys. Because of Ronnie Woodbine's brothers being members of the Lawrence Park Gang, there were strained relations and threats from them also. Because of one guy (Gergen) looking for someone to trip with, and one girl's goofy infatuations, three gangs and many individuals were at each other's throat. It could all ignite at any moment. We needed to get to court before any more disintegration. Don't ever kid yourself if you believe your personal drug use or choice of friends doesn't affect everyone around you.

We will all have our day before the Judge

Finally, the dreaded day arrived with all of us dragging one or both of our parents to the Media Court House for a juried trial. The day would become a test of justice.

None of our band had agreed on a common story. All of us were still arguing self-serving stories. Steve and I had not committed to any one version, saying we would roll with the best lawyer defense as it presented itself. None of us knew the order of procedure or questioning for the day. It was in this spirit of 'who knows what's going to happen' that the five of us stood outside the courtroom dressed in suits like we were going to a wedding, long hair trimmed and slicked back to make our appearance look more innocent (lawyer instructions).

After complimenting each other on looking so dapper, someone regretted not bringing a few joints along to relax our strained nerves. Steve and I burned a few earlier while going over which story to present under various scenarios, then split up to ride to the courthouse with our folks. So we already had a fair buzz going. Wash thought it would be unique to thumb our noses at the judicial system by burning a few doobers in the courthouse restroom and came prepared. So, after getting zonked in an empty basement men's room, we grinned our way into the courtroom to watch justice unfold like a confused Alice in Wonderland story, cynical of everything the justice system represented, thinking what a farce the whole ordeal was, Mom sitting by my side, my mind wandered to all the contradictions present in that room:

Ronnie was lying to her mother.

Gergen was lying to us.

Ric, Will, or Mike were lying to their lawyers.

The lawyers would be presenting those lies to the jury.

Steve and I were about to lie as witnesses.

And a jury had to sort through it all and determine guilt. Good luck!

The following is what transpired. The chronology of who spoke when may be in error with the passage of time, but you will get the main points clearly.

After the charges were read, a lawyer from each side had the opportunity to explain to the jury their client's side of the story. Gergen was first called to the stand by Ronnie's attorney to describe Ronnie's state of mind when he found her alone and upset at Westgate Field. The defense chose not to cross-examine at this time, but instead put their clients on the stand. The other two defense lawyers seemed in agreement to let Scarfo's high profile lawyer lead the way. I can't recall the lawyer name so I will call him Mr. Snake. He dismissed Gergen's testimony as if it was irrelevant when asked if he wanted to cross-examine. I was just glad I wasn't called up next.

Mr. Snake called Bill Scarfo to the stand, but did not ask a single question concerning what went on that night. Instead, his lawyer asked Will questions about his dating Ronnie *previous* to that night.

"Did you and Miss Woodbine go out with each other prior to the night in question?"

"Yes we did," Will replied.

"And how many times would you say you went out?"

"Four times."

"And during any of these four dates did you have sexual relations with Miss Woodbine?"

"Yes."

"How many times?"

"All four times."

"Could you please describe to us what kind sexual contact you engaged in?"

Objections were overruled as we all sat through the detailed description of a sleazy date, which was dittoed as the pattern for the following three dates if you want to call them dates.

"Now, were there any other sexual encounters between you and Miss Woodbine after those first four date nights?"

"Yes."

"And when did that occur?"

"The night we met at Westgate Park." (date clarified)

"At any time did Miss Woodbine object to the way you were touching her?"

"No, not at all," Will said adding shyly, "That's sort of why we got together."

"Did any of your other friends present in this courtroom go out with Miss Woodbine prior to your dating her?"

"Yes, Mike McNicol went out with her once."

Mikey was put on the stand next, but I don't remember by which lawyer. That Mr. Snake used this opportunity to further defame Miss Woodbine was clearly remembered though. Scharf's lawyer was confidently setting up precedence of sexual behavior which Ronnie (and her naïve mother) never counted on being exposed. I can't imagine her lawyer not warning her, so I guess she planned on denying all her previous sex history. And we all knew denying could work. Ronnie was now sitting next to her mother wiping away tears and letting her hair cover her face from the jury and her shame. Probably nerves letting loose.

Mr. Snake's point had been made and he was emphasizing for effect, which the judge didn't want to sit through anymore. It was painful for all present to watch the Woodbine family agonize over the truth just spilled about their daughter. Not painful for me or my friends.

"Yes, your honor, if I may..." furthered Lawyer Snake.

But the judge interrupted, "Let it be noted that the same pattern of sexual relation was maintained on this occurrence. No need for further details, Mr. Snake."

There must have been cross-examining, but I can't recall. There were objections, there were over-rulings; our side was looking good. Steve and I cast nods to each other from our seats. We would support Scharf's lawyer, truth or not. He radiated the polished, confident lawyer; dressed the part, looked the part, and probably picked up on the judge's familiarity with rape cases. They guy was masterfully cutting Ronnie's reputation to shreds and ceased when the judge alluded to fewer details. That was council Snake's victory signal.

The judge cut short the agony of everyone sitting through more sleazy testimony due to the sobbing from Ronnie's mother hearing how her daughter was being defamed. At this point, I think Mrs. Woodbine believed both boys were making it all up. She was in for a bad, bad day.

Rape cases are very rarely won by the victim, but at the time we didn't know that. The reason being in many cases that a good rape lawyer can establish promiscuous behavior in the woman pressing charges. This promiscuous behavior is established to insinuate leading the accused on. This presents reasonable doubt and a hung jury if there are any men on the jury, which there always are. In court, a sharp lawyer will whip up her previous promiscuity and she looks like she made up the rape. Sperm samples and physical bruising or proof of a struggle needs to be in evidence for the victim to have any chance of winning. Ronnie had none of these proofs.

Miss Woodbine was called to the stand next by Mr. Snake.

The Bailiff swore her in, "Do you swear to tell the truth, the whole truth, and nothing but the truth, so help you God?"

She muttered an unconvincing "I'll do my best," The judge caught it and leaned over to her like a father to explain to her now was no time to hide the truth, that lies always get found out in *his* court and only make matters worse.

"Just tell the truth, young lady, and this will quickly be over," he advised assuredly.

She answered "Yes" to the oath and hung her head.

Mr. Snake treated her like a daughter at first and asked her about her Catholic upbringing. He reminded her of the commandments she learned; Thou shall not lie; Thou shall not bear false witness, convincing her the best path is always to tell the truth. Ronnie shook her hanging head in solemn agreement.

Then he morphed back into professional lawyer mode.

"Miss Woodbine, did you voluntarily go out with Will Scarfo four times previous to the night at Westgate Hills?"

"Yes, but…"

"Just answer the question please." He anticipated every "But" that tried to come out of her mouth, snuffing it like wind on a match before reaching the bomb fuse. Watching him in action like this, he was worth whatever they were paying him. I was in total zonked fascination of his craft, even forgetting about getting called to the witness stand.

"Did you allow Mr. Scarfo on any of those occasions to place his hand under your brassier?" he continued, knowing to start small. "Remember you are under oath."

"Well, yes, but…" Ronnie was quickly snuffed at "but" by her interrogator.

"Did you allow him to put his hand down your pants?"

"Yes, but we…" snuffed again.

"Did you allow him to remove your pants?"

"No." Snake feigns a puzzled look with this reply.

"Then how did they come off?" (This is where she says he forced her garment down; directing Snake into a line of questioning whether she called for help, fought back, showed her mother any bruises when she got home, etc., determining no proof of struggle. That led the jury to believe she really didn't try too hard.)

"On any of these occasions, did you remove Mr. Scarfo's pants?"

"You make me look so awful!" she said, now breaking down into hard tears of humiliation.

The questioning was more detailed and brutal than I'll present here; you get the picture. Ronnie's mother was first in shock, then shaking her head like she was in physical pain. Her ears couldn't believe what she was hearing from her daughter so young. Though I had despised her for putting my friends and I through this ordeal, I actually felt sorry for the girl sobbing on the stand. However, I now had confidence for the first time in the last few months that everything was going to come out fine for our side. Fortunately, this line of questioning was about to be abruptly halted by the Judge.

"You're not letting me explain myself," she finally snuck in before Attorney Snake could intercept, but it didn't matter; he had a laundry list of humiliating questions stocked up in case such a "But" slipped by him.

"Is the way you presented yourself on these dates appropriate for a 16-year-old young lady as yourself? Yes or No please."

"No" was just audibly squeeze out under her sobbing. There were objections here and there, but the questioning hit the desired mark. She was looking to her mother for some rescue and the judge was looking for this familiar signal he had probably seen many times before in similar examinations.

The judge broke in at this point.

"OK, I think we have all heard enough testimony, I am calling a halt to any further questioning until after lunch. Court dismissed for an hour and a half." He stood up showing a hint of frustration, turning to the Woodbine's table; I would like to speak with the Woodbine family and both counsels privately.

It was a mid-April sunny day as I strolled to lunch with my mom. The world had taken a beautiful turn and everything seemed right again. Steve and I now agreed to support Scarfo's story 100 per cent; the heck with the other two guys. Mr. Snake had our full allegiance after seeing him in action. We let Will know this as we left for lunch; things were looking up. My mom, after hearing the reputation of Ronnie from her own mouth, fully believed that my friends had not forced themselves on her. She represented the sentiments for most of the jury I'm sure. I loved the Snake.

Who'd have thunk Ronnie would sit there and tell the truth, *nearly the whole truth and nothing but nearly the whole truth*? It was completely unexpected. Hadn't her lawyer asked her if she ever went out with Will and Mikey before, or how she conducted herself on those occasions? It seemed as though all of this was new to her mother, like she wasn't warned how ugly rape trials get by going into the victim's past history. Her lawyer appeared totally disgusted with her testimony like he was clueless too. The other scenario is that Ronnie had told her lawyer nothing happened on those previous dates, or there were no previous dates, then buckled under the *Oath* and *Catholic up-bringing* emphasis from the judge and Snake upon taking the stand. I believe that is exactly what happened. I also believe it was her mother who insisted on taking this ordeal to court and not Ronnie. Parents, if you want the truth on the big questions, look your children right in the eyes when they answer you.

So as it turns out, Ronnie Woodbine was a better person than we or she thought. When it comes down to it, she may have been loose with her body (which often is the result of peer pressure rather than desire), but in a final analysis, honesty was a virtue she chose not to compromise, no matter what it cost her. Obviously, she had been going through a similar agony as us over the last few months. Whether to hurt her mom and tell the truth of what happened that night when she got home—THAT would have taken a Herculean effort for anyone—or lie her way out with a fabricated story; the logical choice and easy way out for any young teen accustomed to lying to their parents. Hey, *I* was lying to my folks to protect myself *and* them. I imagine that witness stand must have a certain power and awe of its own once you are standing there, sworn in before a judge who has seen it all. And we will be standing there some day, in a higher court, with a higher judge, under the purest truth.

In Ronnie's case, the bad choice was to listen to Joe Gergen advising her to claim rape. But once it was out of her mouth, she faced the next agonizing route—admit to mother she lied just before going to trial or follow through with her lie. Either way, her predicament was worse than ours. I get the feeling one of our guys may have forced himself on her, but she had allowed herself in a position, which put her as much to blame as him. The blame is history now.

Back in court after lunch, the judge addressed us all. "I have spoken with the Woodbine family and they have agreed to drop all charges of rape against Mr. Scarfo and Mr. McNicol."

I was elated, it was over, we had won! Almost.

"However, the charge of xxxxxx against Eric Frielicht still stands and we will now proceed."

I was shocked, it wasn't over. I may have to testify under Wash's flunky lawyer or Ronnie's attorney. Oh Ma-an!

Wash's lawyer put him on the stand and attempted to do the same thing Mr. Snake had accomplished but to disastrous results. When I say this guy was not sharp, he reminded me of the stuttering character in the movie *Office Space* who had his Swingline stapler confiscated. That was Wash's lawyer. I sat above, to the side of Wash's counsel, observing him write notes during the trial. He printed in large slow print you would literally expect from a 9th grader. I have no idea how he ever got licensed but here he was butchering Ric's defense to the point of comedy. He and Ric were openly arguing like a teenager with his parent; the judge had to warn them a few times.

This lawyer could not find his notes when he wanted them, lost his place, lost his train of questioning until Ric would tell him what to ask, which the judge wouldn't allow; he should not have been a lawyer. As long as we knew Ric after that day, we would imitate his lawyer for fun.

Shortly, the judge had enough of this clown's shenanigans and dismissed him for being unprepared. Ric was eventually assigned another court-appointed counsel to prepare a defense and the case was adjourned a few months. In the meantime, Wash was guilty of probation violations and had his probation extended again, which had him furious at his flunky lawyer. We found it all very entertaining.

A few months later, Steve and I had to go back to court again but since we only had to witness for Wash it was easy to support his version of his story. His probation was upheld (for another year, I think), but none of the other charges stuck.

The Ronnie Woodbine affair was the beginning of the end of our brotherhood at Manoa Lanes. It forced us to realize everyone was out for themselves. You couldn't trust a fellow hood when the chips got down. At the same time, drugs had now become more important than friendships. Members were ripping each other off and stealing from each other when they could get away with it. Cliques had now formed within our gang. What concerned me most though, were the hand guns turning up. First Mikey got one, then Steve, and others did likewise. One never knew when a gun was among us. This had me concerned when considering the tempers, logic and, track record behind those trigger fingers.

Add to that, we really knew nothing about guns; none of us were hunters or anything along those lines. When Steve showed me his gun the first time, we decided to shoot it at a hand drawn target taped to a concrete wall in his 12' X 16' basement to see if it worked. The bullet ricocheted off the wall, went through the ceiling, and a bedroom wall. We laughed like an errant rocket went off wrong on the 4th of July. We were idiots with a gun.

After the Woodbine trial, I took a hard look at where I was heading. My friends and I had dodged the bullet again, but the next bullet could literally be a real one and it might not miss. If our guys were carrying guns, it was only a matter of time before they used them. That was a fact. I had been high every day for two-and-a-half years and everything seemed to be in a constant mental fog like I was sleep-walking. There was no direction in my life; I was a wandering goofball. The path I was on had no edge, no boundaries. There was no tangible truth to hang my hat on. I knew with certainty some of us would wind up dead or in prison if we continued this path. It seemed like I was the only one at Manoa Lanes who verbally anticipated this. If I tried to talk about this stuff with Steve or anyone else, they would tell me I think too much. I hated the way they all stuck their heads in the sand without seeing our future as clearly and obviously as I did. I guess I was the only one thinking deductively in this crowd. We always placed ourselves in situations where there is trouble, therefore, we will always be in trouble. From our early days until now, the trouble kept getting progressively more serious, and by sheer luck, none of us had died yet and only a few had spent short stints in county lock-up. Reason tells me eventually the luck ends. My friends carry guns, therefore, someone will get killed. We have no control over our drug appetites, therefore, someone will fatally overdose. To me, the handwriting was on the wall, but I was caught in the trap and couldn't escape even if I wanted too.

What was the alternative? Live the mundane life of common folk? Go straight? My spirit for excitement was slowly destroying me. But, on the other hand, I had to feed it. Unless I satisfied my desire to walk this knife edge, I felt I wasn't getting the *most* out of life. I remember going home at 2 a.m. or 3 a.m. after being out all night, looking at all the dark houses thinking, "Man, look at all these people doing nothing, what a waste of their lives, no one in this town got as much out of life as I did tonight." And that made me feel more important than everyone else. Like most of our gang, I'd rather be dead than bored, and if I wasn't living in the fast lane, I was bored. I tried to stop drugs a few times; my longest success lasted two days and I was miserable. Is there a way out? God help us, there has to be a Way.

CHAPTER 10

The Best Night of my Life

Age 18, summer 1972

For some of us, there is a single event where we can specifically point to a life-changing epiphany and what ignited it. My epiphany occurred while sitting in that Media, PA, courtroom during opening statements, stoned, with my clueless 53-year-old mother sitting next to me. A consuming question locked onto my mind and set me on a path for the answer to that question. What *is* Truth? Particularly, I was so curious about how the truth would be either honored or butchered today in this courthouse—the House of Justice. But first you must have truth. This day in court ushered in the event that awakened my spirit to search for truth.

Here I was sitting in this Hall of Justice. Robes, law uniforms, lawyers in suits, oaths, the seriousness of it all reflected the pall of truth. If justice is to be found anywhere, *this* is the place, right? However, nearly all the accused and witnesses were prepared to lie. And it was up to 12 poor saps to sort through it all and come up with the truth. Furthermore, who determined the **standards for truth** and what *is* justice? Someone send me the blueprints, please! From what I had learned so far in my short life, truth and justice were shifting intangibles determined by changing minds and shifting cultures. Truth seemed to be a moving target. Last year, killing babies in the womb was illegal, this year (1972) it is the law of the land. I mean, if we can redefine murder, OF CHILDREN, is there ANY absolute truth? The hunt was on.

Sitting in court that day before the room was brought to session, I thought to myself, "Everyone here is ready to lie through their teeth. If this is our best hope to determine truth, and this is representative of human justice, mankind in general is in capital trouble. Is there no keeper of the truth?" It really comes down to who can fool whom, which shell the truth is under. What mankind needs is an impartial judge who is the keeper of the real truth, a referee. Maybe that's who God is, but that would mean accountability, maybe judgment, and that would bring some kind of reward / punishment, heaven and hell back into the picture; and we all know they are fictional places, right? Scary thought arose; if *my* life was tested on the balance of justice, I didn't stand a chance. My bad deeds would certainly outweigh my good deeds. Yet I don't see myself as a bad person—who does? At least, not bad by *my standards*. I was very impressed with the final outcome of this day in court. An experienced judge saw through it all and was swift to rule properly, but as we have all witnessed from the O.J. Simpson trial, consistent justice does not always prevail.

In our case, no matter who won in court, justice would not be served unless someone beat the tar out of Joe Gergen who was responsible for the whole lie. To me, that would be fair justice, which I left to Ric to deal out via *our gang justice*. Even though we won, the judge didn't serve any justice to Joe Gergen who just skipped away. The law of our land doesn't see it that way. Our gang justice was beginning to look more legitimate than ever. Come to think of it, isn't the whole world just a bunch of gangs warring with each other trying to impose their own brand of justice? So what's so wrong about our little gang getting into the throw of it?

You, the reader, have been reading along with your own judgment of my stories, *you* belong to a gang—oh yeah, you don't get off Lilly White thinking you're not a gang member. A gang is nothing more than a group of people with the same shared prejudices who prefer to be with others like-minded. *You* figure out what gang you belong to: The gang who hates gays and lesbians? The gang who rejects a political party? The gang who can't tolerate pro-lifers or Christians? Islamist Fundamentalist? The gang who donates their energies to the environment and nothing to their needy fellow man? The gang who resents the rich and thinks they should to be taxed more because *you* don't have what you think you deserve? The gang who hides inside a vice? We all have our secret prejudices that allow us to be our true selves only amidst the gang of like-minded individuals. You feel safe among that gang. How about the gang of social indifference? Spiritual indifference? Many of us sport lifetime tattoos for those gangs. Pick your gang(s) and set the rules for your justice; there are way too many to choose from and new members are joining every day. I was far from being alone.

Short Tangent Story

Ironically, a few years back, I was on the jury side of a very similar court case concerning sexual improprieties between an adult man and 15-year-old boy. The lies were flying thick in all directions. The lawyers by way of omission were avoiding the truth. After two days of deliberating, our jury was hopelessly hung and informed the judge as to our stalemate. He sent us back to the jury room for further deliberation several times, saying two days was not long enough to conclude we were a hung jury. Our jury had a list of five items that made no sense from either side's testimony and raised doubts of guilt or innocence; we couldn't get satisfactory answers to these five questions. However, I had it figured out plain and simple but was keeping a low profile after my initial statement after the first day of testimony, when I stated to my fellow jurors, "I think they're *all* lying to us," it was received with raised eyebrows around the jury room. Now with a hung jury, I figured there was nothing to lose. So I asked, "May I present this crime as I see it?" They gave me the floor.

I explained that the sex was consenting between the adult and the boy, not forced, for a mutual reward; a job at a store on the boy's 16th birthday as presented in testimony by the boy, which was reneged on. Once the adult reneged on the reward, revenge set in, the boy told his mom to tell the police he was assaulted, and here we are in court listening to lies. The boy couldn't give us a good reason why he had repeatedly returned to the accused man's place of business after being assaulted several times. Though he was promised a job there, he couldn't admit he was trading sex for a promised job once he turned 16. The lawyers couldn't answer the big gap questions because the truth would condemn both of their clients. This is a paltry short explanation to you, the reader, for sake of saving time but I hope you get it. Both accused and victim were lying, as were the lawyers by omitting the truth. Once the boy told his mom he was assaulted, and she called the police, there was no turning back unless he wanted to tell the truth, that he consented to doing sexual favors in return for a job at the store.

I told the jury foreman to review the five-question list with the other 10 jurors again and see if my scenario fills in all the gaps. They were all amazed and we convicted the guy within 30 minutes on two counts of corrupting the morals of a minor and some other counts I don't recall. One of the jury-women hugged me in tears while asking, "Why didn't you say something earlier?" To which I answered, "The judge told us to determine guilt or innocence based on the testimony presented; the scenario I just presented to you is based **not** on testimony given, but on testimony omitted."

I'm not telling this to sound like Johnny Cochrane. All I did was revert to my old self at age 18 and reconstruct a more likely scenario pooled from a little street smarts, which assumes people lie to save their skin. *No one on the jury could bring themselves to imagine both parties and their lawyers had lied* or omitted truth on such a grand scale under oath, so they couldn't think far enough to reconstruct the real truth. Had I not been there to show them, it would have turned out like the O.J. Simpson trial. Just think of all the O.J. trials that don't ever get the truth presented. Human justice is a travesty and that is the best we have?

In human terms, it is so easy to deceive justice. If there is no great score-keeper or eye in the sky, then what does any of your good deeds (righteous-ness) *or lack thereof* matter? Daniel Webster coined it best when he surmised:

If there is no God, then nothing really matters.
If there is a God, then nothing else matters.

I was coming to that point in my life where I realized there had to be a God. If not, then murderers, pedophiles, child abusers, and all the Pol Pots, Hitlers, Stalins, Mansons, Bundies, etc., that were never brought to justice, got away with their atrocities. So do you and I. This cerebral puzzle now became clear in my head; my epiphany at the Ronnie Woodbine trial—there has to be a God. Without God, we are all just matter in motion for a moment. Matter that doesn't matter. Taken further, life without meaning.

Within the next few months, instead of criminal activity mellowing at Manoa Lanes as a result of the Woodbine case, it accelerated. Along with guys keep-ing guns in their cars, my friends were graduating to needle drugs one by one. Heroin and Meth had found a new home at Manoa Lanes. The pressure was on to keep up, so was the temptation. Not yet 19, I was at another one of life's proverbial crossroads; do I graduate on to the needle with my friends? So far in my life I had taken nearly every wrong fork in the road I came upon.

Other circumstances also came into play. By February 1972, I was devoting more time to selling drugs than my college studies. So I dropped out of college but never told my parents or the college; I just never went to another class, business was just too good. Of course, I had no trade to market myself in the workplace; neither were employers hiring long-haired, dope smoking, maggot-infested, fm radio types with an attitude (a tip of the hat to Rush there). A new recession was rearing its head. For the first time since

The Great Depression, America was shutting down big industry up and down the Delaware River industrial basin, creating a region known as the Rust Belt. Forget about getting a decent job, thousands of unemployed, experienced workers were in line ahead of us young kids trying to enter the work force. Selling dope was one of my few viable options.

Friendships at Manoa Lanes were fracturing as different cliques vied for more power within the gang. Steve and I had been like brothers for the last three years, but we came to a major clash. There is a certain pecking order established among close friends as you grow up together for 12 years. Steve knew never to challenge me in a fight, but because of a disagreement over girlfriends, Steve came at me and a fist fight ensued. So in the graveyard at St. Dennis Church, I quickly dispatched my good friend's feeble effort with a strong emphasis on, "Don't ever try something this stupid again." Fist fighting with a longtime close friend leaves an empty feeling in your heart; win or lose, you lose. I remember once punching JoePec in the stomach when we were very young. He sat there crying and I starting crying because I had made him cry. I tried to apologize, but he ran home crying and so did I. We never fought each other again. After Steve's challenge, things were never the same between us. He started hanging with Tom Harvey and I started hanging with Joe Peca, my Glendale friends, and a few other guys who left the Alleys. Most of us had steady girlfriends by now and hung at the Alleys less, not wanting to bring our girls up there. That's not to say I quit the Alleys yet; I'd still hang out with my old Alley buds a few times a week, including Steve.

A few months after my fight with Steve, he was driving his car when he stuck a nine-year-old boy, killing him instantly (story told at end of this chapter). Again, I was thinking, 'Where's the justice for this boy's family?' Steve made a bad choice to cut school that day, now a child is dead. I was getting a bit angry with my intangible and seemingly disinterested God. Seemed to me like he created this mess called mankind, said "Oops!", and exited to another solar system. I was also thinking about some close calls in my own life where I stood a good chance of never making it home again. I realized how fragile our existence is; for the first time I saw my own vulnerability. So one evening while lying on my bed, contemplating these many thoughts as confused teenagers are so apt to do, I sprung to the edge of my bed and came to a very obvious conclusion concerning God and me.

With SO MANY religions in the world, all claiming to have the answer, how was a simple man like me supposed to sort through it all to come up with the truth?

Therefore, it is not MY responsibility to find God but HIS responsibility to find me. So for the first time in my adolescent life I knelt down to pray, addressing the following prayer to the generic God of this universe whomever he may be. I didn't care if it landed in the ears of Allah, Mohammed, Jesus, Mary, or Joseph Smith, the biblical God Jehovah, Buddha, the Dalai Lama or even Elvis, whoever was listening and could reply. However, I pretty much discounted Jesus as a prime candidate for listening since I had prayed to Him throughout my childhood and didn't get replies. Plus, the nuns were 'married' to Him and I had a bad vibe for nuns. Elvis really was never really in the running either.

The Prayer:

"Hello God, this is Rich Bonnett. I don't know if you are real or not but if you are, you have a *big* responsibility to us all; but for now, here's all I ask of you. I need you to make yourself known to me in any tangible way you see fit because *I* can't find *you*.

And in return, **I make this solemn oath before you on my knees with all the sincerity of my being**: If you *are* real and you reveal yourself to me with your unmistakable presence, it would then be obvious to me that nothing else on this earth, in my lifetime, will matter except following you, which I will *gladly* do. So if you get this message, great. If not, any responsibility *I have* to seek you any further is null and void due to your lack of response when I was at my most sincere. Either way, don't take too long in answering since, as you should already know, I'm at another one of these crossroads

I'm so good at choosing. Good talking, hope to hear from you, if not, I'll be a guilt-free junkie in six months. Amen."

Even though in black and white the prayer looks a bit blasphemous, I was 100 per cent sincere in motive, and God knows our heart. Unbeknownst to me, God had already promised me I would find him in Deuteronomy 4:29 "If you seek me **with all your heart**, you **will** find me". My prayer was said with all the sincerity of my heart while humbling myself on my knees. I figured if God is God, He is not looking for flowery words from a specific location, like a church, He just wants me to speak in plain talk from the heart; He should be able to understand any language, especially that of the heart. God knows my Rosaries and other memorized prayers I'd parroted since Catholic school had gotten me nowhere. Afterwards, I distinctly remember feeling unburdened concerning what is truth, what matters, and responsibility for my lifestyle. I figured that either way I'm the winner in this proposal. If God exists and reveals Himself to me, along with what He wants from me, I'll gladly do what He says. If he doesn't answer, I'm free to live my life as fast and short as I want, as I have, without any temporal or eternal consequences I will ever need to answer for.

Though drugs take you to a dead end, they *do* take the scenic route. I mean, if there is no accountability after death, why not deal max quantities of cocaine, become Snorty the Clown and make lots of money while enjoying the scenery for this short ride? A nine-to-five office job was definitely not in my future. My high school guidance counselor once asked me in my junior year what my interests were; she was trying to help me pick a trade for my future. In my mind, the only true reply I could think of was, "Good dope, and good friends to do good dope with."

Anyhow, I was very curious if my prayer would get a response. For the next several days I'd wake up each morning thinking, "Another day and no answer", I was only half expecting a reply. Then at the end of the week I was at a party where a jock friend from high school named Jim Bianco had captured the attention of a small group of people I knew vaguely. Someone invited me to sit down and listen to what Jim was saying, so I did. I had a lot of respect for Jim, having won the State Championship for wrestling a year earlier. He was straight as an arrow, but a quality guy who didn't pass judgment on dopers. Back in high school, Jim had been in my gym class where we used to wrestle for fun (we were both in the same weight class), becoming friends that way. Tonight, Jim had gathered the attention of a handful at this party, speaking about Bible prophecy and what the Bible said about the return of Jesus Christ. He seemed knowledgeable on the subject, at least from my perspective of knowing nothing. What he said got my attention, but afterwards I thought, 'No deal, God. If Jim is your answer to my prayer, you'll have to do a whole lot better. Granted, being God you should be able to know the future." Little did I know He was just warming up.

A week later, I was sleeping over Joe Peca's house since his folks were away for the weekend. As expected, we threw a party which I don't remember much about until the early morning hours after everyone had left. Joe and I were flipping around the available three TV channels looking for something decent to watch, killing time until sleep arrived.

On comes a preacher who was saved from a gang-land background. The man was talking to a large crowd in an outdoor arena somewhere in California; the "Jesus First" movement was just gaining momentum out west among disenfranchised hippies. This preacher started describing his life before Jesus saved him; he was describing *my* life. Better yet, he was describing how I thought, and why I thought that way. Then he told how Jee-sus changed his life and he was able to walk away from the drugs, the misery and the pain of being trapped in a lifestyle—"You know the end thereof." The man was a powerful speaker who knew how to reach his audience in this targeted 1 a.m. time slot for zonked American youth. I couldn't change the channel, I had to know where this man was taking me; he definitely had my attention. Never had someone so clearly spread my life before me and clearly presented Jesus Christ as I was hearing Him tonight. At the end he gave an invitation to all listeners who identified with his message to surrender their lives; hook, line and sinker to the Lord of all, Jesus Christ. I froze on the sofa like I was made of stone. Not me, not tonight, not *this* way; something is reaching too deep inside me and *I'm not ready*. It was all clear to me for the first time in my life, why God sent his Son to die for my sins as if I was the only life worth saving. The very Spirit of God was reaching into my heart and calling me out…and I knew it, and I was scared to death of this challenge to my soul. I can't win this fight against God; to win *against* Him is to lose my soul forever. But I successfully resisted because I'm stubborn, thick-hearted, and afraid of losing my selfish life to God's plan instead of my own plan. Are you like that?

The program ended, Joe and I sat there thinking but not saying anything to each other for lack of what to say. That guy pointed directly into my soul, identified my life, and tried to direct me concerning the truth about my sin. I was turning away. "*Not enough evidence, God,*" I said to myself, ever the skeptic. That guy just had his lines down well and knew his audience. Then I remembered my prayer of a few weeks ago and I became more afraid. Was God replying here to my prayer? This was just too much. I was looking for a physical answer, not God speaking to my heart; this was just too awesome in a fearful way. I had no idea *this* is what could happen. So I choose to put it out of my head, just the same way many of you have some time throughout your life, all of your life. Though I tried to stick my head in the sand, I had to concede to God that He had successfully reached into my being.

"*Wait, one more final deal,*" I prayed, "*I concede that you **are** trying to reach me God, but **I have to be sure**. So God, come across that strong again within 24 hours and I'll know it's you, and Jesus Christ is your answer. But there is no way I'm caving in to some TV preacher.*" After all, we are all above that chicanery for sure. I Corinthians 1:21

I asked Joe what he thought of the TV preacher's message. He replied something to the effect of it being accurate as far as describing our generation. I asked him if at any time he felt like God was in the room talking to him through that preacher.

He said, "No, but if you want to read more about it I have this book you can read."

"You're kidding me," I replied, feeling the fear creep back, knowing Joe's house had always been barren of anything resembling religious literature since I'd known him.

He got up went over to the trash can and fished out a book titled *The David Wilkerson Jesus Manual*, which I still have to this day. He handed it to me.

"What is *this* doing in *your* trash?" I asked apprehensively, considering my 24-hour deadline deal.

"My mom has been trying to get me to read it for the past few weeks. This afternoon before they left on their trip, she shook it in my face and said: 'Joseph! Either read this book or throw it away, I'm tired of asking you to read it.' So I grabbed it out of her hand and threw it in the trash…then she left, now it's yours."

Let me explain something here. Joe's folks did not own a family Bible or have a shred of Christian literature in their house for as long as I had known them. Neither had they been to church for as long as I had known them, except weddings or funerals. His mother was a rock-solid believer in the justice of God and though Catholic, thought all denominations were a hypocritical sham. Her giving this book to Joe was her rare but loving attempt to try to direct Joe towards God in his erring years. So what do you think the chances are this book would be here tonight, to get fished out of the trash, after the preacher's 1 a.m. TV program, which prompted my 24-hour extension deal, two weeks after my "God, show thyself" prayer? Exactly what I was thinking.

Did you ever in your own life make it Priority One to sincerely ask God to get your attention for what he wants with your life? I'll guarantee you this: He WILL answer your prayer; probably why most people are afraid to ask Him. Feel free to use the exact same prayer that worked for me a few pages back (less the last line). Take a chance, what have you got to lose?

"He who loses his life will gain it forever, he who keeps his life will lose it forever."

I then told Joe about this prayer I said a few weeks back, and that now I'm afraid God is answering me, that my life is on the verge of a big change and I'm not sure I'm ready for what's ahead.

Joe replied matter of factly, "Well, something has got to change; you can't go on like you have been."

"Do you mind if I read this book, Joe?" I asked by the trash can while flipping through the pages. I had discarded God's Word to the trash heap of my life until now. Here, He was taking it out of my trash heap and putting it directly into my hands.

"No, go ahead; read it out loud so it can put me to sleep. TV is off the air."

(For those of you who don't remember TV with three main channels, the stations signed off around 2 a.m. and the TV went blank until 6 a.m.)

I was a few pages into the book and was stunned to be reading practically verbatim the same message I had just heard on the TV. I quickly flipped to the part of the book that talks about the author. Turns out he has a ministry in NYC to gang members. This is more than coincidence, Rich, it's time to make a decision. So I decided to continue reading where I left off. The truth became crystal clear (along with my perspiring) with each paragraph and Bible verse I read. I was stalling, God was confronting me face-front with the convictions of my sin before His Holy (means perfect) Spirit of truth. It was the truth I had been looking for and He was setting it in front of my soul to see if I would grab on for Life, forever. He would not force me, but was placing His truth in my heart for this moment of trial to clearly see He was true and not an errant emotion or trick of the mind. I was not surrendering though, and God is not one to be jerked around. His presence in my soul was telling me he was ready to depart; that this revealing is how he had chosen to show Himself to me and never would He return to put his life in my heart again if I turned Him down now. He could not illuminate *my* understanding of **His** plan any stronger than at this very instant in my life. If I don't get it now, He can't make it any clearer for me. He had answered my prayer without an iota of doubt. It was at this final moment of revealing that I collapsed into his will and surrendered my life to Him who is Author of all Life and Truth.

I had been reading His Word out loud, now it was time to confess my sin to him out loud. I had grown up with Joe Peca through some very personal circumstances, it was only natural that he knelt by my side and prayed with me when I told him I was going to pray to God and surrender my life to Jesus Christ.

"Dear God, I know now who you are and why you came to die in my place by becoming Jesus Christ. You became a man to take on all my sins—past, present, and future—so I can stand Holy (perfect) before you and I can walk with you forever. Please take all my sin on yourself and forgive me, I am ready to follow wherever you lead. Teach me this new truth in Christ."

In that moment, the Holy Spirit came into my life and set up permanent residence to start cleaning house. God definitely got the raw end of this deal, but this is His plan of love for us—unconditional love for the vilest offender as well as for the seemingly righteous man. All come before Him in the same condition, sinful. *The degree of sin* has no bearing on His love returned. I cannot describe the joy, understanding, clarity, and awe of that moment; that is impossible. I do, however, remember picking my best friend up off his feet in a hug and spinning him around saying, "Joe, do you understand what just happened!" Joe looked at me bewildered. It was my first indication, which I would soon learn, that I can't save my friends or family for them. Everyone has to come to this point of salvation in their own time or not at all.

So here I was, a new born-again Christian with a lifetime of bad habits to correct. I had no idea what lay ahead but I knew this: Jesus Christ will be with me every step of the way for the rest of my life and even death would be wonderful. I also realized this Jesus Christ living in me was not the one I had been instructed about all my life through the eyes of those who do not know him. The first thing I couldn't wait to do was throw away all my drugs and paraphernalia. This would not be a mere matter of a few flushes down the toilet; oh no, this would require an industrial strength effort. Boy, was I going to blow some minds and have fun doing it. Second, it was appointed unto me to tell all my gang and non-gang buddies, and girlfriends I was through with the drug lifestyle and had surrendered my life to Christ, whatever that meant, because I wasn't quite sure yet. Our family didn't even own a Bible *and* I had no idea where to start learning about this Jesus. So I just kept re-reading the booklet from Joe's mom, over and over for the first few weeks.

That morning—May 19, 1972—I awoke with a joy for life I had never known. Joe accompanied me on my first venture—a trip to Darby Creek to get rid of my pipes, bongs, rolling papers, posters, and, best of all, my hash stash. I was skimming ¼ ounce buttons of black hash down the creek bed just like skimming stones, and laughing as hard as I ever did on drugs. Joe's eyeballs were popping out. The last time Joe had been that shocked was when I got him stoned and showed him I had taught my pet mouse how to swim around the house plumbing*.

Bongs and corncob pipes were floating down the creek in a row like discarded bottles for target practice. I tossed the remainder of the mescaline tabs, then a few bags of pot fluttered into the stream before a better idea hit me! Seeing Joe's reaction, I knew I had to do some master goofing upon selected die-hard dopers who just won't believe I quit. Let's have some fun with this.

Within the next few weeks, I had alienated nearly all my friends by telling them I was done with drugs and they needed to surrender their lives to Christ. The phone stopped ringing and my social stock was in the toilet, yet I was the happiest I had ever been. Before I continue to tell you how I blew some doper minds, let me explain my own frame of mind.

This illumination, this born-again confidence that I was now a child of God for eternity, made me a bolder individual for Christ than I had ever been for any cause in my life. I didn't care who you were, you were going to hear what Jesus had done for me and the same gift of salvation is available to everyone, just as I had received. It just made common sense to me, seeing my friends who were all doped up and miserable for reasons I understood; to explain that God had a better way, a *perfect* way for them. Boy, was I naïve. That message to my friends went over like a lead zeppelin. I'm sure some time in your past you've known some obnoxious bearer of the Good News after they've experienced Christ. Try to be kind to them; they err on the side of love and are 90 per cent enthusiasm and 10 per cent knowledge at this point of their early emerging. The only ones really happy for me and glad to listen to the gospel were the girls I knew.

No one really took me too serious about quitting drugs; they figured it would pass in no time and I would soon be back to my old self. Time would be the only teller. So getting my point across to some Doubting Thomas's took extreme measures and a lot of dope, which I chose to dispose of in a most peculiar way. I had plenty to get rid of anyway, why not have fun?

It started with *Beau Gerhart*. I invited him to my house to get high and listen to music a day after my conversion, but before I made it public. Once he arrived, I explained I had just become a Christian and wouldn't be doing drugs anymore. He laughed—a reaction I had anticipated since we were always playing practical jokes on each other. He was so convinced I was goofing on him, he shut me off and said, "I ain't buyin' it, Rich, no matter how hard you try." He lit up his own joint and every time he tried to pass it to me I told him 'no thanks', then shared something else about Jesus I had read. He would stare into me with a zonked transfixed glaze, which approached believing me, then snapped out of it to laugh, "NO way, No way, man, you're just trying to blow my mind here, Rich. You've gotten over on me before, but this is good. What did you do, rehearse this stuff? Come on, I'll light up another. Have you pulled this on Wash and the other guys yet? I wanna be there when you do."

After sharing what I knew about the gospel, I realized the only way to convince him was to put my 'other' plan into action. As they say, seeing is believing.

"Beau, buddy," I said in foreboding tone like I had something even crazier to present, "I've got a new way to get high that's going to absolutely blow your mind away. You wanna try it?"

"Sure! Now you're talking, lay it on me man, you had me worried there for a minute! What is it?" he asked, rubbing his hands together as if preparing for a good meal.

"Follow me," I motioned him up to my room. Pulling an ounce bag out of my lock box, and grabbing a double album cover (vinyl record days), I led him into the bathroom where I poured the ounce out on the album cover and started to clean away the seeds and stems. For those uninitiated, cleaning an ounce involves the removal of all but the leaf heads. Normally, you would hold onto the stems and undesirable parts to smoke when the fine stuff ran out, or toss them, so Beau wasn't too surprised when I sorted the seeds and stems into the commode. Then I started messing with his mind.

"Whoa, I don't like the color of *that* head," I said as I nonchalantly tossed it in the hopper, "nor that one," I added.

"What are ya doin', man, that's good smoke you're tossin!" Beau reacted.

"Be cool, man. Did you ever try this weed?" I added to change the subject.

"What's it called?" he asked curiously. Back then, the smoke had to have a name: Michoacán, Acapulco Gold, Viet Green, Panama Red, whatever.

"This? This is Heavenly Blonde," I improvised.

"Oh man, that sounds good," he said in anticipation. By now I had cleaned the ounce so generously that half was floating in the toilet.

"Aren't you going a bit overboard on the cleaning though?" Beau asked concerned, straining his neck to see in the toilet.

"I don't know about that; I've only done the first stage of cleaning," I countered as I flushed the toilet.

As we both leaned over to see how much was going down the toilet, I tilted the album and the rest of the ounce slipped into the kaleidoscope of twirling green. I jumped up in exaggerated exhilaration, exclaiming, "Halleluiah! *Now* it's clean, and so am I! What a rush! I told you this stuff was good. How'd you get off on *that*, Beau?"

Beau was stunned. "Whatareyadoin! What did you just do! You've flipped man." But at least he was smiling.

"Now do you believe me?" I asked.

"I don't know what to think," he said shaking his head, "you're really flippin' my wig, man, Just don't waste any more dope, give it to me," pleaded my friend.

"Nope, can't do that, Beaumont," and went on to explain the obvious reason I couldn't give or sell it either. Shortly, Beau left my house very confused and still not wholly convinced. I knew the word would spread now.

He finally got the message. The next half a dozen times I saw him, the first words out of his mouth were, "Are you still straight?" To which I would gladly reply, "Yes." That was the question most often asked of me for the next few months. No one thought I could quit; and they were right, Rich Bonnett couldn't, "But with God all things are possible." Not only did they think I'd fail but they desperately wanted me to fail. I was the pariah in their midst, proving what God could do. They hated the idea one of their own could turn his back on a lifestyle they so venerated. Eventually, it took a year and only a few slip-ups before God removed the desire for drugs from me completely. I haven't touched drugs since then. For those next few weeks, I had fun handing out super joints with half-inch firecrackers rolled a few tokes in, sneezing on ounce cleanings, spilling loaded bowls, and using my imagination to eliminate the remainder of my drugs among the die-hard non-believers to convince them I went straight.

Farewell to Manoa Lanes

The first task Jesus had was to rid me of drugs. This was the hardest thing I ever had to do. The first few days were easy and actually fun; getting over on my friends by throwing away dope in a variety of goofs. But the next few months were very difficult. I wasn't physically addicted to any one drug, but I was solidly addicted to the doper's lifestyle and everyone I hung out with did drugs. I had been high every day in one form or another for well over two years, with maybe three attempted straight days in that time just to see if I could do it. Now, being clear-headed was a novel experience I had forgotten about since I was 16. Until now, everything had revolved around dope and the gang. My money came from selling drugs; how would I keep my VW Bug on the road now? Going straight made the old gang very uncomfortable around me; they couldn't trust me anymore. I was now on the outside, representing virtues they despised. Going to the Alleys to hang out was a difficult habit to break also. Besides, did God want me to abandon my friends or tell the lost about His Plan for man? This gang was now my mission, but after a month the guys had enough and decided to let me know in no uncertain terms. The task fell to Will Scarfo.

Steve had 'borrowed' Will's Mustang to pick me up and head back to the Alleys. As he approached the bowling alley where the guys were hanging out, he asked me to go sit on the front hood and tease Will to come get his car. As Will approached his car, Steve would drive in reverse faster than Will could catch him while I edged him on. It was standard, cheap, guy entertainment performed many times before. Only this time Steve never put the car in reverse. Scarf came up accusing me of stealing his car and round-housed me up the side of my head, knocking me stunned to the ground. Next thing I knew, he had his foot on my neck pinning me to the pavement with everyone gathered around. Fighting back was useless.

With everyone's approval, Will looked down at me and said, "Get used to it down there because that's where you'll wind up if ever you come back here again." He said it matter-of-fact, as if it was a task that someone finally needed to take care of. He wrenched his foot off my neck for emphasis adding, "You're out of here, Rich. Don't show your face or someone will have to finish where I left off." Walking home, I was at first shocked at the realization that these 'friends' were not really my friends and what I thought was a brotherhood was really a sham once the drugs were removed. Then I saw God's hand in it and thanked Him for showing me the truth about my 'friends'; that the truth will not always be as I had perceived but is what's best for me; that truth will often be a tough pill to swallow.

So that should have been the end of my Alley days. But ironically, every few weeks someone from the Alleys would call to see what I was up to and test me to see if I was still straight. It is hard for friends to just drop each other.

I had become an enigma amongst them. On the one hand, they were fascinated with my transformation and found my preaching entertaining; on the other, they hated everything I now represented. They enjoyed high times poking holes in religion, while I tried to define having a living relationship with Christ, as opposed to being religious. I would drive around with them preaching, earning their nicknames like Reverend Rich, Deacon Dick, The Preacher, Father Fool, and god. It didn't bother me; a few would even admit they were glad for me and there may be some truth to some of this Jesus stuff, but weren't ready to make the jump I had taken— "No way". To which I would reply, "Well, you've gotta admit, at the rate you guys are going, you're not going to live to a ripe old age." To this they nearly all agreed. Up until now, none of our guys had died. But someone has to be first, and that would be Timmy Dougherty.

Timmy was a flaming red-headed Irish boy of 17 with freckles and a temper. However, he was one of the few guys at the Alleys with enough common sense to know he should get out before it was too late, admitting the same to me in candid discussion. Problem is that no one knows how fast tomorrow will get here, and we will all run out of tomorrows eventually. Such was the case for Tim.

I surrendered to Jesus Christ in May. As a dog returns to its vomit, so would I every few weeks to visit my friends at the Alleys, but I was always straight (no drugs). The difference now being I was no longer a trusted member but more of an outside curiosity. These occasional visits to the Alleys came to an abrupt end one August weekend in Wildwood, New Jersey. Steve, Washel, Scarfo, Peeps, Timmy, and I went down the shore for the weekend to pick up Scarf's car, which had broken down in Sea Isle City N.J., two weeks earlier. It was a typical wild weekend of drugs and drinking which, since I didn't participate anymore, looked uglier with each occurrence. I'd nurse one or two beers all night just to say I had something in my hand to shut them up, and steer clear of any lame plans they had while they would do their best to implicate me in whatever they were up to. I remember praying to my new Lord on the last night down there as they trashed the hotel room, "Lord, get me through this weekend and I'll never hang with these guys again; I know being with them is wrong. They have heard your message and my time with them is done." God honored that prayer but had one critical soul on "short time" to reach that weekend—Timmy Dougherty.

Timmy, Peeps, and I spent a sunny Saturday sleeping on the beach. Around 2 p.m., Steve, Wash, and Scarf said they were going to Sea Isle to get Will's car. Peeps got up to go with them, but Timmy was out cold on the sand recuperating from a dusk-to-dawn drinking session. I told Steve I'd watch over Tim until they got back. Steve and Scarfo looked agitated that Tim wasn't getting up to go with them and tried to wake him up, but he was out. After a warning to Tim (and not me) that they were leaving, I should have caught on something was fishy. They left, saying they would be back around 5 to pick us up. Five o'clock came and went with no sign of the guys. Tim was now up and feeling better. When I told him the other four went to get the Scarf-mobile in Sea Isle, he looked at me disgusted, "There's nothing wrong with Will's car," he hesitated, then came his lament, "Oh man!" With that lament, I knew I'd been scammed.

"You saying we've been dumped?" I asked with hope fading quickly.

"No, *you* got dumped, I was too toasted to follow the plan," he said, upset with himself for sleeping through their signal to leave. The plan was to invite Rich down the shore and leave him there. "Well, if they left, they won't be coming back, so we better start looking for a way home," I concluded.

Sometimes at the shore we would run into some girls or guys we knew on the beach, so we started walking down the beach with our only possessions—a beach towel and sunscreen. Neither of us even brought a T-shirt to the beach today. After walking the beach for an hour, chances of finding someone we knew faded with the evening sun. Since my friends had trashed the hotel room the night before, all of us had loaded our stuff in Steve's car that morning with no intention of going back to the room. Our last option was to thumb it home.

So, there we were after another long hour of walking to the entrance of the Garden State Parkway; standing in sandy cut-off jeans, no shoes or shirt, shoulder-length salt-frizzed hair sticking out in all directions, towel over our shoulders, no money or wallet, trying to hitch a ride back home as dusk fell. It was going to be a long night; no one in their right mind would pick up two derelicts like us. And that is exactly who picked us up—two guys nowhere near their right mind. The two souls that picked us up, hitching north, were so high they thought they were on their way to Maryland (south), in the opposite direction. I have no idea where they made their wrong turn, but at this point I wasn't about to tell them they needed to turn around to head the other way; we'd lose our only ride, which took us over an hour to get. It was now dark and Timmy had anticipating stealing some food out of a 7-11 and sleeping on the side of the highway 'til morning if this ride hadn't come along. Not only were these guys too high to know where they were going, they were too zonked to drive, swerving all over the road. I think they were on Quaaludes, the equivalent of being very drunk. I pressed the driver into letting me drive, pointing out he and his friend were in no shape to be behind the wheel. Content to light up in the back seat and continue their high with Timmy who had jumped in the front seat, I took over the driving. I felt obligated to get these guys heading toward Maryland since they were good enough to pick us up. I figured they had missed the last Cape May Ferry and were trying to locate the Wilmington Bridge. Right about the time, one of them saw the Atlantic City sign for the AC expressway and wanted to know "Where the hell are we?" It seemed like the right time to tell them.

"Yeah, you guys messed up somewhere and needed to take the Cape May Ferry or 95 south to get to Maryland," I informed them, "and I don't think the ferry runs at night, so I'll get you to 95 south and you can take it from there."

"Hey man, how far away from Maryland are we?" the owner of the car asked.

"Like two hours at least." I sort of chuckled.

"Oh man, we *did* screw up," he chuckled to his buddy, too high to care. And with that, they hunkered down to sleep saying, "Wake us up when we get to Maryland. Deal?"

I checked the gas gage, "Deal. I'll get you to 95 south and wake you up, but you better crash for a while so you'll be able to drive," I said putting his mind to rest.

With our new friends conked in the back seat and time to kill, Tim and I began an interesting conversation in which he let down his guard concerning his views on God and Christ. He initiated the conversation, having been trapped in this situation because he missed his opportunity to dump me back at the beach as planned.

"So Rich, is this what it's like being a Jesus freak; your friends dump on you and you just shrug it off? That's not the Rich I knew."

"Pretty much so," I replied, "but it's a blessing in disguise because you learn who your real friends are and who are just doping buddies. Most of your friends at the Alleys are just doping buddies, Tim, whether you see it or not. Tell them 'you've seen the light' for a few days and see who still calls," I chuckled. "But it's not as bad as it seems, you trade in one group of lousy friends for one perfect friend who will never let you down for the rest of your life."

"No thanks." Tim thought for a while, lighting up a cigarette from a pack he found on the dashboard. "You're right about one thing though," he conceded, "I need to get out of the Alleys before someone gets me killed or some of us wind up going to jail or something. I can definitely see that coming. And (un-named persons) are shooting up regular now, ya know," he said, feeling me out to see if I knew which guys were now using heroin.

"Oh yeah, I know, they like to rub me about it and tell me I don't know what I'm missing," I said, then shifted back to his first statement. "So, do you plan on leaving then?"

"Nah, I'm still having too much fun. The only way I could leave would be to split off with a few guys like Tommy and Mini-brute." He said mulling the thought around.

"Well, that would be a start at least," I encouraged him. "Do you mind if I ask you a bigger question? Like what are *your* thoughts on Jesus Christ?"

Timmy exhaled after a long drag on his cigarette "Ya know, I don't have a problem with what you're saying about who he is, it's just that it's kinda scary what has happened to you and I'm not ready for that. I think about God though and I know the stuff we are doing is messed up, that bothers me sometimes," he thought some more, "but there's plenty of time to deal with that later, right now I'd just like to get home, take a shower, eat something, and sleep for a day," he said, weary with our present predicament.

For the next hour, we talked about spiritual things, no arguing or macho facade to overcome; just two guys discussing God, Jesus, and religions. It would turn out to be one of the few uninterrupted conversations with an Alley member I'd ever get a chance to have and I was very surprised at Tim's openness about God. The conversation tapered off to discussing our girlfriends who knew each other from their shared neighborhood.

"I *really* like Anne," he startled me in confidence. "Someone like Anne could change my life; I might leave the Alleys for a girl like her," he said in a rare moment of candor.

221

I thought of his statement, "Well, Tim, that's kind of what letting Christ in your life is like," I said, trying to point out the similarity. "It's letting someone who loves you more than Anne take your life and change it, leaving your old ways behind for Him."

"Hmm?" he said thinking that through, "Doesn't sound so bad when you put it that way." I laughed. "No, it's not *bad* at all Tim, I love it!" I assured him, "except this part," I said alluding to our present calamity.

Our Quaalude buddies woke up around the Philadelphia airport on I-95 south, forgetting our previous conversation and demanded to know why I had them in Philadelphia. They got belligerent and kicked us out. (Previously, it would have been us throwing them out, but Timmy knew he wouldn't get support from me for that action anymore and wouldn't chance it solo.) From the airport, we were able to bum a dime to call someone who gave us a ride to Scotties, a burger hangout near home, where we ate with borrowed money from guys we knew there. The same guys gave us a ride home around midnight. That was my last time hanging with the Alleys crew. I'm telling this story about Timmy because his time on earth was much shorter that either of us would have ever imagined that night. Assuming you have tomorrows to sort out your spiritual life is Russian roulette every day.

Our hitched ride home occurred in August; less than three months later Timmy was dead. He and a few other guys from Manoa Lanes cut school and got too high. *Teddy Condracki* couldn't drive at all so Tim was driving Ted's car trying to make his way to Steve Sisca's house six doors down from my house, to sleep for a while. In front of my house, he struck a woman driving a station wagon head on-with children (pre-child safety seat era), putting everyone in the hospital. Tim was DOA, having his jugular severed by the steering wheel. Ted survived because he was asleep in the back seat and never knew what happened until he woke up in the hospital. Joe Peca was the first one to the accident. He said when the driver door was finally pried opened, blood poured out over the door jamb, to the curb, and down the sewer grate. That is an analogy that has never left me, a young life thrown down the sewer.

At the time, I was struggling again with the idea of going back up the Alleys, even after my "get me out of this weekend" promise to God in Wildwood. Here was a clear message to me from God, in front of my house of all places (I'd call that strategically placed); to return to the Alleys would bring me to the same end. "Richard, don't waste any more of your time with this group, your days with these people are over. You have completed what I asked you to do among them, now you must leave, *they* will be watching you." It was closure among friends I needed to be sure about, Steve in particular.

I often think about the circumstances leading up to and concluding with Timmy's passing, as being the event to conclude my final departure from Manoa Lanes. How God brought us together that weekend in Wildwood when Tim missed his exit queue on the beach; the ride God provided for the way home so just Timmy and I could talk alone; our conversation on the way home; his dying in front of my house of all places. I don't know if he ever made a decision for Christ, but his passing sealed my final break from the Alleys.

One last closure concerning Timmy's death and my final days at Manoa Lanes occurred the day he was buried. All of us from the Alleys attended his wake the night before. The next day he was to be buried at a cemetery in West Conshohocken. I wanted to attend, but was starting a new job with Teamsters Union that day and couldn't miss my first day of work. A friend of my Dad had landed me the job without even an interview, so I didn't want to chance losing the job by taking off the first day. Also, I had no idea where West Conshohocken was. On that morning I got in my car and started following the directions my dad's friend had given me, when I noticed the final destination was in…West Conshohocken. Ironically, my route brought me right by the cemetery, recognizing the name from Tim's obituary information. From there, I hung a left up a steep hill to my job at W.F. Altenpohl, a scale manufacturing company three minutes from where Tim would be buried in a few hours. These uncanny coincidences started consistently occurring in my life since May 19 and would continue for the next year. At lunch break, I was able to jump in my VW Bug and zip further up the industrial lane where I could look down on the cemetery from West Conshohocken Industrial Park, which sits high on a hill. A line of cars was snaking into the cemetery below on a beautiful sunny day as I struggled with the emotions of this contrary morning. This was my first day on a job that would later become a career for me, a new beginning. Down below me, with many Alley members in attendance, Tim was being lowered into the ground, a final end to a way of life neither of us would be part of again.

My thoughts as I watched below:

Tim was a victim of his choices, which destroyed him; my choice had saved me. We live by our choices and die with them. Six months ago, I was no different than Tim; yet here I stood, praying for his family and Manoa Lanes because I had sought the truth and, as clichéd as it sounds, that truth had set me free from what was going on below. I thought of the conversations we had that night hitching home from Wildwood; how God had found a way (not to my liking at the time) to throw us together via calamity, which allowed Timmy to open up a tender heart that was hidden behind a leather jacket, gang, and drugs. I could only hope that God's work was not in vain and I would see Timmy again someday. God only knows.

After Timmy's passing, the death toll at Manoa Lanes started to accelerate; the floodgate had opened. A few months later, Mikey McNicol excused himself from the dinner table, went downstairs, put a shotgun to his heart, and ended his days. When his father ran downstairs to investigate the bang, the sight of his torn-up son put the poor man in cardiac arrest. Two years later, Mike's brother would take his life using the same gun.

Phil *Sheridan* died in a similar way shortly after Mike. He worked with his father, riding to work together each day. One morning before leaving for work, while waiting for his dad, Phil went out by the family pool, put a pistol to his head, and pulled the trigger. Phil was the friendliest guy at Manoa Lanes, but had a tragic event haunting him. When he was 13, while playing with a gun at his house in an upstairs bedroom, his friend accidentally killed himself playing Russian roulette. The friend didn't want to play, so Phil put the gun to his own head saying, "See, it's not loaded" while pulling the trigger a few times. Phil handed the gun to the other boy and told him not to be chicken. When his reluctant friend took his turn, the gun went off, knocking him off the other side of the bed, dead to the floor. Phil was the only person I ever met who even as a teen was legally prescribed Quaaludes as a sedative by his doctor.

I can't remember if Woody or Dave was next to die, but Manoa Lanes was bound for extinction through attrition. Lori and I were going to wakes and funeral services every six months until we got married. Noticeable is the number of suicides among these 'tough-guys'. Also, you may be interested to know that few of these guys discussed their intentions or made a plea for help. The violent certainty of their method, shotguns and pistols, indicated the assuredness of their intention. There were no failed sleeping pill attempts or half-slit wrist. Once they made their decision to take their life, they chose a guaranteed method; no crying for attention or help. It is a testament to the futility of living life in the fast lane in order to satisfy a spiritual need. A wild lifestyle will satisfy for a season, but once that lifestyle becomes just another part of their problems, they saw nowhere else to turn for satisfaction.

For me, the saddest of all was watching my close friend, Steven Sisca, painfully follow these footsteps. His is a classic case of spiraling down so deep until living looks hopeless. Some of his story has to be vague because he got caught up in running drugs from Florida for organized crime. I can't go into detail about that since he was careful not to tell me much for my own sake. A series of events in quick succession started when he was 18, just before his graduation. Though we were the same age, Steve had to repeat a year so was still a senior in high school while I was at Community College.

The first tragedy occurred while he was skipping school one day. He pulled into my driveway as I was leaving for my daily commute to college and asked if I wanted to cut classes that day. I had to decline since I had already missed too many classes. He continued around the corner to pick up Tom Harvey. I had no idea how close I avoided tragedy that day.

They spent the day driving around since it was an early spring day. While my friends were cruising down a wooded residential street, a nine-year old boy on his bike came flying down his driveway on a collision course with Steve's '63 Chevy Impala. The boy bolted out from behind bushes on the passenger side before Steve had time to react. The child flew off his bike on impact; his head went through the windshield while his body flipped onto the roof and rolled behind the car, just a shred short of full decapitation. It was over in an instant. As soon as Tom and Steve jumped out and looked behind them, they knew the boy was dead. They have both described to me their hopelessness of the circumstance. There is absolutely nothing you can do, nowhere to go. The deed is done and there is no turning back the clock.

The victim's little brother came up to Steve, looking at the busted bike in front of the car but not seeing his brother yet.

He told Steve, "Ah mister, it's not your fault—he does that all the time, my mom is always yelling him not to ride in the street." Then the boy saw his twisted brother behind the car and ran to get their mom.

I can't bring myself to describe Steve's account of the poor mother arriving on the scene and waiting for a useless ambulance to arrive. Tom has to review this book and I don't want to make it harder than it has to be for him. Tom and I are still very close friends. Steve later told me he wished he was dead instead. In an instant, both of their lives were forever changed. You never get over something like that. Steve never did.

Since there was no witness to the event other than the one boy seeing his brother disappear down the driveway, there didn't appear to be any legal ramifications about the accident. It was pretty much an open and closed case of involuntary manslaughter. That would change, but for the time being I have to pause this tragedy in order to keep events in order. Up until now, no one at Manoa Lanes had died or taken a life as a result of our carryings-on. The passing of this child was the first. Had Steve not cut school that day, the boy would be alive. He voiced his opinion to me about this several times concerning his guilt; he could never get the picture out of his head. It was shortly before this accident that Steve and I started to drift away as a result of the fight I explained earlier. Our bond gets more distant at this point and without my voice of reason to steer his half-baked ideas, he was a greater magnet for trouble and getting caught. Steve started to unravel, even spending a short stint in county lock-up with Mikey.

Steve's next tragedy was similar but not fatal. A year or so later while working for SEPTA as a mechanic, he had improperly jacked up a bus for work. The bus rolled off the jacks, pinning a fellow worker, severely crushing his legs. Steve was investigated, found negligent, and fired. However, notice that both these circumstances were accidents and not intentional trouble. Either way, Steve needed money for lawyers and started running cocaine up from Florida for a Philadelphia crime racquet. He was regularly in and out of court concerning the two accidents for a few years and stated to me at one low point, "My life is nothing but trouble to everyone around me, I'd be better off dead." He was serious. At Timmy Dougherty's funeral, they morbidly laid bets on who would die next. Steve's name was a good bet. Though he wasn't next, he wasn't far off.

In no time he was rolling in the kind of money a 20-year-old can only attain by illegal means or inheritance. One morning he pulled up my drive-way in a new Cadillac Deville to gloat. When I asked how he could afford it, he popped the trunk to show me two kilos of cocaine, street value $100,000? At that point, I knew Steve was in too deep and not wise enough to consider his future.

In the case with the dead boy, a false witness stepped forward a year later to say Steve was speeding (the car) that day. Steve had been introduced to some mob soldiers whom he asked for help concerning the false witness. His mob friends visited the witness, *convincing* him to drop his testimony. For this favor, Steve owed the mob, and they would collect in due time using him as a mule to run cocaine up from Florida. And so deeper and deeper he went until one afternoon he came to my house to feel me out for advice while still half-bragging about the money he was shaking down. His complexion was pasty gray. I could see he was high as a kite, and very nervous. He owed the wrong people a lot of their money for a squeeze deal that went bad.

A 'squeeze deal' can be pulled off with other people's money between the time you collect their deal money for running drugs, and a day or two (especially if driving back from Florida) which you can 'squeeze' in your own deal using their money. Steve used mob money to finance his own squeeze deal without their permission; Steve's deal went bad and was about to be reprimanded (mob style) for dealing on the side and losing their money. I told him to leave town and start over somewhere safe. I was serious. He nervously laughed and said it was over, but I didn't get what he meant.

"What do you mean *over*?" I asked, "You think they'll kill you?"

"It don't matter, it's too late," he nervously laughed again while standing there waiting for me to come up with the answer to his problem.

"Steve, you **know** what I'm gonna tell you," I finally said, expecting the familiar reply. "You need Jesus Christ, no one else can see you through this." There was hardly any convincing in my voice since I knew what he believed. But he was standing there so desperate; I thought maybe it was miracle time.

"God?" He asked almost insulted. "There is no God," he stated, as though it was a known fact, waiting for me to come up with a plan B. Steve didn't say that to insult me, he was feeling out his trusted idea man for a good plan or a way to get money to bail him out of his predicament. I really don't know.

"F*** it. Maybe I'll see you later," he quipped with a sense of finality, jumping in his Cadillac. And that was my last conversation with Steve. Sadly, in those two words he was expressing the futility of accumulated bad choices over the past few years.

A few days later he made phone calls to a few close friends, asking them to be pallbearers at his funeral. That same night he pulled his Cadillac over to the side of the road near Lansdowne Ave., locked the doors, and put a pistol to his head. He didn't die instantly, but blindly groped around the car trying to unlock the door to get out until he finally lost consciousness. When the police arrived, we suspect he was still alive, but they wouldn't open the locked car, pretending the situation was a murder. They wasted time looking for bullet hole entries into the driver's compartment and taping off the area while allowing Steve more time to die. It was their way of revenge, but that is only my opinion.

That night I came home late, unaware of Steve's suicide. My mom came down from her bedroom in her night gown; she had been sitting up waiting for me. She sat down with me in our kitchen and told me Lori had called her earlier to pass on a message about Steve. Mom told me what little she had learned from Lori; just that Steve had shot himself in the head and died. Mom teared up as we sat there; she had watched Steve grow up with Joe Peca and I since pre-school. I was shocked but not surprised. Then mom added, "He called here tonight after dinner but you had left already." She wanted to ask me more questions as a caring mother naturally would, but she left me to my thoughts in the kitchen. There would be time to discuss it with her tomorrow after I learned more. In the stillness of a late-night kitchen, I wondered why he called. My mind wandered from boyhood good times to dark times. I'd learn tomorrow he had been calling his pallbearers.

Steve's suicide was three years after I was saved. I always look at that time in terms of where I would have been versus where I was. I finally understood the term, "There, but by the grace of God, go I."

Well, for a chapter titled, "The Best Night of My Life", things aren't ending up too rosy. What do you say I share some good news in this next chapter?

The following is a list of Manoa Lanes members and their current status. Only *italicized* names have been changed. Out of courtesy, there is no mention of who served any prison time. 'Manoa Lanes' bowling alley and the gang no longer exist.

D = *Deceased,*   **A&W** = *Alive and Well (put former ways behind them)*
UK = *Unknown, don't know where they are or what happened to them.*

The Young Heads, *late 1969 to 1973:*

Name	Nicknames	Status
Rich Bonnett	Pelican or Pel, Bonnyboy, Dickieboy	A&W
Ted Condracki		UK
Robert Connaboy	Gumby	Became a missionary to India
Timmy Dougherty	Doc, Brillo	D
Ric Freilicht	Wash, Washel	D
Beau Gerhardt	Fat's	UK
Tom Harvey	Harve, Harvard	A&W
Michael *McNicol*	Mikey	D
Tommy *McNicol*		A&W
Dave McConnell	Mini-brute, Snoot	D
Billy Peterman	Peeps, Frogeye	D
Will *Scarfo*	Scardeen	A&W
Steve Sisca	Bruin', Spic, the Sisco kid	D

Not members but often hung around the Lanes:

Name	Nicknames	Status
Keith Black		D
Greg Barry		D
Henry Condracki		D
Kevin Sorenson	Shakes, Rattles	A&W
Jill Chaffee		D

The Old Heads:

Name	Nicknames	Status
Bob Dougherty		UK
Jerry McNicol		D
Joe Sullivan		D
Woody McElvane		D
Phil Sherman		D
Joe McLaughlin		UK
Mark Sorenson		D
Bob Connelly		UK
Steve Underhill		UK

There are a few from both groups I don't list for reasons undisclosed.

How they died: This emphasizes the futility of gang life. Most died before their 22nd birthday, the rest by their late 20s.

- Timmy Dougherty: Died in a car accident in front of my house. Tim bleed to death while unconscious.

- Mikey McNicol: After dinner one evening, Mike went down to his parents' basement and put a shotgun to his heart.

- Woody McElvane: While celebrating the 1974 Flyers Stanley Cup victory, Woody fell off the top a party van and fatally broke his neck.

- Joe Sullivan: Got hooked on heroin in Vietnam and overdosed a few years after he got back stateside.

- Mark Sorenson: Burned to death in a fire started by a Molotov Cocktail through the kitchen window at his parents' home. Most of the home was destroyed.

- Steve Sisca: Suicide. His story is told in chapter 10.

- Dave McConnel: Fatal car crash on an icy road.

- Jerry McNicol: Shotgun suicide.

- Phil Sherman: One morning before going to work with his father, Phil walked out back to the family pool and shot himself..

- Ric Freilicht: Drug overdose. A friend injected a dose of heroin directly into his spinal cord as per Ric's request.
- Billy Peterman: Struck broadside by drunk driver going 70 mph. Billy was just starting to get his life straightened out.
- Jill Chaffee: Some say brain hemorrhage, others say differently.
- Henry Condracki: Drug overdose.
- Greg Barry: Alcohol-related liver failure.
- Keith Black: Suicide. He was the only fatality to make it past his 20's

CHAPTER 11

OLD NEWS, GOOD NEWS

"And the truth shall set them free"

Born again, now there's a phrase bound to raise a suspicious eyebrow, a term thrown around very loosely today for a variety of second chance and revitalizing experiences. In the next few pages, I will attempt to explain what happened to me on May 19, 1972, when I was born again in the biblical sense. The term too often insinuates that a person who has gone through the experience is better than the person who hasn't; let me assure you this is hardly the case. Any of you who know me will certainly agree; I am no better than any of you.

Certainly, you have heard the saying, "God is no divider of men." It means He does not view one individual or group any better than another. He does not say, "This person over here is deserving of my love, so I'm going to divide him from this creep over here who I don't want anything to do with." In God's view, his love extends equally to every human being, all men are equal during the Earth part of our journey. There is no degree of human power, value, good works, or sin in our lives which increases or decreases our stock with Him. Hard to comprehend, isn't it? In His eyes we are all equal, and equally loved by Him.

Even when it comes to the Jewish nation, He does not set them any greater than, say, people from New Jersey. What He does say about the Jews is that they are His Chosen People. Chosen for what? Chosen as an example. He set them before the rest of mankind to observe. The Jewish Nation is set before us as a microcosm of the human race, an example of how God deals with mankind; what becomes of them when they love and obey, or what becomes of them when they ignore Him to follow their own choices. Israelites are the people He chose to entrust His instruction manual, the Old Testament, through his prophets. All that God will do with mankind, He does through the Jewish nation first, not because he loves them more, but because they are the chosen focus point of his plan for all of us to observe. Israel, their nation, is a focal point. The Bible is the record of God's dealing with this group under the magnifying glass in every conceivable situation under the sun, by all nations. Examining how He deals with *them* is to examine your own life. This examining of one's own life, therefore, requires reading the Bible, His Word, which we, by *our* nature, are inclined **not** to do.

By now you have probably concluded that I was a prime candidate to be born again; being far off the center line of normal moral behavior. This is why I mention that God is no divider of men. The degree and frequency of our sin has no bearing on God's love for us. He loves the harlot as much as the heroine.

To write this book and leave out the mechanics of the single most important event in my life would be negligent. In order to understand being born again, and what happened to me that day, you will have to step back, clear your head and throw away any pre-conceived prejudices about organized religion, Christianity, or those who have insulted you like TV evangelists (most of them insult me also). It may even be better to imagine the term 'born again' has nothing to do with religion. Experience has shown me that people have such a misunderstanding of the term that I deem it important to try and shed some light on it. In order to do that, I have to go back to the term's origin.

The first person recorded to ever use the term 'born again' was Jesus himself. So, we need to take a close look at **when** and **why** he said it, **who** he said it to, and in **what** historical and spiritual context. It is important when studying any part of scripture to always look at the who, why, what, where, and when. Trust me, this is not boring stuff if you can keep up. Read on, it only lasts a half dozen pages.

When & Where

In Jerusalem, early in the ministry of Jesus. In the third Chapter of John the Apostle, a man named Nicodemus comes to Jesus in secret (at night) saying, "We know that you are a teacher come from God; for no one can do these miracles unless God is with him," to which Jesus replies, "Unless a man is born again, he will never enter the kingdom of heaven." John 3: 1-8

To even the casual reader, Jesus' reply to Nic's greeting seems to be out of left field and completely unrelated to the salutation Nicodemus just gave Him, so we will have to look closer and read between the lines to see what is really going on between Jesus and Nic. The reason the reply by Jesus seems unrelated to Nic's statement is because it is! Jesus was looking past the superficial salutation into Nicodemus' heart and gets right to the real reason why Nicodemus was there. Let me explain with an example: A guy you know of (Jack), but never visits you, is sweet on your little sister (Jill), but she is too young to ask on a date. Jack's other friends inform you he has an infatuation for your sister. One day Jack shows up to approach you on the topic of maybe asking your sister out and starts with, "Hey, I saw you catch that long pass in the Thanksgiving football game last week, what a great catch."

You reply, "The answer is NO, she's too young." You saw through him as to why he was there so you got right to the point. This is what Jesus has just done with his reply to Nicodemus.

The real question in Nicodemus' heart, based on Jesus' reply, was the same we have all asked, "How do I know if I'm good enough to enter the kingdom of God?" THAT is the question to which Jesus is replying. *Why* would Nic be coming to Jesus with such a question? Ah, in order to really understand that, we have to stop and look into *who* Nicodemus was and why he came in secret, which involves a short lesson in Jewish Temple custom. Nicodemus, spiritually and authoritatively speaking, would today be the equivalent of the Roman Catholic Pope. You decide. So as you read this, imagine the conversation is between the Pope and Jesus.

Every year the Pharisees and Sadducees (think college of Cardinals), the 'who's who' of the Jewish high priests corporately known as the Sanhedrin, would choose one priest among their own, usually the most respected and qualified priest among approximately 2,000, to enter into the 'Holy of Holies' to present a sacrificial lamb for the whole nation of Israel. This sacrifice known as Yom Kippur is the most important event of the Jewish calendar. The Holy of Holies is the name given to the innermost chamber of the Temple in Jerusalem, entered into just once a year by this chosen high priest for the purpose of presenting the national sacrificial lamb to atone for the sins of their nation. Inside the chamber rested the Arc of the Covenant, the manifestation of God's dwelling place on Earth. To help you better imagine the solemnity of this event called Yom Kippur, let me describe a bit about the Temple.

At that time, the Temple in Jerusalem would make the most beautiful of Cathedrals in existence today look like your backyard shed. Not said lightly, I have been to the great Cathedrals of Europe and researched the first-century Temple. It was known throughout the world for its beauty and size, not to mention the extensive gold gilding that made it shimmer from miles away. Think more along the line of Saints Peter and Paul Basilica in Rome with its massive courtyard, now enlarge the Temple by another one-fourth square mile. The ceiling of the Basilica in Rome is 150 feet high; the pinnacle of the Jewish temple was 273 feet high, at least 225 feet higher than the next highest building in the city. The massive **outer** Temple courtyard, consisting of many square acres with worship halls, was the place where the gentiles where allowed to enter and worship. Yep, non-Jews believed and worshipped the God of Israel too back then. The enormous **inner** courtyard and its halls are where only Jewish people could enter to worship; no gentiles could pass the Temple guard to enter here. Then there were the priest chambers as you climbed the steps towards the main Temple, and lastly the innermost Holy of Holies already described.

All week-long during Yom Kippur, this special day of the year also known as the Day of Atonement, families from all over Israel would come to present a sacrifice for their individual sins as instructed by Hebrew law. Then on the final day, the chosen high priest would enter into this Holy of Holies to present a perfect unblemished sacrificial lamb, chosen from throughout all of the sheepfolds of the country for the entire nation of Israel, while the assembled masses watched and prayed outside, confessing their sins as a nation (boy, could we use some of that today). There is so much more to this event than I am offering in these few meager sentences, but for the sake of not losing your interest I'll speed along. Jewish historical records (not from the Bible) tell us some priests would fall dead in the Inner Chamber while presenting this sacrificial lamb, either by heart attack under the pressure of standing before the dwelling place of God on Earth, or perhaps, as the Jews believed, because the priest's heart was not right before God to represent the nation. Sort of like going in there all pumped up on an ego trip because you were elected high priest instead of being the humble servant of the people. Either way, records show these high priests died often enough that the Sanhedrin started tying a rope to the waist of the chosen priest when he entered the Inner Sanctum. That way if the priest died, they could drag him out without entering the Holy of Holies themselves to retrieve his body.

Well it so happened, a man named Nicodemus was the chosen high priest at this particular time and the old boy was obviously having doubts about his own spiritual preparedness to represent the people before The Almighty God of this universe. By the way, like the high priest, some day *we too* will also have to stand in the presence of the same God.

Now that we understand **who** Nicodemus is, we'll look at **why** he came in secret; the Bible says he came *"by night"*. Anyone who has read the trial and crucifixion of Christ understands it was the Sanhedrin who hated Christ the most and started plotting early in his ministry to have him arrested. Jesus was exposing their hypocritical ways and represented a major threat to their authority and power base. Remember, this same group will eventually convince Pilate to condemn Jesus to death. Nicodemus is a highly respected member of this Sanhedrin, so if he wants to talk with Jesus, he can't let the rest of the Sanhedrin know he met with the enemy, especially since he is the chosen high priest that year. There is one other possible reason you could speculate why Nic may have come in secret; he may have been *sent* by the Sanhedrin to interview Jesus without the people knowing. But in light of who Nicodemus was, the Sanhedrin wouldn't have sent their Highest Priest; no, this was an individual effort on Nicodemus' part, especially when we look at the response from Jesus. He sees through Nic and gets right to the point by answering the real question on Nicodemus' heart, who will soon stand before the Presence of God in the Holy of Holies (not knowing that while he was standing in the presence of Jesus he was already standing in the presence of God).

So get the picture. What we have is Nicodemus, the most religious man of the time, the holiest man the Israelites can produce, one of the holiest men on the planet, schooled from his youth concerning Hebrew law and righteous living, the most knowledgeable and respected leader of his people who has memorized the Torah inside out, visiting Jesus, an outsider who has already overthrown the money-changers and chastised the Sanhedrin at their Temple. **Why?** To ask in secret if he, the high priest, is worthy to stand in the presence of God. But before he gets the chance to present the question, Jesus answers him with "unless you are born again" Whoa! Jump back Jack!

Now, looking at this from Nicodemus' point of view; if he IS able stand before God in the Temple and survive, he will certainly be going to heaven when he dies. But Nic *isn't confident* he is going to heaven and is petrified to enter the Holy of Holies for fear of death! Now, if *anybody* should know if they were going to heaven, it would be Nicodemus, don't you think? And if a guy like Nicodemus isn't sure how to get to heaven, how in the world can *you and I* ever possibly figure it out?

I would think it safe to say that at this point in Jesus' ministry, Nick was at least convinced Jesus was a prophet due to the miracles Nicodemus himself had witnessed, or he wouldn't have bothered to come to Him this night. So being a prophet from God, Jesus **would** be the one source to ask the question, "Am I going to heaven?" While we're here, what would y*o*u say is the single most important question in life? Bingo.

Did you know that the term Bingo in Hebrew means: Who am I, Why am I here, Where am I going? Just kidding.

Jesus repeats his first response with more emphasis, but it is still a mind bender for poor Nic. "Verily, Verily, I say to you, unless a man is born again, he cannot **see** the kingdom of heaven." Notice there is an implication concerning those born again which Jesus throws in there with the word, see. The implication is that from the moment one is born again, not only will the person *know* he is going to heaven, but they will begin to *see* (understand) the kingdom while still here on Earth through the indwelling of God's Holy Spirit. Jesus' first reply was "**Enter** the kingdom." It is a given that if you "enter a kingdom" you are also seeing inside it. So why, on the second Verily, Verily does Jesus say, "**See** the kingdom"? Because enter the kingdom is future tense, see the kingdom is present tense. In other words, in order to **know** you are going to heaven in the future, you have to *see* (understand) you are going to heaven now (1 John 5:16 – "that you may know you have eternal life"). And that is what old Nic wanted to be sure of NOW, before he entered the Holy of Holies (God's presence), how he can see now. Uh oh, I'm getting too deep; I don't want to lose you though. Go back to where I may have lost a few of you and re-read till you're caught up, I'll wait here.

You good? Back to Nicodemus. He is boggled by this saying and replies, "How can a man be born when he is old? Can he enter back into his mother's womb to be born"? (Seems like whatever elective body chose Nic as high priest didn't pick the sharpest knife in the drawer.)

So Jesus comes back with a deeper explanation of his first two replies, "Verily, Verily, I say unto you, unless one is born of water (1st) and the spirit (2nd), he cannot enter the kingdom of God. That which is born of the flesh is flesh (refers to the first birth, water breaking) that which is born of the Spirit is spirit."

Side Note: Whenever Jesus says, 'Verily' twice in a row, it is the same as saying, "Here is a core truth, listen closely to this core truth." The American Standard translates it as "Truly, Truly".

Read the verse again. Water refers to flesh, or our first birth, we are all born out from our mother's water breaking; that begins the first birth, our life as we know it. Spirit (capital S) refers to Holy Spirit (from God) giving birth to spirit (small s), *our* spirit. That is exactly how it is written in the Bible: "That which is born of Spirit is spirit." In order for our spirit to awaken unto Life, we need to surrender our sin to Christ and ask God's Spirit (the Holy Spirit) into our hearts, this is the beginning of a new creation, a New Life, God dwelling in us, being born again, our second birth. This is why you exist, for this very act of transformation from the world of material existence to the world of spiritual existence.

I love to read the Bible. If I don't understand a verse, I pray and read closer, pray and read even closer, and sometimes pray and walk away as ignorant as my first attempt to understand a passage, returning to tackle the verse at some later date after more prayer. It is not a matter of God hiding understanding from us, or the Bible too difficult to understand. It is more a matter of one's Christian maturity in God's Spirit allowing us to understand Bible passages as we grow spiritually. A six-year-old kid picking up a book on

American History for the first time will get something out of it but nothing like what he can glean from the same book 12 years later, or 20 more years after that. My point is: I couldn't figure this stuff out on my own, but once I was born again the Holy Spirit of God living within me revealed it piece by piece. Whoops, am I scaring you? Remember, it's just me. Relax, I'll be stepping out of preacher mode shortly and getting back to my stories.

Clearly, Jesus is referring to two kinds of births. The first we can all understand, it is the physical vessel by which we all entered into this world. People can't be spiritually born until you first have a physical body. We have Mental capacity and Spiritual capacity. 1Cor 2:14 tells us our mental capacity can't understand the spiritual things of God (they are foolishness) until we download the spiritual app (born again). The second birth is the one we struggle to understand because it is a choice, intangible to the uninitiated. Not only a choice, but one we are wary, even afraid, to embrace. And let me add this; it is perfectly normal to be afraid of the second birth. We often fear that which we don't understand. However, that fear stems from losing personal liberties and self-centered living, which we seem convinced, is better than God's plan for our life. That's what we're afraid of; the full surrender to loving and serving Jesus Christ.

Perhaps though, by sending us all back to the womb for a moment (as Nicodemus implied), the concept of being born again will become clearer. Go ahead and imagine being nice and warm again in the comfort of the 98.6° watery womb. Forget all the knowledge you have, you haven't been born yet, no worries. Think strictly elemental warmth and coziness. You're in the womb, you have no cares, you don't even understand what a care is. *All your needs are provided for by your mother whom you vaguely know but is always very near. You can't visualize her form, you have no concept of form to compare to, but you elementally understand you are an image of her. You don't know anything about her, other than her being the one source of all you needs and the constant accompaniment of her steady heartbeat (presence). You don't quite understand it, but instinctively know you can't exist without her.

* Now go back to the last asterisk and substitute the name of God wherever you see 'mother' or 'her'. You may get an idea of the difference between life as you know it versus life through Christ.

Much like your present life outside the womb, God wants to provide all your needs, give you life, but you vaguely know Him, perhaps you have a very vague notion that He loves you. You have never met Him though he is eagerly awaiting your spiritual awakening. You don't quite comprehend it but suspect you are dead without Him.

While you are in the womb, it is the only world you know. However, you are sure there is something bigger going on outside your safe little world because you can hear muffled sounds, feel poking and prodding from beyond. You have no idea what this other world looks like though, or even that it is a world of atmosphere and color instead of the water and darkness you now float in. *Given a choice*, you would stay in your womb as long as you possibly could, perhaps forever, afraid of what is in the other world. But no matter how long you stay in the womb, the world on the outside is the **real world** that awaits you. If you choose to stay in the womb, think of all the wonderful things you would miss—the senses of sight, smell and taste, and all the experiences that accompany them, friendships, love and laughter, discovery, music, learning and growing, sadness and pain, the wonders of our planet, sunshine and clouds—in essence you'd *miss life*.

Even as safe and warm as the womb is, none of us would want to go back there once we experience the real world. This is why Christ so carefully chose to liken spiritual birth to a second birth because of the *new life* we experience after seeing that the world as we know it, is but a dark womb compared to what we are spiritually born into. Once one is born again, they become babes in a spiritual world they never knew was really in existence and, therefore, couldn't see. A relationship with Jesus Christ was all folly before they received sight. It is a second birth, but unlike the first birth, it is a choice, and for too many a choice they will never make, even though their life depends on it.

We think this Earth life is the only existence we can be sure about. Yet there are occasional muffled sounds from another world, poking and prodding our conscience, particularly when loved ones die to prick our minds that there is yet another world. We are by nature drawn and apprehensively curious about this world on the other side but know little about it, or assurance of its reason to exist. Relax, my friend, this is all part of God's Great Plan. He has made it so simple to find your way, in fact, that many people have trouble believing His Plan because of its simplicity. A plan so simple, so as to be understood by the least common denominator of humanity.

Earth is but a round womb. Eternity is the real world; the entrance into that world is a *spiritual* birth which only God can provide and requires a second birth. It is a radical change for most, not as radical for others. How radical the "born again experience" depends often on the age (meaning Earth years) at which this change occurs. Young children who are born again are not as startled at finding God, as are adults. Young children are not as confused about God to begin with. On the other hand, adults with their skeptical hearts hardened by jaded experiences become awed and dumbfounded when finally surrendered to Him. To put it in today's lingo, Jesus Christ is the Spiritual app downloaded to your heart for knowing God. No matter what age this occurs, everyone I've met who is born again can point to a specific age, or time, or place, or period, often to the hour, they entered from this world into the next; where Jesus Christ who is Lord above all, Creator of the Universe, God in the flesh, Author of Life, Ruler of an unknown, unseen region called Heaven, whose Kingdom there shall be no end, came into their hearts forever. Those who have been through this change, even decades later, still tear up when they consider that moment of God's grace in their life. Sorry, sorry, getting carried away again. Two more pages then story time again.

Seeing that Nicodemus is still confused, Jesus tries to describe the indescribable. "Do not marvel that I said to you, 'You must be born again.' The wind blows where it wills, and you hear the sound of it, but you don't know from where it comes or where it goes; so it is with everyone who is born of the Spirit." Translated means: A person born again knows the Spirit of God (wind) has come to dwell within them but doesn't see the change coming or where it will take them; it is a 100 per cent step of faith, but they know (the wind) is real because of the objects it moves (lives changed). We see the results of the wind, but we can't put our hands on its physical presence; I see the results of the Spirit in my life, but I can't put my hands on Him to physically produce evidence. It is all by faith.

This is the best I can do trying to describe the impact on one who is born again. It is like trying to explain being in love to someone who has never been in love. Matter of fact, that's exactly what the comparison is; a world without God's love compared to an eternity with His love.

"All right," you may ask, "how does one know if they are born again?" Simple, if you don't know, then you aren't. If you are, you will definitely know it. If Jesus Christ isn't constantly on your radar throughout each day, chances are you haven't handed him the tiller of your boat. A more material way to ask yourself if you've surrendered is to follow the money trail. For example, if you spend more money on your monthly car payment than any of His causes (church giving, feed the hungry, etc.), you haven't quite gotten the point that all you own is His. If you are middle class and throw a $20 bill at any global collection plate each week, you need to examine your heart. Your money will follow your heart and His leading.

Stingy giving = dead heart; Hilarious giving = awakened, trusting, happy heart.

Ministry doesn't have to be through a church. If you are giving your time and talent to Him weekly, it is because you have a relationship with, and love for your Savior; if you don't give freely of your time each week to His causes, it is because you don't think it is important in your life. That said, giving money and time to the church or secular good works **does not** save a person, but is often a fair indicator of where their heart is.

Those are a few basic indicators of where your relationship with Him stands. Now, I better back off a bit. Political correctness is not one of my virtues. Who can be saved? Anybody. Who can't be saved? Nobody. You want a good definition of a born-again Christian? They are a Nobody, telling Anybody, about Somebody, who can save Everybody.

Disclaimer: As John 3: 1-8 states, Nicodemus is named in the gospels as *a priest* of the Pharisees. Hebrew records list a Nicodemus as *High Priest* near the time of the conclusion of Jesus' life. Though many Bible historians link both names to conclude the Nick that came to Jesus by secret was also high priest that year; that link is not 100 per cent conclusive. However, the gospels reveal that several temple priests met with Christ in open and even had Jesus dine with them at their homes. Nick is the only one recorded who meets the Lord in secret. Other priests had the luxury of doubt as to whether Jesus was the Christ (God with us) or not, but the High Priest better be sure before he enters the Holy of Holies. Nick came to Jesus **to be taught how to get to heaven.** To do that in daylight would be admitting to the Sanhedrin that they had selected the wrong High Priest to enter the Holy of Holies.

Jesus shook Hebrew religious power from top to bottom. It would only make sense the highest authority of the Sanhedrin (the high priest) would seek the Truth, the Highest Authority of all mankind, of all Existence, of the Universe.

Maybe as you've been reading along you've concluded as many have told me, "Rich, I could see why *you* needed to turn to God to get straightened out, but my life is pretty good and I never did the things you did." Or in other words; you the reader don't need God's salvation. If you get nothing else out of this book, make sure you get this (a verily, verily coming). *It is not the severity*

(degree) of our sin that determines our need for salvation; it is the quantity.
And a quantity of **one** sin separates you from God forever. We've all sinned
once (an hour). "For All have sinned and come short of the Glory of God."
Thanks for being patient through the last pages. Time for a break from the
spiritual stuff. Time for a few stories about walking out of the womb into
another world.

Immediately after being saved, I had three big questions for God—
questions which God knew I had to have answered before moving on for Him.

Question 1. So God, you're telling me Noah and the Ark and all
that fairy tale stuff is true? Okay, I'll believe on faith for
now but you have some 'splaining to do, and soon.

Question 2. Where do I get more instruction on my new life and
how to grow? I had no idea the Bible was the place to
start. Nor did I know where to start in the Bible if I had
one, which I didn't.

Question 3. Where are the other people like me or am I the only
one around here? I didn't know a single born again
Christian, but I knew they had to be around because I
saw them in the TV show arena that night at JoePec's
house. Was I to go to California to join them?

In the next few stories, God answers my three questions in a most
wonderful and direct way. I didn't know *any* born again Christians to direct
me, all my friends were dopers. My parents were devoted church-zombies,
but not Christians; I was surrounded by a 100 per cent Christian void of fellowship. There was no one to direct me to start reading the Bible, specifically
starting with the book of John; I was clueless. Neither did I own a Bible. So
God found a special way to get one into my hands.

About a week after giving my life to Christ, while waiting for the right
time to sit down with my parents and tell them Jesus Christ has turned my
world right side up, I came home to see a stack of new Bibles on my dad's

stereo console in our living room. Being Catholic, our family had never owned a Bible, ever. My mother remembers the RC church teaching (1930s in Canada) that owning a Bible is forbidden; only a priest had the training to understand the contents there-in . I picked one up to smell the newness of the pages and wondered if someone had dropped them off for me. One Bible would have been enough.

"Whose are these?" I asked my mom.

"Ask your father," she said, busy in the kitchen getting dinner ready.

Dad was coming down the steps for dinner after changing out of his business suit. "What are you doing with these" I asked, standing by the stack of Bibles.

"It's a job we're doing," he said to dismiss my question.

You see, my dad started his own printing company after WWII and was just about to sell his equipment, dismiss his 20 employees and broker his clientele in order to retire; Urban-Renewal in Philadelphia had just bought his building and the entire city block for demolition. This Bible work, as it turned out, was one of the last big jobs of dad's career.

"You're printing Bibles?" I asked, the hairs on my neck starting to stand up as I began to see God's hand on this whole ordeal.

"Part of them," he replied, "A co-op of printers worked on different parts; I just brought these home from the binder (a company that binds the pages together). Take a look at the work there," he said proudly, coming over to point out the fine printing on rice paper.

"I'm very impressed," I said referring to the circumstance, not the craft. "Is it okay if I keep one?" I asked.

"What are you going to do with it?" he asked suspiciously, probably recollecting I had set the woods on fire, been thrown out of Catholic school, and may now be considering a good old Bible-burning.

"I plan on reading it, Dad. Really!" I said putting him at ease.

"Sure, suit yourself!" he beamed, pleased at seeing me doing something constructive.

Still shocked at the coincidence of my dad printing bibles, I eagerly continued my questioning during dinner.

"So Dad, did you ever print Bibles before?" I wanted to know as much about this 'coincidence' as I could.

He didn't even hesitate when he came back with, "No, actually I was the last printer asked into this job when another backed out," he said, shaking his head like it was as strange to him. "Nick put me on to the job as a thank-you for some business I sent his way, heckofaniceguy, that Nick." Nick was a business associate buying dad's client list.

After a few more questions to confirm I had just witnessed a miracle of Bibles, I blurted out to my astonished parents as I wolfed down dinner, "I can't wait to read that Bible!" Coming from their long-haired, maggot-infested, fm type, dope smoking son of many disappointments, that line brought them to abrupt attention.

"And what is the big hurry to read the Bible?" they inquired with great curiosity.

"Because my heavenly Father just used my earthly father to put this miracle Bible in my hands, so I expect great things are in that book waiting for me," I said, beginning a long pouring out of the last week of events in my life. Tonight also began the healing between my dad and I. Up until that moment, dad and I had a badly strained adversarial relationship and rarely spoke unless to argue. Dad did not believe in sparing the rod, strap, hand, or whatever else was nearby as I grew up. He often disciplined with his temper out of control, to put it mildly. For that I had lost respect for him. In his defense, I believe I would have driven most fathers to the same frustration.

I don't think my parents heard too much beyond the statement that I had quit drugs. I know this was the day my mom had prayed for and was now thanking God for her own miracle. Mom had never given up on me when everyone else had. She was the only prayer warrior in my life and I credit her prayers for my salvation. That her prayers would move God into my life to eventually present the gospel to both of my parents is a bit ironic, but that is the way He works. And to say God doesn't hear the prayers of non-Christians is ridiculous; He hears all our prayers. Answering prayers of the un-saved is one of His ways of proving a desire for a personal relationship with each of us. Anyway, such is the way I came into possession of my first Bible. Question (prayer) #2 got answered. On to questions 1 & 3.

The only born again Christian person I could recollect near that time in my life was a girl named Ruth from my senior year of high school, whom I hadn't seen for a year. She attended a Bible study with a group of do-gooders; they called their group Ranch. Prior to my own salvation, they turned my stomach. She would ask me to join her at their Bible study and told me the kids were all praying for me. It insulted me that some dorks at a Bible study were praying about me, as if they were better than me; neither did I understand why she wanted me to join them and remember asking if she was trying to get me out on a date. When she laughed "no", I made her a deal. I said I would go to Ranch and hang with her nerdy friends if she would come with me for a night to get high and hang out with my friends. Naturally, she declined and I called her a hypocrite. Yet she remained persistent in inviting me out, while I remained persistent on my deal, so that was the end of that. Now, over a year later I wasn't about to go search her out, she was probably off to college where I was supposed to be. Searching back for any possible Christians I may have known; she was the only one.

Out of boredom one evening in mid-June, because all my friends were now dodging 'Reverend Rich', I went for a walk in the neighborhood to do some thinking and praying. As I turn onto Stanley Lane I was reminded of a friend, Joe Paolela, whom I hadn't seen for over a year but grew up on this street. Joe was a few years older than I and had his own apartment when I first met him. I saw him a lot for about four months because he had a nice apartment to get high with my friends, then we lost touch when he moved again. Walking down his street now, I started thinking of Joe when I saw a bearded Cat Stevens-looking guy sitting out in front of his parents' house playing an acoustic guitar. The beard and hair made him hard to recognize and I knew Joe didn't previously play guitar. As I approached his house I tried to identify if it was Joe, and what song he was playing, but it sounded like a praise song, not a rock song. When he noticed me, he abruptly put the instrument down and greeted me apprehensively as I did him. After a little small talk, I asked him what he was playing on the guitar. He took the opportunity and dove in head first, just as I would have if asked such an opener to explain my surrender to Christ.

Here's the short of it: Since I last saw him, Joe became so strung out on drugs that he quit his family business, sold everything he owned to pay debts, including his new Triumph TR6 and, stuck his thumb out for wherever it would take him, ala Simon & Garfunkel's *We've All Gone to Search for America.*

"Kathy," I said, "I'm lost" though I know she was sleeping.

"I'm empty and aching but I don't know why?"

Counting the cars on the New Jersey Turnpike,

They've all gone to look for America,

All gone to search for America. - Simon & Garfunkel,

describing the sentiments of a lost generation.

Joe's thumb took him many places, but the one worth noting is the Astrodome * in Houston, TX. Some Jesus freaks picked him up hitch-hiking a day earlier and talked Joe into attending a Billy Grahm crusade at the Dome. And as you probably already figured out, he surrendered his life to Christ. I told him my story and we had a good ole hootenanny hug fest right there on his front lawn with hearts pouring out in amazement over God's love for us. An evening I will never forget. He had returned home in late May and was attending summer training seminars for Young Life, a campus ministry to senior high school kids. The sessions were every night for four weeks and they were now two weeks into it. He invited me to join him and explained the instructor was a great guy named Bob McCook who would gladly welcome me. So it was settled.

"What kind of stuff are you learning there, Joe?" I asked before I was about to start back home.

"This week we are going to be covering Noah and the Ark," he said, locking me in step. "Bob gave us some really eye-opening stuff to review if you want it. I've read it all through already, it will blow your mind."

"Oh man Joe, it's blown my mind already," and I proceeded to explain the miracle of *this* answered prayer.

I gobbled it up. Since we can't prove Noah built a great barge, what I wanted was scientific proof that the flood was possible and that is what the books Joe gave me covered. One of the books, *Fact or Fable*, was particularly good and presented some interesting facts. Three points to consider about Noah's Ark should you be interested, or you can skip over the next three number points:

- The Astrodome is no longer a sports venue. It was the first indoor stadium in the US.

1. Ark Dimensions: A team of biologists and mathematicians estimated if you gathered in the representative pair of every land dwelling (unclean) animal kind on the earth, and seven of (clean) species as the Bible account directed, all of those animals along with their necessary food storage would fit very comfortable into a freight train 140 boxcars long. Of course, the fish stayed in the water and avian species kept heading to high ground until the final stage of the flood when they could take shelter among the miles of floating flotsam islands. The representative number of mammals of the North American continent would only require 18 boxcars! If you mathematically computed the volume of 140

railroad boxcars into a boat, it would be the dimensions of the Ark as recorded in the Bible, the size of a small seagoing oil tanker.

Ship engineers can only build wooden ships to a certain length before their own bulk will cause them to break in the middle on high rolling seas. That is the same length which God directed Noah to build the Ark. Amazingly, the dimensions written thousands of years ago match the same dimensions determined safe by modern shipbuilding engineers for wooden structures. But that would take forever to build back then? Exactly 108 years to build, according to God's testimony.

2. Water Volume: If it rained for 40 days and 40 nights, the ocean levels would barely rise to any significance. However, the Bible tells us the "wells of the deep gave forth their waters", along with the rains, which would have melted the ice caps also. Geologists now know there are aquifers and great underground lakes below. Our knowledge of 'the deep', both land and ocean is very limited. Fewer men have been to the far ocean depths than have gone into space. Watching *Blue Planet* a few months ago, oceanographers are just finding boiling, streaming water vents along the Great Rift. What else don't they know? It is commonly known among geologists that sea floor fossils can be found on the highest mountains and the lowest deserts. Most of the scientific community also believes the Earth was at one time engulfed in ice *and* water in separate epochs. Perhaps the Earth was relatively flat before the flood and the majority of the planet water was underground? Perhaps it was the weight of the land, once these "wells of the deep" emptied, that collapsed the massive subterranean voids and created most of our mountain ranges, possibly starting the continents drifting in motion and colliding. All we have is *theories* about our planet's early geologic history. We try to teach

it as fact because of man's vanity at being so ignorant, but truth be told, theories of new earth geology are as accurate as the weather report. We examine what is present today and draw logical conclusions, but that doesn't mean we are right. Science is perpetually disproving old theories and creating new ones as technology broadens the window of our vain understandings.

The deepest scientific bore hole ever drilled was by the Russians. It operated for decades, then abandoned in 2011 because six miles down, they hit a lake too deep to stabilize the drill. All theories before that said water can't permeate the density of rock at that depth and that large water deposits could only be found above the permeable Earth table (from *World's Most Massive Projects*, or some series like that on PBS). Oops, that theory was proven wrong, on to the next. On the other hand, the Bible author (God) sure had it right about there being "great wells of the deep". So science once again proves out the Bible.

I'll bet when God reveals this all to us on the other side, we'll all laugh at what was being taught by "the experts" concerning not just Earth geology, but the whole cosmos. Heck, until recently, we couldn't figure out how man built the pyramids just a few thousand years ago; even with the original structures to work with! Whenever some fool expert starts in with "millions and billions of years ago *we believe* xxx happened. . ." I just chuckle inside. He's just another weatherman with his finger in the air, trying to leave his mark in a scientific journal.

3. Mt. Ararat: The Bible says the Ark came to rest on Mt. Ararat, which is on the present border of Turkey and Russia. It is the highest mountain in Eastern Europe and Europe at 17,000 feet and reasonable distance for a boat to drift in 40 days from the Tigris and Euphrates Rivers, generally acknowledged as the

cradle of civilization. The top 5,000 feet of the mountain is locked in ice year-round. Expeditions have been going up there to locate the Ark for generations. Turks who claimed to have found pieces of the Ark over the ages say it is locked in the glaciers. But now we have satellite imagery, which has not been able to turn up any large structure so far. There is one account of finding the Ark worth mentioning though.

Ararat is a nasty climb touching the Russian border. With the advent of airplanes in the early 19th century, the Russian Czar sent an aerial survey group to fly around the mountain looking for the Ark. They reported a small part of a larger structure hanging out of the ice, so the Czar sent a lengthy military/scientific expedition of over 50 men to investigate in 1917. To cut the story short, they found a portion of the Ark, walked among the remains, took photos and wood samples to bring back as evidence, then jubilantly set foot for home. Only home had changed in their long absence. The Bolshevik Revolution had defeated the White Army, killed the Czar and replaced religion with atheism. The news of the Ark's evidence did not fit well into Comrade's atheistic dogma so the expedition was parceled out to various labor camps (gulags) to silence the discovery. However, a few fortunate souls served out their time or escaped to other countries. An Ark researcher later tracked down four survivors individually in the late 1950s. They had established new lives in various countries, never to see other expedition members again. The accounts of finding the Ark from all four men agreed with each other, in detail. It's enough to make one wonder anyhow. Also, Noah did not have to round up animals from all over the world; God brought the animals to Noah. Well, if he made the universe and all creatures; rounding up a few animals would be like you calling the dog to come in. I've learned not to limit what God can and can't do. Perhaps Mt. Ararat was only a 2,000 foot bump at the time the Ark landed and still rising geologically? And when the wells of the deep gave forth their waters, the collapsing underground voids formed the first low mountain ranges. With these new fractures in the Earth's crust, tectonic plates would begin to shift, raising land masses and mountain ranges faster than they do today. Naturally, the water would recede as the land rose. That would certainly re-write the world climactic patterns, maybe kill off gigantism (dinosaurs) with an Ice Age? Who knows, you certainly can't rule it out. However, if you remove God from the equation as evolutionists do, yes—you DO have to rule it out.

So that is how my first three big questions were answered; My dad brought home Bibles he was printing, Joe Paolella introduced me to other saved kids my age, the summer training with Young Life satisfied my Noah's Ark question and a lot of others. Coincidence? Forty-five years later and I could never list all of the co-winki-dinks of God moving in my life.

So began my discipleship in the word of God. Of course, the first three questions, once answered, were quickly replaced by three more, then three more, then three more, unto this day. What about other world religions, are they all wrong? Why is there such suffering? Where did the other races come from? Who did Cain marry? Well, those are questions that require other books, one of which, has been around for a looong time. Pick it up and try reading it; start with the gospel of John. God took loving care to answer three questions on which my spiritual growth depended. He is a God who answers prayer. To this day, I am still amazed but expectant at my prayers being answered to His will.

The most astounding change I noticed about my New Life was my ability to clearly comprehend much of what I was reading in the Bible. Because of this new comprehension, many new Christians get addicted to their Bibles. This is good. Stuff that was Greek (Latin actually) to me through my Catholic upbringing was now easily understood. I hadn't been bestowed with more brains, that's for sure. It was the Holy Spirit of the God of the Universe who was opening these myriad new truths to my opened eyes. And *nobody* is prepared for that first awesome introduction to God working through his Word, directly in their puny lives. God teaches us; whosoever believes is a direct heir to His kingdom, none of us are puny in His eyes. Amen brother!

The big statement, "Whosever Believes" is taken too lightly in understanding the full surrender God is looking for from us. He is looking for 100 per cent *trust in Him* with nothing held back from us. That includes 100 per cent trusting God's plan for you, His timing, His hand-picked hardships and trials, His seasons to test us, His plan for mankind, His plan for Earth, His universal plan, His Word, His judgments, His promises, and most of all, His personal love for each of us individually. Us, allowing Him to be our father in all things. But reality is that we only trust Him for maybe 10 per cent at best on a part-time basis and trust in ourselves the other 90 per cent on a full-time basis. That is not the relationship in your life that will work with God. If you entered into a marriage with that degree of trust on one side, there isn't a chance of that union working; you're heading for divorce court. Yet that is the degree of trust we "trust" God on a trial basis the first time we test Him out in our young lives. When the relationship fails due to *our* lack of trust, we blame Him and exit stage left. But God never left the relationship and is still there waiting for the true marriage between you and Him. God is offering His 100 per cent; it is we who are falling short in the marriage. But have faith, God has not abandoned us; He has a plan. You always gotta have a plan!

Life in the balance

By providence of God, I was granted a career with industrial scales. This required me to sell, install, repair, and certify all capacities and manufacturers, with numerous certifications to perform such duties within state and federal regulations. One day I might be gowned up like a doctor to service analytical micro-balances in dust-free white rooms, then next day slopping around in coveralls under a railroad track scale, replacing rusted steel or load cells. Because of my early years of erring in the fast lane, and many more years now on the side of God, joined together with a 40-year career of weighing stuff, I, hereby, by all the powers infested in me (yes, infested), declare myself an expert on matters of weighing life in the balance of justice. Care for me to certify your balance? I'll go easier on you than the real judge. Let's look at our scales of justice.

Mankind has become frustrated with religions and particularly wars in the name of God. While often abandoning the religions of our birth with just cause, we instead tend to subscribe in some measure to a more generic universal religion as our personal back-up plan. Since you and I can't trust religion (and you shouldn't) most people have adopted an 'alternate' faith based on logic and your own moral justice. Some of your moral belief may even stem from a religion you half agree with while tossing aside the other half. The belief system of this universal religion has two basic tenants:

1. *It is impossible to wade through all of these religions, so you have pretty much given up on one religion and accepted all religions as different paths to God;* or more simply stated, whatever floats your boat. Even if you haven't given up on religion and try to cover bases by participating in some faith-based institution, you really don't believe much of what they teach and have adopted a personal back-up plan as follows.

2. *Should I have to answer to God someday for my actions, He will be fair and judge my good deeds against my bad deeds. I'll take those odds based on my believing I'm not a bad person. I'll trust my* good deeds will tilt the balance in my favor, outweighing my bad deeds.

This second tenant can be expanded further and I have coined a name for this universal religion; I call it 'Life in the Balance', or LIB. All religion set aside, most of mankind subscribes to the logical belief of being judged by their deeds. Also, that there is *probably* One True God (or Intelligent Design Master we are hearing so much about lately). He is a God of Love and Justice who will probably judge us individually for our earthly deeds someday. If not, then tens of millions got away with murder, rape, child abuse, etc.—the list goes on. Since he is a God of love, LIBer's believe we all should go to some form of eternal peace (let's just call it heaven for now). But being a God of Justice, we also believe some will *not* go to heaven, but neither do they go to hell which is a figment of man's fears and too cruel a place for a loving God to send us. Since we deny hell, let's meet in the middle and call it 'not heaven'. Certainly, pedophiles, marketers of sex slaves, murderers in general and the baser sorts, will not be in heaven, along with those who practiced from an elite list of unforgivable sins per man's laws. At the end of your life, God will weigh your good deeds against your bad deeds and you're fairly confident you'll measure up on the positive side of the ledger. Or, as long as you haven't participated in that elite list of unforgivable sins like those people over there, you'll be granted eternal peace somewhere.

If you are a LIBer, then by default you have to believe you exist forever. Why else would you be judged if not for reward in your eternal existence? What value is there in judging if there is no reward?

If this is how you generally believe it will go down, you are a LIBer, believing in **Life in the Balance**; that's fine, most of us are LIBer's at some point or to some degree. I applaud LIBer's logic and reasoning. But fortunately for us, love operates entirely outside the bounds of logic or reason; did you ever notice that? Since God is love, he too operates outside of the bounds of logic**, or so it would stand to reason. Dolt! There, I just used logic to reason love. Stop - Rewind - Proof Read - Let it be - Move on. Why do we always hurt the ones we love? Illogical. A man mistreats his wife and she still loves him? Illogical. Your daughter rebels in every way she can, yet you still love her. Illogical. You would give your life to save your wayward child, right? None of these are logical but we do them out of love. (In nature, animals will abandon their young if the choice is them or their offspring; live to breed another day.)

* Mt 5:44 Jesus speaking: "But I say unto you, Love your enemies, bless them that curse you, do good to them that hate you, and pray for them which despitefully use you and persecute you." True Love is Illogical.

Similarly, God's love also operates entirely outside the bounds of human logic or reason. He loves us though we continually disobey, ignore, insult, use His name in vain, and generally hurt Him. He turns the other cheek. No logic there. However, for the sake of argument, let's continue with the *logic* of 'Life In the Balance' and see where it takes us.

The cornerstone of the LIB plan rests on the assumption that God judges us by logic; eye for an eye, tooth for a tooth. However, that logic rests on a very misquoted Bible verse. Ex.21:22-24 refers to a specific case in Hebrew law concerning an injured woman who is pregnant. If a woman endures a miscarriage because another person injured her, that woman's husband shall determine a fine for the judges to approve. If any other injury came to the woman as a result of beating, that man shall be punished in kind as to the injury to the woman, an eye for an eye, a tooth for a tooth, hand for hand. Interestingly, the very next case (and verse) goes on to judge a man who beats his servant or handmaid so as to blind them or knock out a tooth; the punishment is to set the slave free, not eye for eye or tooth for tooth. So the eye for eye and tooth for tooth logic we like to quote is really case-specific for a few cases in the Bible, not a universal logic God judges us by.

In order for LIB to work universally, you will need universal standards, which apply to *all* people. Universally, this standard has been the Golden Rule or the Ten Commandments, which are accepted by all religions of the world because of their universal fairness *and logic* more than their origin. Yes, they came from God. No, they were never intended as a means to *earn* our way into heaven or measure your righteousness. Quite the opposite; they are God's yardstick by which we see how impossible it is to *earn our way into heaven* or save ourselves by obeying them. Anyone who truthfully examines the Ten Commandments will readily admit to violating all but two on a regular basis. The two exceptions being Murder and Adultery. Did I assume too much just then? Okay, let's make it all but one. However, if you take into account Jesus pointing out that we commit murder in our hearts, (I'll admit to mentally rubbing out one politician per week) we don't really keep any of the commandments. At best, we keep some of the commandments some of the time, for short distances, when convenient.

So I guess from personal experience, since I was an LIBer, the LIB scorecard would go something like this; I'll use stealing as the example. Johnny stole twice this week versus the 10 times he resisted to steal; that's pretty dang good in my book! Johnny is tipping those scales in the right direction this week, baby doll! 10 W's vs 2 L's! Johnny is a very, very, good boy! Just wait a second kids, let someone else do the examining.

Did you give *willingly* and *generously* to the needy or your church this week? This month? Oops, you robbed from God, of all people. Did you study any Godly instruction or spend time in prayer each day? Oops! No time to seek His ways! All right, forget about God, He expects too much anyhow. Did you volunteer any of your *time* to a worthy cause to help a brother or sister this week? Oops, robbed from your fellow man. Did you get to work a few minutes late, stretch your lunch or work break a bit? Don't we all? Oops, robbed your employer. Did you shop online those 20 minutes while you were supposed to be running those reports? Oops, robbed the employer again. Downloaded or 'borrow' any software or music illegally? All right, so you didn't take home office stationery this month, go to the head of the class? See my point. Judge yourself by your own standards and you will always come out smelling like a rose. Let someone else judge you by higher standards, and perspectives change Big Time. Let God judge you from His standard? Okay, I guess it's time to go there.

Since God is the one judging us on this industrial-sized celestial balance of our life's deeds, we really need to look at ***His standards***. Forgive me while I quote a few verses to explain God's standard, but I think it only fair we let Him have a few words here.

> *"For **ALL** have sinned and come short of the glory of God" Rom 3:23*
> *"But we are **ALL** as an unclean thing, and **all our righteousness are as filthy rags"***
> *Is 64:6*
> *"Thou (God) art of purer eyes than to behold evil, and **cannot look on sin**" Hab 1:13*

I'll stop there with the Bible verses. God says that even the most righteous man that ever lived stands before Him wearing his best deeds as "clothed in filthy rags". All have sinned and God can't look on sin or have a relationship with us while we are still wearing our sin (filthy rags). Looks like God's standard is a teeny-tiny bit too high for our 'Life In the Balance' plan. Whoa! So what do we have to do to win this balancing act? Very simple; walk away from the side of the balance where you're busy stacking up your good deeds and go over to the other side of the scale (think scales of justice) where you thought bad deeds were piled and tell me, what do you see? Go ahead, I'll wait. Hmm, hmm, hmm, nothing? You sure? Go back and look again. Okay, what did you see? Absolutely nothin'! Say it again, y'all. War! Hmph! Whoa-woe-woe-woe. What is it good fah,… Sorry, every time I see or say those two words together I just can't help hearing that song; it's an old habit. But that is exactly what you are stacking your good deeds against— Absolutely Nothing—while all this time you expected to see your bad deeds on the other side of the Balance. How then, if your good deeds are sitting high in the balance, can NOTHING out-weigh it on the other side of the scale. Read on, I'll 'splain.

The Standard

So seeing nothing, you can now start to comprehend what the problem is; you never saw or understood the **standard** which to work towards. Now go back to your good side of the balance so we can start over and do it right. First, I want you to sweep away all those good deeds you had piled up there on the scale so we can replace them with something much lovelier. Next, reach inside yourself and pull out every sin you ever committed in your whole life. Yep, even *that* one, go on now, don't be afraid, ain't nobody looking but God. Now slap that hefty hunk of steamin' junk on down where your good deed pile of filthy rags was. WOWzers! Couldn't help it, just had to peek. Had no idea you were THAT bad. Don't feel bad, my pile was higher. Ignore that very large crowd of people behind your pile; those are the people you hurt with your sins throughout your life (witnesses), most of whom you never even knew you hurt. They're just there to testify against you.

"Now hold on there, Rich! I never killed any border guard, what's **he** doing in the crowd, I don't recognize half of these people!?" Well, Cosmo, even our smallest sins have big consequences; that border guard is one of several murders you were part of. Remember that ounce of pot you bought the week of April 6, 1976? Looks like one cent of the cost of that $80 ounce was 'hit money', which went towards the murder of that Colombian border guard and the innocent pilot that died with him. You are listed as an accomplice in that one. You really don't want to know any more about the others in that crowd, but God knows. Our sin reaches so deep that the Bible says the sin of one generation (person, family, **or** nation) has multiplying affects upon future generations. We tend to mentally sweep the severity of our smallest sins under the carpet.

Flashback

"I don't see where smokin' a joint in the confines of my folks' home or with friends is hurting anybody." Correct, you don't see.

A young lady from a loving family makes a bad choice to boink some heartthrob out of wedlock. She runs away from her critical parents when she finds out she is pregnant and has to find more sinful ways to get by and raise her child, or abort secretly. That baby's life has been forever changed by her mother's (and father's) choices. Their sins are visiting their child's future, future siblings, the parents, the grandparents, the tax burdened entitlements others have to pay for…and on and on.

OK. The new pile is in place. Now, the object is get the sin pile down to the size of the pile on the other side of the balance (in the weighing industry we call it back-weighing), which, as we already noticed, is Absolutely Nothing. Why is it nothing, you ask? Aha! This is the meat of it. That empty side of the balance is God's sin. *Now* you understand why it is empty. "Come on, Rich, you gonna try to tell us the Balance of our lives is being measure against the perfection of God. THAT'S IMPOSSIBLE." No, I'm not gonna say that, I'm going to let God say it, and remember *"with God all things **are** possible"*.

> *Gen 17:1 I am the Almighty God, walk before me and be thou **perfect***
> *Lev 11:44 ye shall be holy for I am holy. (Holy is the same as perfect in these applications)*
> *Matt 5:48 Jesus said, "Be ye therefore perfect, even as your Father in Heaven is perfect"*

However, since most of mankind doesn't take much stock in what the Bible says, I shall not borest thee with more verseth about God requiring thou to be perfect; we'll stick with logic for the time being. But I will add this: I find it fascinating the way God goes out of his way to repeat something in His Word over and over again just in case we're not getting it. Just like any good Father repeats himself.

The task before you now is to use your pile of good deeds sitting next to you (not on either pan of the balance) to whittle down your heaping dung-pile of sin, to balance out God's nothing-pile on the other side of the balance. That, my friends, is how the real Balance of God's justice works. **You** are judged against God's perfection. Hurry now and shovel, that stuff hardens up fast and then you'll be needing to bring in the chisels of generosity, then jackhammers of volunteerism and lastly, the dynamite of lighting motif candles or financing the psychic hotline.

You see, with the LIBer standard you only had to balance your good deeds a smidge past your bad deeds on the other side of the balance. But with God's standard, you have to weigh your life's deeds, bad and good, against His standard of perfection.

You can't leave even ONE sin on your side of the balance. As Mom used to say, "You can't get up from the dinner table until every last pea is gone from that plate!" Just one sin separates us from God. Sorry, that's God's standard, according to His Word. Hope you didn't plan on *earning your way* into His kingdom via the LIBer plan.

———————————

By spending a 43-year career in the weighing industry, I've learned a thing or two about standards. Truth #1 – Standards don't change. A kilogram is a kilogram no matter what country you go to, just as a US dollar is 100 cents or a yard is 36 inches, etc. These are universal *standards* that we live by. Countries go to great measure and expense to maintain truth in standards. For my job, I used a set of weights that range from .01mg (0.00001 of a gram) to 25,000 pounds. These weights are called **standards** and are used to calibrate industrial weighing apparatus. My weights (standards) are tested each year at the Pennsylvania state lab in Harrisburg for accuracy. The master set of weights in Harrisburg is tested against a Federal Master set of weights at the National Laboratory in Maryland. In scale lingo, this means my weights are NIST traceable (National **Institute for Standards** in Technology); or more simply put, my weights can be traced for accuracy back to the federal lab master set for our nation.

God's standards are similar in that they are universal and never change. His standard is perfection. God's empty side of the balance is an absolute zero, a total void of sin. What was sin 5,000 years ago is still a sin today because universal standards don't change. So it also stands that the standards of righteousness, forgiveness, and justice are the same today as at the beginning of time.

At the complete other end of the spectrum are our individual human moral standards, which change laughably from person to person, day to day, generation to generation, culture to culture, etc. Since man's standards of behavior change with the wind, the only universal standard to level the field for everyone is God's standard. By God's provision there is a physical standard by which sin can be removed from the sinner, by which the oppressed can be victorious over the oppressor, by which the slave can be set free. There is only one standard to remove sin and it is one word. You are *not* going to like the word…not one bit…but there is only one word to describe this standard by which men are set free. Are you ready? Now don't throw the book! The word is 'blood'. Told you, **you** wouldn't like it. But apparently, mankind *loves* this blood standard for freedom and has embraced it open-armed like a love affair since history began. Don't want to believe me? Read on to test the argument.

Someone violently breaks into your house and within 30 seconds they make it perfectly clear they are there to kill you, take your life. You have two choices: Diplomacy, which means negotiating with the invader; Zzzip, he slits your throat and you're dead. It may be a moral victory but you're still dead by the shedding of blood. To continue living, you really only have one choice, the second choice; fight back with every ounce of life in you. If you choose to fight, you have just adopted into the blood standard. You will fight to your last drop of blood to regain your freedom from this oppressor over you. And very likely spill their blood also. This bloodletting will allow someone to emerge victorious over the other, but not necessarily you, the assumed person in the right.

Now, say, we look at the reason that person came into your home to kill you. This may be a bit far-fetched, but I am tired. There has been a major war and you are boarded up in a basement living by yourself, hoarding a year's stash of food. The person who just tried to kill you was trying to liberate his family from certain starvation. Both of you are justified in your cause, willing to lay down your life (blood) to liberate yourself or family from your oppression (starvation). It doesn't matter who is right in the cause, the point is: there is only one standard by which the matter will be settled, blood. Now I'm sure well-intentioned peaceniks will argue there is another way, a negotiated settlement. Even if you were killed while negotiating, that was your choice of how to risk your blood to liberate yourself from the oppressor. This object lesson is after all negotiations have been expired; negotiations fall under peaceful resistance. If one who did nothing wrong is willing to *shed his blood as a lamb* for peace or liberation, that is fine; either way, the final solution is still blood, will always be blood, has always been blood.

Blood has been the standard for *perceived* freedom throughout history. Nations throughout history have spilled millions of cubic yards and liquid tons of blood to achieve their perceived freedoms over and over again. It is a fact of our existence as plain as the nose on our face. Since day one, blood has been the symbol of life, our life's blood. It is the standard by which we protect our life. In 1863 America, when the South said to Congress: We will not be governed under new laws that we believe oppressive, destroying our slave-based economy, they chose the standard of blood, *a lot* of blood to settle the matter. Revolutions, civil wars, religious wars, even neighborhood brawls have all been settled by this same standard of precious blood throughout history. A battlefield lament sung by soldiers burying their dead and made popular by Crosby Stills & Nash during the Kent State killings tell it well. The students were protesting for freedom when they paid the blood price.

> *Find the cost of freedom,*
> *Buried in the ground.*
> *Mother earth will swallow you.*

Lay your body down. - From Four Way Street
The Bible tells it much better.
Lev 17: v11 For the Life of the flesh is in the blood: and I have
given it to you upon the altar to make atonement for your
souls: for it is blood that makes an atonement (setting free) for
the soul.
*v14 For it (blood) is the **life** of all flesh; the blood of it (the flesh)*
*is for the **life** thereof...*

When the Bolshevik Revolution overthrew the Czar to conclude a bloody war to establish Communism, the standard of blood was used to liberate the oppressed from an oppressor. Forget the ideology of it, the idea of *perceived* liberation under the banner of a blood standard is the point. I could go on and on for volumes stating examples of the blood standard liberating men and nations from their oppressors.

For my Christian friends, consider this: Judo-Christianity is a faith solely (or souly) based on blood sacrifice, both animal (lambs) and human (Christ). In the Old Testament, all the Hebrew instruction from God to present to him an *unblemished* (perfect) lamb, bull, doves, etc., is pointing to the individual and national need for ***perfect (unblemished) blood*** to remove their sins, pointing to the perfect sacrificial Lamb of God (the Christ) yet to appear. God is saying as clear as possible that perfect blood is His standard. Don't bring Him the lamb out of your flock that has a bum leg or is blind; He wants your best, for He will send His best (in Jesus). To the outsider it certainly looks barbaric and superstitious, right up there with the Aztecs. Then, when the Son of God *IS* sent to us, God sacrifices His own blood in the Perfect Lamb, Jesus, the Lamb of God who taketh away the sins of the world. In appearances, Christianity just took blood sacrifice a BIG notch above the Aztecs by sacrificing their God! How does that look to modern man!? Well, considering the standard of bloodletting by which all history of perceived freedom is based upon, it makes perfect sense, even logical that God's blood would be given to free His creation from their sin. At least try reading the last few paragraphs through again before calling me crazy. And if you have time, read about the Passover. It is the story of how each Jewish family was instructed to spread the blood of a lamb over the doorway of their home so the angel of death (God's wrath) would bypass their home. Certainly, God knew where the Jews were living, but he wanted His people to see for all of history that unblemished innocent blood protects them from His judgment. We will look more at blood a little later, but for now we need to return to the standard by which God will be judging us—perfection.

The whole reason for our existence is for us to be with God forever. Everything else—the economy, environment, education, spouses, families, friends, kings, and kingdoms—are just infrastructure to support that one reason for being. Not just to be friends of God, but a humanly inconceivable love relationship with Him forever. He loves us, and we love Him, by choice, that simple. To miss this understanding is to fail at Life completely, miss the boat altogether. Remember what ole Dan'l Webster said and worth repeating.

If there is no God, nothing matters.

If there is a God, nothing else matters.

We are created in God's image. And like us, God is particular about who He hangs out with. Like it or not, we are all, by conscious choice or unintentional, prejudiced about whom we hang out with. Look at who you hang out with. I'd venture that if you're financially well-healed; nearly all of your close friends are in the same boat. You may have a few old neighborhood friends still struggling financially, but you don't make new friends with anyone in the poverty bracket. If you are white, most of your close friends are white and you don't really go out of your way to befriend other ethnics even though you may work with and like them. If you are a religious fundamentalist, you tend to surround yourself with like-minded friends. If your life revolves around hunting or sports, so do your closest friends. If your life revolves around your career, many of your friends will be career-minded or same professional level. I'm not criticizing, just stating the obvious for the majority of us. We tend to gravitate towards those more in common with our own social-economic-intellectual standards because we can relate to them. We have *certain standards* that new acquaintances must meet in order to qualify as a friend. And so it is with God, but only on a much higher degree of expectation. He can only hang out with those who meet His standard of being without sin, 100 percent sinless, because he has absolutely nothing in common with sin.

"*Thou* (God) *art of purer eyes than to behold evil, and cannot look on sin*" Hab 1:13

Question from mankind: How can God have a love relationship with us if he can't look on us because of our sin?

Answer from His Word: He can't, unless we are sinless, which none of us are. Our sin is the gulf between Him and us.

Q: Then why did He create us sinners?

A: He didn't create us sinners. He made us perfect (without sin in the Garden), which included free will. WE choose to be sinners.

Q: Why did He give us free will then, if He knew we would choose to be sinners, isn't that the same as damming mankind from day 1?

A: Without free will, we are just mind-numb robots. Love is a choice, not an automatic program. God wants our love relationship to be one of choice. He loves His children and only wants us to return that love voluntarily. Would you force your children to love you? *Could* you force your rebellious teen to love you? Good luck with that. Hopefully, that teen will someday mature and recognize his parental love and begin to love back, even apologize for hurting mom and dad, asking their forgiveness to start over.

Q: Still sounds to me like God created sin by giving us free will. If that's the case, isn't God the original murderer by condemning us to death because of our sin?

A: Oiy-Vey. Why did I ever allow this line of questioning? OK, I'll play along as devil's advocate.

Devil's Reply: **God** made man sinners and is, therefore, guilty of murder like the man just said! I just think mankind should be allowed to judge Him (God) fair and square by the laws of man. I'd like to see Him tried for murdering your sad race, which by the way, I have been a big fan of man since the Garden, always was. It's time we got all this straightened out, fair and square, once and for all.

Rich: But what would putting God on trial prove?

Devil: You just keep writing, you pin-head, and I'll tell you what it proves! You see, if God is guilty, then all of mankind is off the hook (and so is Satan) since *He* gave you free will to sin, not me. I Looove mankind! I would never hurt any of you! You're not sinners, you're just,… normal!

Rich: All right, Satan, say, man finds God guilty by your crazy line of logic; the consequence for murder is to be put to death. Are you actually suggesting that man then put God to death?

Devil: **Now** you're talkin'! And why not put Him to death? Fair is fair. He's guilty of the same against you. Git 'er dun!

Rich: Done. Now go to hell, Satan, you lose.

Devil: Hey dork, you don't tell me where to go! I don't lose! And what do you mean by "Done?"

Rich: **You Lose.** *God became flesh (and blood) and dwelt among us.* The highest religious order in the world tried Him and had

Him condemned to death, even though he was sinless. He died in my place and the place of all mankind that will believe and choose His gift of salvation. He has made a way for our free will to still choose Him through the perfect blood of Jesus Christ. Like you said, Satan, His death gets all believers off the hook.

Devil: "DOLT!" And exits, defeated by his own reasoning.

Disclaimer: I do not support the above argument (the part of God's guilt). I included it to carry out to the conclusion an argument some people have that God is responsible for our sins by giving us free will. He is not responsible for our sins. That thinking is typical of today's mentality of not taking responsibility for one's action. I teach my children not to steal and set the example by not stealing (all right, all right already, need a set of cheap tires?). It was their choice to steal; my choice was for them *not* to steal and I set the example.

That last argument ran off on a tangent so let me get back to the original question.

If God requires us to be sinless in order to have a loving personal relationship with Him, how can we ever be sinless? Finally, I thought you would never ask.

The answer: **We** can't do a thing to save ourselves. Bummer. But, God can, and has provided the way, the only Way.

No way, Rich! Way, I'm tellin' ya, in Jesus Christ, the Way! John 14:6

No matter how good we try to be, we are slaves to our sin. Slaves need to be set free, but are in bondage to their master. His name is Satan and the bible says he is the present master of this world. God bought us out of Satan's world of slavery by providing the standard for freedom; His perfect, sinless blood. We're back to that blood standard again. Is your head spinning? I'll try simplifying.

God creates man with free will.

271

Man uses his free will to turn from God and sin, thinking our way is better than His way.

Man is separated from a perfect God by sin.

Man is now slave to sin; Satan is the author of that sin and lord of this world.

Though we don't realize it and may not consciously make the choice, Satan is our master by default when we ignore God. There is no gray area in between.

Satan has us in slavery to the **three sources of all sin**—the lust of the eyes (I want nice things), the lust of the flesh (I want more than things; hubba-hubba, wink-wink), and our pride (everything revolves around me; power, vanity and greed).

In order to be set yourself free from your slave-master, you must enter into the blood battle. Remember, blood is the only standard to set one free from his oppressor.

Your blood battle has already been lost because *your* blood is sin-blood—blood Satan already owns since the Garden. As a sinner you cannot be in God's family. Satan, on the other hand, can only hang out with sinners and has adopted you until the day you surrender your sins to Christ. If you die in your sins, you are permanently adopted into Satan's family, Forever. You have tried your futile battle with Satan, but you always lose as he cackles with delight because you don't understand that you are trying to put out a fire by throwing gasoline (sin-blood) on it.

Enter the water. (John 4:14 – the water I shall give him will become in him a spring of water, welling up to eternal life.)

Since God can't die, He has to become a man, since only man can die.

God becomes a man with perfect, sinless blood in the person of Jesus the Christ (Savior, Redeemer) for the soul purpose of going into blood battle with Satan in order to set us free from our oppressor.

If Satan can get Jesus to sin just once, he has turned Christ's sinless blood into blood like ours and Satan would be the victor. I did the math: Perfection + 1 sin = Imperfection.

The battle rages for 33 years until finally, a frustrated Satan who can't get Christ to sin, resorts to the last tool in his arsenal to separate Christ from God. He throws all of the sin of mankind, which he rightly owns, at Jesus while on the cross.

With that, the most beautiful act of love ever to occur in the history of the universe took place. Though sinless, Jesus allows Satan (and God by not interfering) to put all of the sins of mankind on himself, Jesus.

By doing this, Satan and God have entered into *thee* blood battle for mankind.

And this was the whole reason why Jesus came, to pay the perfect blood standard *in our place* so we can stand sinless again in the eyes of God.

The next part is beyond my literary explanations.

The blood battle begins with the scourging, then on to the cross as sin destroys the body of Jesus where, as a last resort, Satan throws at Christ the one thing he knows can kill a man—sin, not just one sin but all of man's sin, which is exactly what Jesus wanted. But sin has no dominion over the Holy Spirit, God in Christ. However, Jesus' sin*less* blood has dominion over our sin*ful* blood owned by Satan. For three days, the blood battle continues in hell with Satan. That I can't explain, other than Love is victorious over Hate. But I do know, personally, very personally, that because Jesus never sinned, He was able to resurrect His body, becoming the first man completely victorious over sin. And because He has promised all born again, washed in the blood standard, that they are heirs to all that is His, that He will resurrect all the sin destroyed bodies of believers to perfection in His Kingdom, God's Kingdom.

I have no idea what Jesus did for those three days before He raised himself from the grave, but I suspect it was still part of the blood battle. Jesus resurrects himself, the first resurrected man, proving death and sin have no

OLD NEWS, GOOD NEWS

power over Him. Since He is sinless, he cannot die. Sin is the author of death. Jesus is the author of Life.

It wasn't until the disciples saw Him alive after His crucifixion that they finally understood why Jesus came:

To die in our place,

pay the perfect blood standard for our sin,

so that we can be set free from sin-slavery while on Earth and forever,

so we can stand sinless (perfect) before God, serve and love Him all our life,

so we can be in everlasting love relationship with Him,

and return to the new Garden as intended.

God's perfect plan is perfected.

And the good news (gospel) spreads around the world. Scoffers laugh. Believers rejoice.

Are we pawns in this battle? Most definitely; pawns with a choice in our own outcome. There we are with free will again. Free will got us into the mess, and God has provided a Way, a Redeemer, His life for ours, by which our free will can choose out of the mess. But the blood of Christ only has power for those who use their free will to believe and trust him. As in any relationship, trust is the key that determines success. Not trust as in 80 per cent sure, or even 99.99 per cent sure; but hook, line and sinker, 100 per cent, no doubt sure, by surrendering your life completely, on your knees, to the Life that can save you. It is a choice. God will not force you, but he made sure you could see the Way.

274

The choice is simple. Admit you are a slave to sin, surrender your life to Christ who gave *His life* for *your* sin, get saved (born again or whatever term you prefer), and live the rest of your life with Christ in you. Now that He can only see you as a sinless new creation, you're gonna make a great pair, believe me. Believe Him.

Jesus is heir to all that is God's, always was, the first verses in the book of John tells us as part of the Trinity (I won't go there *) he is co-creator and co-equal with God but separate.

Now that the sin gulf between us is removed, we, His children who believe and accept this blood sacrifice, are heirs to all that is Christ's. We are heirs to His Kingdom, His Life, His abundance forever, never to be judged for our sins because they have been removed as far as the east is from the west. God will never even ask me about my sin on the final day because He has no knowledge of its existence. Christ has removed all account of it.

* All right I'll go there for one short paragraph. We are made in His image (Gen 1:26)**. We have a body, spirit, and soul, just as God has a Body (Jesus), Spirit (the Holy Spirit) and Soul (God Essence). Your soul is that part of you that never dies, your essence. Your spirit contains your God made individual personality. It is yours to keep as you see fit or surrender to God through Christ. Luke 9:24, Jesus speaking: *"whosoever will save his life shall lose it, but whosoever will lose his life for my sake, shall save it."* And that's all I have to say about that.

* Actually, In Gen 1:26, God says, "Let *us* make man in *our* image." Those are plurals. He was talking with Jesus and the Holy Spirit at creation.

Does this mean you won't sin anymore? You wish. However, it does mean that all future sin is covered by the same blood and forgiveness. "Great! A license to sin!" you're thinking. Don't be such a knuckle-head. The Holy Spirit which now dwells in you and is instructing you in new life is also convicting you about sin like you never knew before. You will lean on the Holy Spirit to fight sin in your life before it happens because you love God and now understand this love relationship is a two-way street. God asks you to surrender a bad habit and you do it because you love Him and want to please Him; ever mindful of how much He loves you and the price He paid for you. Too hard to convey in words, it's a love thang. The good news is that you now have victory over any future sin and no longer need be a slave to it. The Holy Spirit is able to help you overcome any sin. This is a life-long effort that is only completed the moment you pass from this Earth. Christians are still sinners, excellent sinners at that.

A quick side note: The term redeemer has an interesting history worth telling. In Jesus' time, the Roman armies would return to Rome after conquering a nation. In tow would be a large population of non-Roman citizens (now slaves) from defeated countries. These hundreds of thousands of slaves would get parceled out to different areas of the empire so as to weaken their previous national unity. From there they would be scheduled for the auction slave markets. Every once in a while, a wealthy Roman citizen who abhorred slavery would come to the auction to purchase slaves to set them free. Word would quickly spread through the crowd that a redeemer was in their midst. The main conversation and hope among slaves in those days was of a redeemer saving them from the slave auction. This redeemer would buy a group of slaves, issue them certificates of Roman citizenship, and tell them they could live freely as citizens of their new land. Their debt was paid and they were free to go. When the first 10,000 Jews (now termed Christians) at Jerusalem got saved after Pentecost, the new converts likened it to a redeemer saving a slave from the slave market (of sin) and granting them new citizenship in a new land (heaven). Thus, the name of Jesus the Redeemer was added to His growing list of names.

Understanding More about the Perfect Blood

Hang in there. Get through the next few pages and we're back to more stories.

All of my rambling about standards, blood, and Life in the Balance is going somewhere believe it or not. Let's gather up what we have looked at so far.

- The Ten Commandments teach us that no one can keep them. Symbolically, in their stone form, they were broken before Moses even had the chance to deliver them. Spiritually, they've continued to be broken since delivered.

- Since no one can keep the Ten Cs, all men are sinners. To deny this is to lie to yourself, a violation of the commandment not to bear false witness. So there.

- God can't be in fellowship with sin because he is perfect. We live by standards. Standards don't change. The universal standard to liberate one from their oppressor is blood. This is a history proven standard.

Following the reasoning that we are all removed from fellowship with God by our sin nature *and* blood is the standard by which we are liberated from our Oppressor(s), it stands to reason that the only way to defeat this sin, get back to the Garden and fellowship with God, is for the historically proven standard of blood to overcome our Oppressor. Call me crazy, but I'm just following the logic path here, folks.

Just who is our Oppressor? Well, sin has a face and that face is Satan.

"Okay, Rich, now you just left your argument of following logic with that last line, AND, I don't buy into the Satan stuff, so the book just got thrown back in the trash can!"

Give me a chance to explain.

Science, logic, and even karma teach that for every force there is an opposing force, for every action there is a reaction; the only reason we have a moral concept of "Good" is because we have the concept of "Evil" to compare it to. Without the concept of "Evil", all we have is knowledge of Good as we did in the Garden, which unfortunately is no longer our estate. If you believe there is a God, intelligent designer, or other form of grand wazoo representing perfection, then by reason you have to believe there is an opposite to God. For convenience's sake let's give him a name—let's call him Satan. Aw come on, what's in a name? Satan is the Oppressor, the source of our sin. The blood battle will be with him if we are to get back to the Garden with God. Satan was the one who conned us into trusting in free will to determine we don't have to obey God; that if we try our own way, it will be better than God's way. Time for a tangent truth to help you better understand how Jesus was sinless, thereby able to offer sinless blood to battle Satan.

This page will take some patience to read because at first it will sound like plain old religious nonsense you heard before and always thought was pretty darn close to fairy tale as fairy tale can get. It concerns the Virgin Birth of Christ. There is a medical fact here that should blow you away and supports the claim of virgin birth.

We have all heard that Jesus was conceived by the Spirit of God and born of a virgin, which sounds ridiculous. Listen closely (that's a verily ver-ily!). This is a Biblical truth specifically given to us living in these end times to fully understand. The medical record supports what no other generation before the 20th century could have understood until modern medicine proved it out. Check with your Doctor or Google WebMD to prove out the following.

Any of you mothers out there who have read up on your pregnancies know for a fact what happens if a mother's blood ever enters the body her baby inside her; the fetus will immediately miscarriage. Less than 100 years ago, modern medicine learned that all of the *blood making abilities in a fetus derives entirely from the male*. From conception, the sperm establishes all blood production ability as the first cells divide to start a tiny fetus, able to manufacture its own blood. Mom's blood NEVER mixes with babies' blood. **Babies make their own blood** in the womb from nutrients sent from the mother's body through the umbilical cord. No one knew this 2,000 years ago when the gospel writers recorded that Jesus was born sinless, with God as the father; or before that time when the OT prophets recorded that a messiah would be born of a virgin. Now that we can understand the blood producing functions in a fetus, we can understand that a woman, virgin or not, whose child inside her was started from God by a means we shall never understand, would birth a child of perfect sinless blood since all the blood-producing abilities came from the male source, God, who is sinless.

Muddy water can't cleanse a muddy face; only fresh clean water can wash that face/soul. Sinful blood can't cleanse a sinful soul, only perfect sinless blood can.

Mary, though virtuous, was a sinner like the rest of us. Her seed was from God, therefore sinless, and her sinful blood is incapable of mixing with the blood of her fetus, Jesus; her offspring was, therefore, the second perfect man with perfect sinless blood, Adam being the first; but Adam blew it when he fell. *"By one man (Adam) sin entered into this world and by one man (Jesus) it was removed."* In order for man to be redeemed to a sinless state again, the blood battle will have to be fought with perfect, AAA grade, God-certified, pure sinless blood, not the cheap back-shelf stuff running in our veins.

Just wanted to try to clarify the Biblical record on the emphasis for Jesus having perfect sinless blood from birth to equip Him for the world standard of the blood battle with our Oppressor and the cross.

An interesting side note for my Catholic friends with no offense intended. The Roman Catholic Church was faced, in the early centuries, with the dilemma of explaining how Jesus could be born sinless if born of Mary, a sinner. Remember, they didn't know the medical facts of blood production in the fetus as we know today. *They* thought fetus blood came from the mother through the umbilical cord—a logical deduction. Their answer: Mary had to be sinless. However, there is nothing written in the Bible to support that conclusion. Had the first popes just trusted scripture and waited 1,600 more years, medical science would have provided the answer; Mary's blood never mixed with that of her child. Had Mary been sinless, God would have sent *her* to the cross and there would have been no need to send Jesus at all. And since the RC church teaches that ALL are born with original sin, how could

Mary be sinless unless born under the same circumstances as Jesus, which I think would have received *some* mention in the Gospels.

Three thoughts that may help clarify the chapter:

1. *Without* our sin we would be in fellowship with God and live forever with Him here on Earth as originally intended. Our choice to follow our own way instead of His way is why we're in this mess, and the planet is dying.

2. It is our choosing to sin which creates our physical mortality. In a sinless state with God, in the Garden, Adam and Eve had immortal bodies created in perfection. When mankind chose to sin, we opened the door to imperfection, aging, diseased bodies. So now I'm bald, skinny, with a face that sags like a basset hound; a slow rendezvous with a dead body.

3. **By** natural universal moral code, a wrong can only be made right by *a*) removing the wrong, or *b*) making recompense for the wrong.

   Example *a*: Removing the wrong –I stole your pig and you hate me. In order to remove the wrong, I return your piggy, apologize in all sincerity with a contrite heart, saying I don't know what got into me. You let it go, but always think I'm a jerk. The hurt remains even though I returned the stolen pig. You think like the old saying; "I will forgive you but can never forget". *Our friendship is never the same.*

   Example *b*: Making recompense for the wrong –I stole your pet pig, had a fine backyard roast, and didn't invite you. I feel bad a week later and return what's left of your pig, along with a new pig and a note that explains I was suffering from the swine-flu virus when I swiped your pig. You accept the recompense but you prized that first pig and the replacement is never equal to the first. The hurt remains even though I recompensed for the pig. You still think I'm a jerk after seeing another side of me you don't like. *Our friendship is never the same.*

You see, no matter what we do to make a wrong right, some hurt remains. Recompense can be made for the transgression but forgiveness is a lot more difficult. Even when forgiveness is fully granted, we can't really forget; our trust is never quite the same toward that person, part of our guard will always remain up. Ever been burned in love? Then you know about guards going up. You may fall in love again, but it won't be the same and your self-preservation guard will always remind you that this new love too could very well let you down. That ain't no way to run a railroad, or heaven. Think of how many times we have let God down or blamed him for our problem.

I don't know, maybe God could have forgiven us some other way for our sins without Jesus coming, but He would still be warily conscious of our capacity for sin, our crushing ability to let Him down again and again and again and again. How can we love each other whole-heartedly in that sort of scenario when the guard is always up between us and Him? And what kind of heaven would it be if all the people there couldn't share 100 per cent pure trust and love? We can't trust someone because of their capacity to sin against us. How could we have distrust in heaven? *This distrust comes from the knowledge of our capacity to sin.* What God chose to do, in order for His perfect plan to work on Earth as it is in heaven, is *REMOVE SIN AND ALL MEMORY OF ITS EXISTENCE COMPLTELY.* The Bible teaches that through Christ perfect sinless blood, our sin is forgiven AND forgotten, "as far as the east is from the west" by God. For those of you who struggle with a compass, that means infinity. Infinity, when applied to God's timeline, means past, present, and future. God-love has been returned to man, not by **anything** we have done, but 100 per cent by what He has done.

Show me any parent that wouldn't give their own life in place of a ter-
minally ill son or daughter so that their child could have life. Good News, this
is simply what God did through Christ. He gave his Life to save his children's
soul. Our short time here on Earth is heading for a death trap set by Satan if
we die in our sins. Satan owns the human race.

When Satan conned us into sin, he became victorious over us and has
been our Master/Oppressor ever since. We are powerless to fight against his
power of sin over us, even for an hour. We are slaves to his power over us,
slaves to our sin, slaves to our pride, our vanities, our prejudices, our hate,
our bodies, our lust. And he does this to the point that we no longer even
realize we sin. Even worse, have convinced ourselves we are not in a hopeless
state of sin! We all have become so immune to our sin nature that we have
trouble even recognizing it on a daily basis, having convinced ourselves we
are a loving race committed to peace. Read the headlines, folks, we are slaves
to our sin.

For those who think mankind is inherently good, allow me to quote
some facts from a *National Geographic* January 2006 article concerning
genocide throughout *JUST* the last century; the period in history which we
have considered our race "civilized". We came into the 20th century with a
world population of 1.6 billion and exited with 6 billion. By 1950 there were
still only 2.6 billion. The total population for the century was less than 10
billion. In that time, death from genocide alone took 50 million lives and
continues unabated into this century. Do the math; that is, *one out of two
hundred people born in the last 100 years died just from genocide*, a topic we
rarely even consider among world problems. That does not include abortions, mind you. Worldwide abortions add another 50 million per year to the
genocide numbers. Nor does it include those who have died from non-geno-
cidal wars, starvation, run-of-the-mill everyday murders, or easily treatable
diseases like malaria and typhoid. It's a pandemic that makes the COVID19
virus just an inconvenience. I mention malaria and typhoid because they are
solvable problems in Third World countries we choose to throw a few dollars
at but would rather ignore. So when did we become "civilized man"? I say

this simply to point out that we are not a very attractive race who destroys our own on a grand scale. All are guilty by verdict of allowing it to continue.

Does anyone really believe the answers to our problems will come from politics or any of our corrupt governments? From religions, which have caused more war and hardship than any single empire or source in history and is repeating with Islam this time around? From technology? If anything, technology will destroy us, after it lulls us into thinking our brilliance solved all the problems. Or from a One World Order which the Bible predicts is just on the horizon before the final end? In Revelations, we read that if not for the second return of Jesus Christ to stop the madness, mankind would have obliterated mankind. Not hard to imagine based on all the means we have to outright destroy ourselves, along with mother ship Earth racing towards ecologically collapse. And now we come into the 21st century with very unstable governments building nuclear arsenals to aim at Israel and the west, along with the religious fervor to commit nuclear destruction in the name of Allah, believing they are under his protection. Countries which encourage suicide bombings are not beyond stepping it up a notch to nuclear national suicide bombing.

As Rosanna Rosannadana's mom often said, "There's always something." (I was getting too grim there). It is an ugly fact: Man is destructive and sinful by our chosen nature.

CHAPTER 12

Thrice Lost

I have to stop here for a moment and chuckle to myself. You have patiently read this far and I really owe you a gigantic thank you. But I know you've been thinking all along to yourselves; "Okay, Rich, all this stuff may be well and good but where do *you* get off handing out this unsolicited preaching; we all know you and you're no angel, not even close; you're still plenty rough around the edges." And to that I plead no contest, guilty as charged. When I put my life into the hands of Christ, I imagine He cupped his hands to His bosom while breaking into a broad smile; one of His children had returned. Then He opened His hands to see what kind of deal He got, only to find a big melted M&M chocolate mess. Instead of wiping his hands to be rid of the mess, He beamed back at me, "Rich, I just looove chocolate, I can do so much with this!" Well, He's still working with the mess. But remember, most of you know me since re-construction. To be fair, only my wife and a few old friends can make a proper judgment on how far He has brought me, and how far I yet have to go.

This is my book; I gave it to you and it is yours now. I didn't write it for me, I wrote it for you. Many nights at the computer I wanted to walk away from this project, feeling inadequate and hypocritical to present such weighty spiritual matters. But God nudged me to be patient until it all came together for His purpose of pointing others to Him. Most people won't pick up a book that discusses Jesus Christ (think of the last time you did; see what I mean), and some of us just don't read books at all or don't have time to read. However, a book written by a friend will pique your curiosity enough to read it through. Realizing the stories from my quirky youth might hold your interest long enough to get to the meatier matter; I saw the opportunity to present the gospel to many of my friends who normally wouldn't take the time to listen otherwise. So if you feel I tricked you into reading this book, I plead no contest again. And if I erred in doing so, please consider that I erred on the side of friendship, out of concern for the people I care about.

My decision to tackle this project was made on that night at the Optimist Club meeting after I ran into Officer Bernie Romic (see Introduction). Typically, over the years, when my old friends and new friends mixed together, one of my old friends would reminisce on some goofball event from yesteryear and the new friends would want to hear more. It dawned on me that I could use those days and stories to point people to Christ. The night with Officer Bernie put it over the top so I decided to jump in even though I seriously doubted my abilities to write a book; and that was always my excuse *not* to tell my story—the lack of ability. I mean, I was a solid D student for 12 years, then dropped out of college. But with God, all things are possible. I learned long ago that God doesn't look for intelligence to do his work, He looks for cheerful willingness.

All right, back to story time. A trilogy, then a closing chapter and you're done!

Lost in the Wilderness

As most of you know, I am a backpacker, canoer, and outdoor enthusiast. Knowing me, you expected any book I wrote would be about nature, birds, bear, and rattlesnake encounters, or a few travel stories—not about Jesus Christ or spiritual matters. So to round out my stories I decided to

incorporate the following three stories about hiking, journeys, getting lost…
and getting found. Only now you have read enough to realize all three stories
also point to Jesus, and how God reaches out to us. I'll leave it to you to read
between the lines, starting with the title at the top of this page.

On several occasions I became hopelessly lost in the backcountry. If
you ever had one of these experiences while alone, you already know it is
thee scariest thing that ever befell you. It is like claustrophobia and panic
teaming up to the edge of insanity. The only way to get past that initial panic
of realizing you are totally lost in the woods is to settle down and tell yourself
you are not going to die, that you will eventually find your way out. This is
life in a microcosm. Some will find the way, some will die in their panic of
realizing they are lost and have missed the way out by following their own
sense of direction instead of the compass provided.

Dan, a very experienced hunter friend, once told me about his experience of being lost in our eastern woods while upstate on a deer hunt. His
story always stuck with me because of his reaction. After firing off a few
alarm shots and calling out to the other hunters he started out with, there
was no reply. Trying to find his way back, he steadily realized just how lost
he had become as dusk began to fall; none of the landmarks were familiar. At
that point he became so freaked out and disoriented that he threw down his
very expensive hunting rifle and just started running as fast as he could until
completely exhausted, but still lost. Doctors call it a "fight or flight reaction".
There was no more logic in his actions; he threw away the one item that
could save him in the woods. And that is just a small example how freaked
out one becomes when they realize they are hopelessly lost and alone. It is
an all-consuming panic and terror at realizing the path back to where you
want to be is no longer available. I imagine it will be very similar to the terror
of facing death someday without having come to the saving knowledge of
Jesus Christ while the way was opened unto us. Though lost several times,
I never experienced the panic my friend Dan described; I always had Jesus
with me. Since his story already described those fears, I'll move on to my
experiences being lost.

Nowadays, I always carry a compass, topography maps, and GPS. Many years ago before GPS technology, while still learning about the backcountry and how to properly use a compass with topo maps, I became hopelessly lost overnight on two separate occasions. I will now tell the story of one of those times. Also on two occasions, I have come across other parties that were hopelessly lost in backcountry wilderness. I will tell one of those stories. Finally, once I ran into a lone man backpacking without food who was lost but too naïve to know it. That's another interesting story worth telling. The following three stories are about finding lost people or being lost myself. All three are very different and bear their own reasons for telling. The analogy of being lost in the woods is parallel to being lost in the busy-ness of our daily lives. These stories offer far better value if you take the time to read between the lines. Without Christ we are lost in the forests of our daily lives; these three stories parallel that truth. Read the stories from the perspective of the lost person in the story, who followed their own way.

Lost - Part I - *"Can anybody hear us!"*

In 1988, Carl Williams and I spent a week hiking the backcountry of Rocky Mountain National Park in Colorado. After hiking in for two days, we set up a base camp just below timberline at 9,200 feet so we could explore above timberline the next day using just daypacks, which avoids lugging our backpacks to 13,000 feet. After spending a long day in alpine meadows photographing wildflowers and the local fauna, we had retreated to our cozy base camp to enjoy a hearty dinner around the fire. Typically, we sit around the fire until 10, read for a while in the tent, and fall asleep. So it was tonight.

Our camp was far enough off the trail (as required by park regs) that you couldn't see our tent. Carl was already settled in for the night when I turned off my headlamp after reading; it was around 11. Just as I turned off the light, I heard what seemed like a very frightened high-pitched voice in the distance. Being this far in the backcountry with no one camped within miles, considering the time of night, and being very tired, in total darkness you sometimes imagine hearing sounds and voices the wind can imitate. So I shook Carl, "Carl, did you hear something?!"

"Yeah, it sounded like a voice," he confirmed as I switched my light back on.

From far off I could now clearly hear a panicked plea: "Can anybody hear us! Can anybody help us!?" Someone was in trouble…and the panic in their voice and time of night put my blood in a chill as my mind raced.

"Yes, we hear you and can help!" I yelled back while scrambling into pants and boots, "Just stay where you are and we will come get you!" I yelled back, knowing they would have to cross a trail-less thicket and small ravine from where they were calling. I followed my memorized route through the brush out to the main trail, turned right a few hundred feet and came upon three dirt-smeared faces I will never forget. Here were three wide-eyed, terrified, sweaty, muddy teens huddled together in the trail; their single working flashlight as dull as a burning cigarette. One kid did most of the talking, one was so dehydrated and fatigued he just stared past me the whole time their leader spoke. Lucky for them, one boy had spotted the faint glow of our illuminated tent softly reflecting off the underside of the conifers' bows. They had been arguing among themselves whether one boy had actually seen a glow of light or was imagining things at the moment I turned off my light to sleep. That is when they called out for help.

"We lost my dad. Where is my dad? Did you see my dad? We have to look for my father!" he blurted out in the rambling of someone losing touch with reality. His thoughts were so scattered I knew immediately they had been in this panicked state for hours and were absolutely spent. When I told them there was no one camped between us and timberline, the boy with the dying flashlight started to walk on like a robot on automatic cruise control, "I gotta find my father…"

"Hold it, son," I said in a fatherly way as to calm him down while stopping him in the trail,

"You're done looking for your dad tonight, wherever your dad is, he's safe. You need to get some food and water in you, get some rest and we'll find him in the morning." The boy didn't want to hear any of it.

This threesome, along with two fathers, had driven up from Texas with great expectations for a father-son week in the backcountry. However, while backpacking up over the Continental Divide, the winded dads lagged behind while the young teens full of piss and vinegar excitedly pushed ahead, getting separated. If you're above extensive Colorado timberline and low clouds roll in, you *have* to use a compass to keep your bearings; there are no trees to form a path through the fog. Most hiking above tree-line is typically the equivalent of short-grass meadow wandering without a trail; only the scale is massive with few reference points. When these young bucks realized it was getting late and their fathers didn't join them above timberline, they started back down to find their dads. They knew that without their father to lead the way, they were lost in the woods (hint, hint). Though the boys had a map, they didn't know how to read contour lines, determine scale, surface geography or distance. In the low clouds, they had gotten turned around and came down the West side of the Continental Divide instead of the East side they originally ascended. When they didn't recognize the terrain or find their dads, they panicked and scurried back up to timberline—a place where you don't want to be exposed when thunder or lightning roll in. Since late afternoon, they had been franticly running around above timberline until darkness and a July lightning storm drove them back down to where we found them.

Carl and I were earlier run off the mountain ahead of an approaching thunderstorm and pitied anyone who hadn't reached the safety of tree-line before the lightning arrived. These boys had been hiking steep terrain all morning and afternoon with their dads, and then while lost another 7-8 hours of frantic scrambling in scattered directions without stopping to eat or drink. They were absolutely spent. The greenhorns had experienced a firsthand introduction course on mountain thunderstorms they will never forget or want to see again. RMNP loses a few souls to lightning strikes every year. When you're lost, you run on adrenaline until spent and in zombie mode. At the pace they were going, I figured they had covered 10 miles since getting lost, maybe another six before that; they were now running on empty and dehydrated, in no condition to make decisions. Most people have never experienced such exhaustion.

It took some convincing before the other two out-voted their leader and agreed to camp with us. I made sure they drank plenty of water and ate something while Carl and I set up their tent for them. We put it up about 20 feet from my tent and they all crawled in after I assured them I would get them squared away with a ranger in the morning to locate their dads. It was about 1 a.m. when things finally quieted down.

In the pre-dawn of morning I got up to relieve myself and was startled to find all three boys sitting huddled outside the entrance to my tent as quiet as church mice but all packed up with backpacks ready to go, waiting for Carl and I to wake up. Turns out they had moved their tent five feet from the entrance to my tent because they were too freaked out from wild animal stories their Texas dads had told them. From the questions they asked as I made breakfast, I could see they were suburbanites that didn't get into the woods often.

Over breakfast, I painted the scenario of what probably happened to their dads so as to put them at ease that bears had not attacked their fathers. I calmly explained that being from Texas lowlands, their fathers didn't have the lungs at high altitude to make it up to timberline. Unfortunately, they couldn't communicate this to their sons, who had gone too far ahead. They probably set up a camp just below timberline on the other side of the Continental Divide, expecting their sons to come back down, which the boys did but on the wrong side of the divide after getting turned around in the clouds. Their dads were now franticly hiking out the East Divide to notify the rangers their sons were lost. We needed to get out to a ranger station on our west side to tell the rangers all were well.

"Probably happens every week in the summer at this park," I assured them.

They were comforted by my confidence and satisfied with my explanation, but that didn't slow them down once we hit the trail out together. There was no keeping up with their youthful pace that morning to get out to the ranger station. So I called them back to mark on their map which turns to make, and to leave a stick arrow at each intersection pointing their direction of travel so I knew they went the right way. That afternoon, a ranger on horseback caught up to Carl and I to inform us the boys had reached the ranger station shortly after noon (they had to have averaged 3.5 mph) and the dads had done exactly as I had said. All was well, and the ranger appreciated our providing them with a plan to get back to their father(s) and offered a relieved "Thanks" from the boys.

So some children just don't have time to wait for their fathers' guidance…and they become lost because they truly think they can find their own way. The *fathers* were never lost; they just couldn't stop their children from wandering off on their own or following the wrong path back to Dad.

Lost - Part II: The *George France* Story

When I first got saved, backpacking was spiritual therapy hand-picked by God, tailored for my still adventurous spirit. It was also the best way to get away from drugs. If I could go away for four or five days in the backcountry without drugs, I could manage another few weeks back home until my next backcountry trip. I kept a trip journal and added up all the nights I spent under the stars. It came to 156 nights in two-and-a-half years, from age 19–21 (nearly half a year) in 18 states and five European countries. If I couldn't get anyone to go with me, I'd go off on my own for a week. I loved it and still do. This next story is one we can all identify with if you ever chose to run away from your problems. Hey, I have my hand up.

On this particular trip, Paul Serluco and I decided to go down to the Smokys in Tennessee. It was Paul's first backpacking trip. This was before Interstate 81 was finished in Tennessee and Virginia when the ride down in a '67 VW bug took two days through backcountry mountain towns on two-lane blacktop. We had picked the Appalachian Trail along the western spine of the 6,000 feet range for a five-day hike. It was my first trip this far south and I bit off more than we bargained for. On our first day we encountered a bear that was routinely charging hikers and shredding their surrendered backpacks. On our second day, we were warned by fellow hikers heading in the opposite direction to watch out for the 7:30 bear the next morning if we planned on camping at Spence Field, which we were. Sure enough, that bear showed up at 7:32, ate our breakfast, and dragged my sleeping bag off into the woods. The last straw was the pack of wild boars that scared the daylights out of our suburban wits. That was it, these mountains were just too creepy and Paul was looking for the slightest surrender on my part to get out of there.

"All right," I conceded still shaking from the boar encounter and looking off into the dense woods to see if they were coming back. "We should be able to reach Derrick Knob by nightfall, then we will only have a few miles out tomorrow." Both of us would be glad to leave the steaming August Smoky Mountains to the rogue bears and squealing boars.

On our way to Derrick Knob we came upon a guy in his upper 20s stocking up on the plentiful blueberries along a field edge (I was 19, Paul 18). He had a fishing pole strapped to the side of his noticeably empty sagging backpack. All packs we'd see on hikers were normally bulging past capacity with accoutrements hanging off. One of the pleasures of hiking is the people you meet, so it is customary to strike up a conversation with passing hikers if just for the excuse of taking a break.

"Hi, how long are you out for?" I asked with a typical hiker's opener as I joined him to pick berries.

A very cheerful thick Brooklyn accent came back with, "Oh I don't know yet…depends on the fishing!"

"Well, how has the fishing been so far?" I wondered for future reference.

"Nothin yet," he replied a bit miffed, "been living off berries so far. Hey, have you guys come across a lake or anything where I can catch fish?"

This question had me a bit puzzled since we were on the 6,000-foot spine of the 2nd highest range in the east; lakes and fishing were 3,500 feet below us in the valleys. When I explained this to him, he did one of those 'Oh yea-ah!' light bulb revelations.

"Do you have your map handy?" I enquired. "I can point you down to Fontana Lake if you'd like."

"Oh no, I don't have a map," he stated matter of fact.

This put the red flag up for me; by himself, living off berries, empty pack, thinks streams run along the ridge crest, no map, no itinerary or return date planned? But he was a heck of a nice guy and I liked him immediately. We made introductions and I further learned he hadn't packed as much as tea or coffee and planned on living off the land in a National Park. His name was George *France* from north Jersey; he had just taken off on a whim and was pretty evasive about any other questions I asked. I was feeling him out to see if he needed our help, which he certainly did. This was his first time in the mountains and he was as dumb as a post concerning backcountry living.

"Look George," I offered, "We have a few spare meals since we're hiking out a day ahead of our itinerary, you can have them and are welcome to hike with us if it suits you.""Yeah, that sounds great!" he jumped at the chance for a good meal and friendship.

That evening as we prepared our dinner and sat around the fire, I learned very little about George other than he had hitch-hiked down here by himself and headed out into the backcountry for an unspecified period to "get away from it all". At this time (1973), this was not that strange at all; many a hippie was thumbing his way across our country, searching for America and themselves. He knew New York City very well and liked that we were from suburban Philadelphia. I offered him a ride back to Jersey as far as the Philly bus terminal if he wanted, and he said he'd sleep on it. Our hike out the next morning was only a few miles. I told George if he wasn't heading back to Philly with us he should at least go into town with us to stock up on food, buy a map, and register his itinerary with a ranger as required. As it turned out, we would spend three days with George and learn some amazing things about him.

Traveling back north, we had plenty of time to talk. If George didn't want to tell us about himself, that was fine; he was very interested to learn about Paul and I. So I naturally told him about my abandoned gang days and surrender to Jesus Christ with Paul as my witness. By way of his questions, I could see George seemed to identify with my gang days. He was particularly interested with Manoa Lanes' reaction to my quitting the gang—whether they threatened me or came after me. Old Georgie-boy had something to hide, but we were getting along great and I didn't care to pry.

The next peculiarity about our traveling companion was revealed the first time we stopped to eat. Pulling in to a Booger King, George said his stomach was unsettled and wanted just to walk around outside while Paul and I ate inside. As I sat in the restaurant, it struck me that he may be broke and too proud to admit it. I went out and told him Booger King was on us if he was hungry. He sheepishly realized we had caught on and agreed to take our offer. We told him as long as our money held out we would feed him back to Philly. He realized he had two new friends and said he would pay us back. That was okay with us, but neither Paul nor I expected to see a penny of that promise no matter how well-intended.

For the next hour, George sat quietly staring out the window in the back of my crammed VW Beetle. When he finally decided to talk about his situation, there was no stopping him. His story was so fantastic as to be unbelievable.

"You guys have been really good by me for the last few days," he started in. "I know I can trust you two and will pay you back when we get to Harrisonburg, Virginia; I have good friends there who will take care of us." The delivery of this statement was directed in a manner of us having passed a test, to be rewarded by the manly code of trusting your friends at any cost. Over the next hour, George told us a fascinating story right out of a Mario Puzo novel. Answering each question we asked, he had either memorized the screenplay for *The Godfather* or he was telling the truth; we could only wonder at this point of our trip.

Here is the short of it: For the last three years, George had been a trusted inside accountant for a New York crime family. By keeping the books, he knew the money trail for all of their endeavors. In my back seat was the Tom Hagan of the Corleone family. Two years ago, he fell in love with and married a French national living in NYC whom he spoke of with adoration. They had a falling out over his career choice, which I assume he had not informed her about before marrying. She tried to persuade him to quit the mob, but as we all know, you don't quit a crime family. Your choice for the rest of your life has already been made. The only other options were: get whacked, go to prison, or run and hide while looking over your shoulder for the rest of your life.

His wife's argument (I'll call her Greta) was for the couple to return to France and disappear into that country in hopes the mob wouldn't bother to track him down there. George was a native New Yorker with no desire to immigrate to another country. Also, he believed that if ever found in France with her, retribution would include his wife to keep her quiet. Our new friend was in a bad fix.

Recently, Greta had given him an ultimatum. She was returning to France, with or without him. So off she went back to France while George was left to ponder his decision. She hadn't left him; she loved him very much and was hoping her leaving for the old country would prod his decision to follow her if he loves her. Greta could not *force his decision* if he was to love her for the rest of his days. His life was at a major crossroad between *love*, even though it may cost him his life, or a lucrative illicit career in his native surrounding (hint-hint in those last few lines). Greta was the salvation provided to George to start a new life. I should mention here that George didn't have any problems about working for the mob; just that he couldn't live in two worlds. The parallel here is very much like the choice to follow Christ when we are presented with His truth. Choose to follow Him for the rest of your life (love and the right thing), even though it will cost you your lifestyle as you know it; or choose your present course where you are comfortable and familiar, apart from Him, set on your ways.

George could not run this by his crime bosses to help him decide; that would be suicide. However, the Family had somehow received word of his predicament and had called him in for a meeting once they found out his wife had returned to France. Not ready to meet *their* ultimatum, he dissed the meeting, deciding to get out of Dodge to clear his mind, somewhere no one could find him. He chose to hitch-hike for fear they were watching his car. Literally, he left town with the shirt on his back and the cash in his pocket. Next, he spent his pocket cash on a cab ride to PA, bought a backpack, some non-accountant looking threads, meals, and several hotel nights. One of his hitched rides on the Interstate had painted a nice picture of the Smoky Mountains in his mind, so that is where we met him, naively trying to live off the land after his money gave out.

He assured us his employers wouldn't be on his tail down here, but were waiting for him to come in and declare where his allegiance stood. As long as he decided to leave his wife and continue serving his boss, he was okay; probably would even get a promotion. Leaving his wife would solidify proving his Family is his family, not Greta.

Even though I had only been a Christian for a short time, I now tended to look at situations like this from a much broader view. I could see George's point of view, my point of view, the mob's point of view, and the Viblical point of view; or in other words, what would Christ do. For me, Christ's point of view trumps all other points of view so I advised George with absolute certainty to leave the mob and join his wife no matter what the consequences. Of course, having a captive audience for so many miles gave me the opportunity to share my story and the basis for my advice. George and I clicked well; he could relate to my small-time gang dealings and was intrigued with my recent emersion in Christ. He really needed to talk through his predicament with somebody so Paul and I were the appointed listeners. For me, George was just one of the many colorful life forms God would continually place before me to share the gospel over the years.

Not having money for a camp ground or hotel tonight, we opted to push for George's promised Shangri-la on a farm outside Harrisonburg, VA. The farm had some sort of business relationship with the NYC Family and George had to stop down there regularly on business. That is all he would tell us about the place. Grinning with anticipated surprise, he promised we would like the people on the farm, stating "They're young hippies like you guys" followed with, "and I know you guys doubt most of what I'm telling you, but that's okay, you'll see when we get there; my friends at the farm will back me up".

About 11 p.m. we found ourselves wandering down dark back roads of the Shenandoah Valley, which George knew like the back of his hand. "This is it!" he grinned as we pulled into a dirt lane and up to the back porch of a dimly lit farm house. He tapped on the back door strictly out of courtesy then opened the door and called out a few names. "Jack! Gary! It's George!"

Out of the living room came two brothers in their early 20s. They were dressed like farmers but had long hair typical of that era but hardly common in rural Virginia yet. And they definitely contrasted George's quaffed accountant look as much as Paul and I did.

"George!" they exclaimed in surprise, "we didn't know you were in the area! Come on in and set down, what can we get for ya!"

Introductions were passed around while snacks and beer were brought out. George was treated like a third brother. The brothers asked George broad questions about 'business' and his 'friends up north' while casting a suspicious eye toward Paul and I, then back to George as if to ask if we were 'cool'. George assured them they could speak openly around us. Once everyone's guard was relaxed, George enquired if anyone from the New York family had come calling, then proceeded to explain his AWOL status, asking if he could stay on the farm a few days and borrow some funds. With this the flood gates of generosity opened. He was welcome to stay as long as he wanted and borrow whatever he needed.

Paul and I didn't have to ask any questions to confirm George's history; the natural flow of conversations around the kitchen table was proving him true to his word. Later we learned that George liked to come down to his Virginia friends for routine vacations of fishing and relaxing away from the Big Apple, becoming part of their extended family. By now I had a good inkling as to what they were growing on the farm. George would ask about the crops and the boys would smile and say the 'corn' was over their heads and was already being brought in. What sort of 'corn' they were growing wasn't yet open information even though George said we could be trusted. The brothers used the corn term more as their little inside joke than it was meant to be kept secret from Paul and I.

Well, soon our ruckus in the kitchen awakened a much older gentleman from another room of the house to join us by giving George and his two new friends a warm Southern welcome. A near toothless farmer in his mid-70s with an exuberant character stood in the kitchen doorway and let the cat out of the bag. With a big grin on his face, he looked to his grandsons and asked, "Have ya showed 'em yit?" And with that he disappeared down the cellar steps returning in no time, chuckling at the top of the stairs with his prize held out at his side like he was showing off the fine Christmas turkey he just shot in the woods.

Hanging from his hand was an inverted faggot of cannabis heads clipped about 4 feet from the top of the plant. The stems were banded together to a diameter the thickness of a soda can. My jaw dropped faster than the aroma of cannabis filling the room. I was stunned at the sight of the familiar weed so proudly displayed by this farmer in his seventies and his enjoying the moment. Up until that moment, the oldest person I ever knew associated with pot was maybe in their mid-20s. This guy was jumping the generation gap like Evil Knievel at Caesar's Palace; hope he sticks the landing better.

"Ain't that just purdy now?!" he grinned showing every last remnant of his mouth ivory.

"Oh we gonna have a great season, this is some of the first in so far but there's plenty more ready any day now!"

So without asking for details we learned the farm was a productive growing station not far from NYC. One of George's accountant responsibilities for the NY family was to check on their interest here from time to time and return with estimates of delivery, quantity, quality, pricing, profit margins, etc. I can only speculate but I'd imagine this farm was not the only farm in the area contracted to produce the leaf. I would also speculate that this farm was the collecting station based on George's close relationship here. I wanted to know as little as possible and George already had gathered that was my point of view.

"Well, this definitely calls for an all-night barby-que," said Jack in a lazy Southern drawl while reaching for the phone. "I'll get a few of the boys together." It was now close to midnight. Soon we were at a 24-hour supermart picking up beer, chicken, snacks, and other barbeque favorites. George was excited to be among family again and out of his funk. Coming out of the store he stuck a twenty in my pocket (equivalent of $100 today), which more than doubled any expenses we had forwarded him.

"See! I told you my buddies would take care of us," he beamed proudly in his Brooklyn accent while slapping his arm around my shoulder. "We're in for a good time tonight my friends, my turn to take care of you guys!" By the time we arrived back at the farm house, the big grill was fired up and about a half dozen people had arrived. Pot and beer were a-flowin, but that didn't bother me. I was content eating chicken, nursing a beer and taking in the picture, listening to stories, while meeting all of George's friends. A laidback early-1970s all-nighter was in the works. The crowd grew throughout the night and we learned more of the locals were at a parallel party at an abandoned quarry nearby (must have been a Friday or Saturday night).

So around 3 a.m. the decision was made to move the party to the quarry where we could cool off from the humid August night. I hadn't showered in six sweaty days and was definitely up for a refreshing swim. The folks at the quarry had a camp fire going and lots of friendly people were coming and going among the shadows cast by the glow.

About 50 feet from the fire was a cliff edge where guys and girls were jumping off. I love quarry jumping so I went to investigate. I could tell by the gap between the jumper leaving the cliff top and the sound of impact that it was a good distance to the water below. But with the fire behind me and a big black hole below me I couldn't see where the jumpers were landing at all. Once they jumped, they just disappeared into the blackness and reappeared 15 minutes later behind me dripping wet, huffin' and puffin' from climbing back up.

"How far is the jump?" I asked of those who were wet. I received answers of 40 feet to 60 feet; I figured 40–50 feet. Then they directed me to a 10-foot section of ledge they said was the safest launch point. I stood on the edge staring down into the darkness. "How deep is the water?"

"Oh it's plenty deep, we've never touched bottom," I was assured.

"Is the cliff clearance good all the way down, or do I have to jump out as far as I can?"

"Well, it won't hurt to jump out as fer as ye can," was advised.

"How do I know where to climb back up from down there?" was my final question.

"Just swim aways from the landin' area after ya'll jumped and yell up that yer clear. We'll jump and show you the way up." They were amused that the "Philly Boys" were interested in jumping and were urging us on. I don't remember if Paul and I jumped together or not.

With all the essential questions answered, I was standing on the edge psyching myself up to jump. I knew it would be a new kind of rush like I never had before. I had jumped from RR trestles, road bridges, quarries, and high rope swings before, but never at a strange location on a dark night where I couldn't see the bottom. There is something about that initial jump, while you're suspended a half-second before descending that creates an adrenaline rush which becomes addicting. The anticipation of the unknown surface strike made the experience even more exhilarating. There is no horizon to set your eyes on, no bottom to see coming up at you. It is like jumping into a black void. Most people wouldn't do it intentionally (another hint-hint).

The scariest part is: that on high leaps, your legs and arms work as a gyroscope to keep your body vertical for entry. At entry you have to pull your feet together and arms in or risk a painful landing. If you straighten up as soon as you jump there is a good chance of tipping forward, backward, or sideways and entering on an angle that will knock the wind out of you. It's a timing thing based on vision, which tonight I don't have. And that is what will make it all the better. "GEEERONIMOOOOooo…!"

It was a blast but I only dared it twice. The second time was scarier than the first. Our all-night barbeque wrapped up at dawn. After a few hours' sleep, George gave us a morning tour of the farm but I was too beat to remember much. However, I do remember him showing me cannabis plants growing between rows of corn. Our departure from George was vague in my memory until I went rooting through a few fading pictures of that trip. The last shot is of George on Hawksbill Mountain in Shenandoah National Park. I had told him Paul and I were planning to spend a night or two up there before heading home because it was my favorite mountain; for me, a place of healing. Since it was my favorite, George wanted to see it too so he stayed with us to that point. From there he caught a ride back to the Shenandoah Valley from two new hikers we met on the mountain. Paul and I headed north for home.

I never knew what choice George made concerning his career with the crime family or joining his wife. At our parting he was still on the fence. I gave him my address and he gave me an address of a friend who would forward mail to him where ever he was. I dropped him a postcard w/o return address, but never heard anything back, and never received any communication from Europe. A postcard from Europe would have told me he made the right choice. However, I take comfort in the thought that George was street wise and would have thrown out my address to protect me. I'm sure if he went to join his wife in France, he wouldn't have taken my address with him or chanced communication.

Sitting around a campfire on a mountain top draws out opinions and declarations about life, philosophy, and the universe in general; it just does for some reason. George was interested in my opinion because I was an outsider looking at the facts from a Godly perspective without an ulterior motive of business or losing a friend. He also considered Manoa Lanes' reaction of throwing me out of their circle once I bucked the system for Christ's sake.

My advice to George was from recent experience and pretty simple. That no one in his crime family were true friends once *his* interest and *their* interest go separate directions. As he already knew, they would turn against him and rub him out rather than risk him carrying around a mental library which could put his bosses away for a long time. He'd be fooling himself with fake friendships for the rest of his life and would someday regret a wasted life. On the other hand, he has a forgiving wife who loves him and is waiting to start over with him. From a campfire on Hawksbill Mountain the choice looked simple, but I understood the addiction of adventure to a young man moving up in a crime family. I tried to imagine this friendly Brooklynite whom I had only known in cut-off shorts as a hiker, in lively living room Family meetings, wearing a tailored suit, advising from the financial books and being patted on the back and treated like family. Satan standing with Christ atop the temple tower, offering wealth and power, but not an inch of love. Happens every day. The right choice is often very clear but the decision is often much more difficult.

And we all face difficult crossroads throughout our lives. Should I go to college, what will my major be, should I try drugs, should I marry this person, choosing the right career, should we have another child, should mom go back to work, should I get Cocoa Puffs or Cheerios? *Your life is the sum total of your choices, all choices have consequences, therefore make good choices.* I memorized that line from an experienced pastor who had seen every imaginable result from bad choices you could possibly think of, and then a few. Part of the intent of these stories is to stir you to examine choices you either have, have not, or need to make now in your life. There is a big decision you may have swept under the carpet these many years. It's a spiritual decision. The decision is: What will you do with the truth of Jesus Christ? Ignore it or face it? Make good choices.

Pssst: Greta is Jesus. Mob Family is the lord of this world, Satan, who will do all he can to keep you from Greta. You and I are George.

Lost, Part III - Into the White Wilderness

Do not neglect to show hospitality to strangers, for thereby some have entertained angels while unaware. Hebrews 13:2

After I was born again, I had one friend who particularly enjoyed backpacking trips any time of year. *Mathew* will be his name for this story. I don't use his real name because he is a recovered alcoholic and I don't want his grandkids to know that till he is ready to explain it firsthand to them someday. We spent the next three years discovering the ranges of the southern and central Appalachians down to the Smokys in Tennessee; sometimes taking off for weeks at a time. Seems we were always out of work, broke, and traveling on a shoe-string budget. Those were the good ole days of unemployment checks, 33¢ per gallon gas, and living at home with our parents. Matt witnessed my changes firsthand and really enjoyed discussing Jesus Christ and the Bible on our long travels together. Spend a few dozen nights around a campfire with one person and you'll know them as well as one can. Campfires in the deep mountains are like natural confessionals. Matt and I knew everything about each other and stay in touch to this day.

Matt liked his alcohol and had no intention of kicking booze or drugs. This might be a good place to re-iterate what I wrote back on page 101—*sin will take you farther than you ever intending to go, and cost you more than you were ever willing to pay.*

Like everyone else, he figured it was only a matter of time before I would return to drugs. He watched me closely. Matt respected my choice and was courteous enough not to do drugs in my presence. He could also put a pint of apple brandy away in 15 minutes and still be sober by all appearances. However, at the time neither of us ever thought he was on his way to an alcoholic. Eventually, after several years of hiking trips and campfires, he came to understand and agree what the Bible taught about salvation and a Christ-centered life. But as Matty-boy would often say, "There is no way this early in my life I'm ready to make that decision and miss out on all the fun." And there-in lies one of the biggest misconceptions of living for Christ; that you will miss out on all the fun in life. On the contrary, I didn't know the *joy* of living until I came to Christ. Did a lot of stupid things that *looked and felt* like fun at the time, but there is no comparing the trade-off. I could also write a few books about the adventures and people I've had fascinating encounters with since my salvation. These three stories are just a sampling. No, fun and adventure doesn't stop when you give your life to the God of the universe; that is lame thinking. Stepping out in faith when your natural self dictates, "DON'T" will *always* line you up for adventure with interesting people and God-directed purpose.

Man, Matty-boy and I would get into some deep discussions. As I was learning my Bible, Matt was learning the Bible via verbal transfusion from me. We'd get settled into my VW Bug or Opel Manta for a six-hour drive to West Virginia on a Friday night and he'd sit there a mixing ginger brandy and ask me, "Okay, Rich, fill me in on what else you have learned from the Bible since our last trip." Matt would often read the Bible between trips, even listened to Christian radio each morning, but wouldn't make a decision for Christ. We were great friends (I also seriously dated his sister for the better part of a year) so we accepted each other as we were.

Matt was very much like a lot of people who believe they are Christians today. They have a foundational head knowledge about Jesus Christ, but disagree with most of their denomination's teachings; believe there are other paths to God, but pretty much stick with Christianity because that is the faith they were born into. Once a week, if they still attend church, their faith makes them feel good enough to convince themselves they are in good standing with God. Most people I listen to discussing their Sunday Morning church service speak of going to services as if it is a weekly quota to get out of the way as painlessly as possible. Forty-five minutes tops in church and they're checking their watches. If that describes you, you don't have a living relationship with your Savior; you've been throwing Him a bone once in a while and that's about it. Many of us have no problem dumping our dead church denomination, but never replace it with a living Christ.

As the years wore on, we took fewer and fewer backpacking trips together simply because our lives had gone from unemployed bums on an extended lark, to responsible husband and father, on my part; Matt was still single. I had landed him a job where I worked, so for two years we played and worked together. Around November 1983, we decided to resurrect our traditional three-day Thanksgiving weekend hike, which had been on hiatus for several years since I had moved my family an hour away out to Birdsboro, PA. Matt and I both left our old Philly employer and looked forward to getting caught up on old friends, jobs, kids, girlfriend, etc. Basically, it was an excuse to shed the responsibilities of our lives, get together as old friends, and just enjoy the backcountry to stay in touch.

Matt always left the trip planning to me. So by 6 a.m. on Friday morning after spending Thanksgiving Thursday with our families, we were heading for a remote area of West Virginia not listed in any hiker guide yet; a few valleys west of Seneca Rocks.* Matter of fact, it was one of those spots on my topo maps I had always been curious about. It showed big mountains, but no official trails among them, mostly because parts were on private in-holdings in Monongahela National Forest. During previous trips, I had done a little reconnoiter along some scenic dirt roads in the area and we both thought it would be a good place to discover before a designated wilderness area (created through The Wilderness Act of 1964) was established or a guide book opened it up to the throngs of hikers too apprehensive to do their own pioneering. Trips like this were a 50/50 hit or miss as far as discovering an unknown hiking gem. Among the list of our successes were Otter Creek, Dolly Sods, Cranberry Glades, Seneca Creek, and a dozen other current popular hiking destinations we discovered in the early 1970s before Congress set them aside as Wilderness Areas. By the 1980s, throngs of hikers flocked to these areas we once had to ourselves.

On this particular weekend, we were hoping the approach to 4,600-foot Haystack Knob from Elklick Run up Roaring Creek Valley was going to be a winner. We only had to climb 2,500 feet in five miles so we were feeling confident. Once on top of Haystack we would set up a base camp for two nights and explore north to the Roaring Plains. That was the plan anyhow.

There wasn't much information available at the time for this area. Usually, I would write the local Forest District Ranger for trail conditions and access permission but too often they had outdated information, as was the case this time. I should have reconsidered when the following was all that could be found about Haystack Knob access for Monongahela National Forest:

"This trail is mostly on private property, starting out on a gated jeep road three miles up the gravel surface road along Roaring Creek. The only marking to find the beginning (East end) of the jeep road is a "No Trespassing" sign. Most of the trail is no longer usable by vehicles of any kind. The upper (west) end provides splendid views southwest from Haystack Knob. A side trip along the knife-edged knob is highly recommended. The trail is said to follow an old Seneca Indian route across Allegheny Mountain. Easy to miss spots are,…" the National Forest Service survey goes on to list four places where the trail fades or no longer exists.

None of that was going to stop us; we were seasoned backpackers who prided ourselves on how thoroughly lost we could get. I always instructed my wife not to worry if we don't come home or call on the designated returned date. If we're not home **two** days after we should be, it might be a good idea to alert the district ranger to see if our car was still at the trailhead. After three days, we're out of back-up rations, so call out a search party. Fortunately, none of our trips ever went that bad.

Once we located the trail head, I drove back down the gravel road to the nearest farmhouse to ask permission to park at the "No Trespassing" gate and hike across their land. As usual, I was greeted with smiles and invited in to get acquainted. In most cases and contrary to Hollywood stereotyping, the good ole back-homey folks love it when out-of-staters come all the way down to enjoy the mountains they are so proud of. They hand out so many location nuggets and local history that I need another trip to get to them all! Anyhow, they informed me the branch of their family that used to farm Elklick Valley had abandoned the operation about 20 years earlier (~1963) and that we would see some old homesteads from 1910 up that narrow valley. I was psyched. Farewells and good lucks behind us, up the valley we went.

In no time our sunny day turned to cloudy and damp as a storm moved in. The first homestead we came to hung precipitously over a rushing stream, ready to slide down the slope where the bank had washed away. The last proprietors had propped the back of the house up on posts to try and save it, but the old place was no longer livable. There were only three small rooms in what we would call 'a shack'. It was constructed from forest materials and insulated with multiple layers of newspapers plastered to the walls. On one wall of the main room hung a picture of a deceased pope, on the opposite wall a framed faded newspaper picture of JFK clipped the week of his funeral. The gray sky was visible through the gaps in the roof; below us, the stream rushed past the holes in the sagging floor. It didn't take much imagination to reconstruct the hardscrabble living some family etched out of this steep valley. The terrain is too steep for even a tractor to plow. Eventually, the landowners got too old to stand behind a pair of mules to till the soil. Nothing came easy to these people and finally the encroaching stream ran them out. At times like this, I just had to stand quietly to let the house and experience soak in. It would be great to just pitch the tent in their front-yard but we better make tracks if the Haystack is to be gained before dark. Another mile up the valley we stumbled upon what had to be the original homestead, a two-room log cabin which was falling in.

Soon the narrow jeep trail went off in different forks, which left us to logically guess the most likely route; there being no markers or signage. Next, the old jeep trail turned into a foot trail. A mile later, the foot trail merged with an abandoned narrow gage railroad grade leftover from lumbering operations 80 years earlier. Walking on the narrow overgrown RR grades was easier than bushwhacking, so we followed that NE heading since it took us in our general direction. Soon the RR grade became choked with Hawthorn so thick there was no passing through it. For those of you who never had the pleasure of trying to bushwhack through Hawthorn, you just haven't lived. It's a strong inflexible wood that grows like a shrub in thick impenetrable stands at the sapling stage. The trunk and branches have three-inch thorns as strong as nails. If Jesus was crucified in North America, these are the branches his crown would have been fashioned from. With Hawthorn stopping us in our tracks, our next option was to bushwhack uphill to try and intersect some other abandoned path. Right about now it begins to snow. Soon it is snowing hard, and just as soon, we are lost without knowing how to even get back to the old RR grade for fear of encountering the Hawthorne in that direction. Getting lost in snow is very easy, but we beat the norm by getting lost before it snowed.

Matt had a proven plan whenever we got a bit turned around. He'd pull out his ginger brandy flask, sit down and sip while I went ahead without my pack to scout the best options. If I came back, grabbed his flask for a swig, and said something to the effect of "I don't trust my compass" or "better check the map again Matt", he'd know we were hopelessly lost and start laughing, as he did on this occasion.

"We are so freakin' lost, aren't we?" he'd chuckle without a care while searching my furrowed brow, knowing I hated to admit getting lost. If I got us lost, Matt was never concerned because it was my responsibility to get us un-lost. His job was to laugh or curse about being lost, which he performed with true dedication.

"Well, yeah, we're a bit lost," I'd respond with indifference, "I just don't know *how* lost."

"Well, *I* know how lost we are Bonny-Boy," Matt announced as he searched the best choice of slowly pronounced adjectives while shouldering his pack. "We are: Hawthorn-shredded, snow blowin', mother fartin, low on brandy, have to hump all over this damn mountain to get found, lost!" He'd smile as if putting such articulation to our predicament made it seem clearer. "Am I right?" he turned to inquire.

"You may be off on the brandy part. So what's the problem?" I'd grin back, "We came to do a little backpacking, enjoy some quiet time in the back-country, and that IS what we're doing, aren't we?" I'd ask sarcastically. "What's the difference if there's a few flakes, a gray ceiling descending, and we just witnessed a beautiful grove of Hawthorn? Trails are for beginners anyhow."

"Did you get us lost on purpose? I bet you got us lost on purpose!" Matt would come back half-serious. And that is how we would usually deal with being lost until fatigue sets in and we're out of spunk and banter.

An hour more of hardcore pushing up the steep mountain grade through trail-less brush had us no closer to found…just more beat. When you get this tired, you stop talking and just resolve yourself to mechanically pushing on. You really don't notice that your heavy winter pack is even on your back. You just plod along, each in his separate zone of personal thought.

"What's the plan, boss?" asked Matt after an hour of sweaty silence; meaning he was done for the day.

"Let's just find some level ground where we can pitch a tent," I said knowing it would be dark in half an hour. "We can get our bearings in the morning when rested and fed." Four inches of snow now lay on the ground, coming down heavy without a breeze; the kind of snow that will drop a foot by midnight if it doesn't let up. A level bit of earth big enough for our tent becomes our focus as we continue pushing up through brush.

Even a maintained mountain path is difficult to follow with a six-inch covering of snow. Once the ground is a blanket of white, the tramped earthen way is no longer a guide. A hiker can leave the trail and never realize it for a long time. In our present snowy predicament, we could walk right across a maintained path and never know it. Only a compass, topo map, and dead reckoning can help us at this point, but with dark and snow descending, we no longer had the luxury of a line of site to get a bearing.

Even when lost, there is something serenely beautiful about snow falling at dusk in the deep mountains. It stirs a melancholy chord of times past, while still promising a brilliant tomorrow with a sunny snow draped landscape. Trudging along lost through the steep terrain, with snow falling silently around us, had a very calming effect. The gentle descent of twilight snow limits our visibility so that our world consists of two hunched figures softly plodding through an unchanging landscape, which fades to gray 20 feet in any direction. The falling snow casts a peaceful spell on the landscape and our minds, to the point I really don't care about being lost. To be lost with three days' rations, a North Face expedition tent for shelter, and snow as available water is not a panic situation. If I was alone, the woods would be unbearably desolate under these circumstances, but with a good friend it becomes an appreciated shared silence. My only concern was to find a flat spot to camp without having to climb another hour in darkness before reaching the summit of whatever mountain we assumed to be on. Our topographic map only offered continuous steep slope until reaching the top.

About the time Matt would normally go into his second degree of, "I can't go any further, let's just stop here", we crossed an old grown-over center cog-logging RR grade angling off steeply to our right. I know that when a logging road rounds a ridge, it will always have a small area where the switchback is graded flat. Walking on a RR grade provided needed relief from pushing through the forest under-story. In 15 minutes, the anticipated switchback presented a flat enough open spot to pitch camp. Little things like a flat spot to comfortably camp become so cherished at times like this. I pray for it, it appears.

Sitting against our packs in the snow, letting flakes land on our face, we are too tired and grateful to motivate ourselves to start setting up camp, so we just sit there and pass the brandy; watching the snow fall as night engulfs us. It is only 6 o'clock; there is still a long night ahead. Plenty of time to begin the usual camp negotiations.

"You want to put up the tent and start the stove? Or gather wood and start a fire?" I eventually ask Matt. Someone has to initiate the fact that it's time to get off our duffs.

"You do the fire," he replies as he has scores of times in the past, stiffly gaining his feet. It's a ritual. Both of us execute our memorized camp duties.

If mountain hiking through gentle snow at dusk is melancholy, then sitting around a roaring fire with hot stew and buttered French bread in a snowfall is downright Yuletide cheerful! Backpacking is full of moments of simple appreciation and reward. And so we passed the evening, the snow never letting up. 'Twas a magic night indeed; finally falling asleep to the sound of snowflakes gently sliding down the low roof of my tent while snug in our down bags. I've experienced few comparable earthly satisfactions.

Hours later, in the darkness of early morning from inside my warm cocoon, I could hear the wind had picked up and promised to blow out the storm by daylight. I woke at first light to discover the sides of my battle-worn North Face Sierra tent lying on my down mummy-bag, sagging under the weight of last night's snow. This is the best moment of winter backpacking; waking up to a fresh day of outdoor discoveries in a different land, high in the mountains, miles from anyone; or to lie there a few more minutes in the sanctuary of warm down coziness while listening to the freezing wind blow through the bare branches overhead. Further up on top of the mountain, the wind pitch has a higher decibel level that tells me it would have been nasty up there last night. Lying here quietly, I wonder how deep the snow is now and anticipate the beautiful morning just beyond the thin nylon door by my feet. What new adventure will this day bring? Excitement drives me from my comfort.

Winter camping requires a suit-up each morning, which is a lengthy process. First you have to shove the sagging load of snow off from inside the tent, guaranteed to wake up your tent mate. Tiny ice crystals from a night of two guys' respiration in close quarters has frozen to the inside roof of the tent like very fine sand. It is the first thing you notice while lying there, tiny crystals on the ceiling. The action of shoving the snow-laden walls off my sleeping bag brings down a fine sprinkle of tiny ice crystals on Matt's five-inch circle of face peering out from his sleeping bag breathe hole. If I was nice, I could just stretch out my hand to block the rude awaken of ice crystals landing on his face, but I always cherish his reaction.

"You bastid," he says while retreating further into his bag. "For that you better make me coffee," he chuckles. And he knows I will.

Matt likes to sleep later than me, which works out well because there isn't enough room in the tent for both of us to suit-up at the same time without getting in each other's way. Getting dressed begins with pulling your first layer of clothing into the sleeping bag to warm them up before wearing. If not, that first layer is like putting on a 20° ice suit. Even though the outside temp is well below freezing, a down sleeping bag is most effective at trapping heat if you sleep in nothing more than a thin layer of polar-tec T-shirt, long undies, and wool socks. Next, you have to do the same thing with your boots which have frozen hard overnight from yesterday's foot sweat. So warming and thawing usually takes a good 20 minutes on a cold morning. And it is during this warm-up time that you always realize just how bad you need to make that yellow snow!

Knowing Matt would sleep for another hour, I decided to reconnoiter up the faint path to try to get our bearing from distant peaks as reference points. I unzipped the tent door to a wonderland of white forest. The increasing wind was blowing snow off the branches but all precipitation had ceased; the storm was blowing out. I stepped out with the exuberance of a 10-year-old heading out to sled with friends. The higher I climbed, the wilder the wind blew. My hour reconnaissance hike gained 300 feet in elevation before I met the racing clouds. My quest only confirmed what I knew before about our location. Nothing. I wasn't even sure if we were on Haystack Mountain anymore. The clouds and I shared the same altitude now. The ceiling was only a few hundred feet above my head while sometimes engulfing me. Racing clouds only broke long enough for jaw-dropping three-second glimpses of distant frosted ridges or small windows of brilliant blue sky one only sees out west. Lost or not, the scenery today will be spectacular. Might as well go tell Matt that continuing our climb seems to be our only option to locate a real trail.

Matt had a very interesting encounter while I was away. As I was approaching camp but still 100 feet away, he yelled to me through the unrelenting wind, "Did you see those two guys?!" He was pointing past me. I turned around, no one was there. "What is he talking about?" I thought to myself.

I waited until I got closer to camp before I confirmed. "Did you say two guys?"

"Yeah!" Matt stated incredulous. "Two hunters just walked up in your direction following the same path! There's *no way* you could have missed them!" he exclaimed, thinking I was pulling his leg. "Tell me you didn't see them?"

"Nope. I didn't see them or anything else," I replied as fact.

We went back and forth for a few moments before Matt was convinced I really hadn't seen anyone so he pulled me 15 feet in the direction from whence I had just come. "There!" he said pointing to the ground. "You didn't notice those footprints as you came back to camp?" He was challenging my ego now, knowing how I prided my reconnoitering, tracking, and orienteering ability in the backcountry. He was looking at me with that highbrow of doubt that said, 'If you missed two sets of footprints in deep snow, how do you expect to get us back to the car?' Looking in the direction the footsteps went, I too was at a loss, shaking my head in disbelief at how I could have missed those footprints. Maybe I was too focused on the beauty around me or on Matt once I saw him moving around outside the tent when I rounded the bend in the trail? I really don't know. But *someone* had passed my way, that much was sure.

"Well, let's eat breakfast, I'm starved," I said to divert my error. "And you can tell me all about it."

"Yeah! Well, that's why I sent them off to find you! They are Jesus people like you!"

"How do you know they love the Lord?" I asked with more interest than before.

"Because…the one teenage kid said to me, 'Mister, you need Jesus Christ in your life!' Can you believe that?" Matt said looking at me, waiting for me to acknowledge his astonishment.

"But why would he say that to you out of the blue?' I enquired, trying to put the pieces together.

"Well…" Matt hesitated, a little embarrassed now. "I had just stepped out of the tent and gone right to my pack for a jolt of brandy. Just as I was taking a swig to jumpstart my morning; this kid is at my elbow with a rifle folded across his chest looking up at me and he says, 'Mister, you need Jesus Christ in your life!'" Matt was nervously laughing at the coincidence.

This was blowing my mind up here in the middle of nowhere. So I told Matt to explain everything that happened and everything the two guys said from when they first appeared to when they left. Over breakfast, this is what Matt relayed to me.

As you may have figured out by now, Matt had a drinking problem which eventually will land him in a detox program (he is all straightened out now and a great father, husband, and family man). At the time of this trip, neither Matt nor his friends saw the problem that would require AA five years later. On this particular morning, he was starting out with a wake-up drink and never saw the young teen approach. The boy was just suddenly there, quite startling Matt, even *before* blurting out the Jesus line. And rightly so; who would expect to be approached by anyone this high up (over 4,000 feet) where there are no roads. This was as 'middle of nowhere' as one can get in the mid-Atlantic states. We were parked six miles away at the nearest road access, which is a privately maintained gravel road. There isn't a maintained trail, it was a nasty morning just as a storm is blowing out, and we just spent a night lost on the trail-less side of some mountain. Who would have the luck of coming across us here? As hunters, they would have had to hit the nearest approach trail no later than 3 a.m. in the dark when it was still snowing and blowing, trudged non-stop through this snow *in the dark* for four hours, and climbed 2,500 feet in elevation in order to reach us at this hour of 7:30. I don't know *any* hunter who would intentionally tackle a 12-mile round-trip hunt under these circumstances. And what if he shot a deer? Air lift it out? Hunting season in West Virginia started Friday or Saturday after Thanksgiving. This was the Saturday after Thanksgiving. That was the only thing that made sense—that it was opening day of deer season. None of the rest of it made a lick of sense unless they had a camp somewhere on the other side of the mountain which they had hiked into earlier and spent the night.

Matt's first question to the kid, since we were lost, concerned where the boy had come from; to which the boy replied (verbatim) "My father knows the way" pointing behind him towards an older gentleman moving slower through the snow. When Matt enquired to the boy if they were camped nearby he said no, that they had walked in. So that answered my question about having a camp nearby. Before he could ask another question, the young man pointed to the bottle still in Matt's hand and reiterated his first greeting. "Mister, you need to replace that bottle with Jesus Christ." Better advice could not have been given. That was followed up with, "You need to meet my father." At this point the father came plodding through the snow to join his son. Matt stated to me he was glad to talk to the father because by now, the kid gave him the creeps, that is, made Matt uncomfortable pointing out his weakness for the bottle.

The father starting asking Matt cordial questions—where he was *from*, where he was *heading*, why were we camped *here*, etc. When he told the old guy we were heading for Haystack, the weathered mountaineer pondered for a moment, then advised our approach was from the wrong ridge. We would be better off to descend to the next ridge south and follow that up. After more directions and talk about the weather, the boy implored his father to tell Matt about Jesus Christ. The old man smiled at the boy and asked Matt if he was lost. Matt replied that he thought we could find our way out now. The man replied kindly, "No, son, I'm asking if you're lost" and gently tapped his own heart with his gloved hand.

"Man, you two ought to talk to my buddy up the trail, he's really into that stuff and would love to meet you!" Matt babbled nervously in an attempt to ditch the two towards me. The elderly man cast his gaze up the trail asking, "Your friend, is he a born again, Bible-believing, follower of Jesus Christ?"

"Yeah! Yeah! Years ago he was all messed up in a gang and quit all that stuff for Jesus Christ." He pointed the two in my direction again, stating they would really enjoy talking with me and pointed up the trail to shoe them towards me.

The older gentleman got the message and started to move out with his son. Looking at the bottle now in Matt's coat pocket, he gently advised, "You need to start listening to your friend a little closer," then started up the trail in my direction. Content with their departing, Matt didn't want to chance their turning around to talk some more about Jesus so he abandoned the idea of calling out after them to ask the older gentleman which way they had come in from; so the question never got asked. But he did ask the way back to Roaring Creek Road in the valley before parting company. "Follow our tracks a country mile back down to where the abandoned jeep-trail splits and stay on the jeep trail. Our tracks will show you the way to the jeep trail," he said, pointing back from where he had come. Their appearing and disappearing became a mystery never to be answered.

During breakfast, the wind picked up to an uncomfortable level, requiring us to snug down our hoods. The snow now began to drift and the wind was making it difficult for the stove to boil that second cup of coffee. The temperature was dropping with the arrival of a cold front. As Matt finished loading his pack, I retraced my earlier steps up the ridge trying to follow the set of footprints left by the mystery team. At the next open exposure, the wind had filled in all trace of their passing. It was fruitless to attempt picking up tracks further up. I had expected the visitors to return past our camp during breakfast but that never happened. They were gone up the mountain into wind and deeper snow, not terrain a hunter would choose. Matt was stoically humbled by the encounter and stated the boy seemed older beyond his years. I continued asking for any tidbit or detail he may have left out, but Matt was withdrawing. We both silently considered the coincidence and likelihood of anyone coming along through this high wilderness in a snowstorm to tell Matt he needed Jesus Christ. The more I thought about it, the more I wondered about this whole coincidence. Or was it?

The wind now roared like a jet engine on the ridge above us, a warning to heed from experience. Drifting snow and dropping thermometer were promising a bitter cold night if we continued our plan to the top. We didn't want to chance a night on top of this mountain exposed to arctic conditions; I had done that a few times and it is no fun at all, no matter how prepared you are. So with camp packed and loads shouldered, the decision was made to follow the hunter' from whence they came before the wind obliterated their tracks to the old jeep track split. This would at least give me a good idea how far they had come that morning. Curiosity over how they found our lost camp had overcome my desire to see the top of Haystack Mountain. My mind couldn't comprehend hunters this high up in these conditions or being willing to drag out a deer so far if they shot one. These were steep mountains with an elevation gain of 700 feet per mile for three solid miles before the gradient started to let up. There is no maintained trail, just 80-year-old grown-over cog RR grades for hauling out timber; the rails and center cogs hauled away by 1910.

Here and there, the blowing snow would obliterate the foot prints we followed like hound dogs. Fifty feet later, we would pick them up again. By late morning we had dropped 1,000 feet while traveling a few miles south-west to gain our bearings again, putting us at the head of the same valley our route climbed yesterday. At a long snow drift we lost the hunters' prints for good, but by that point we knew where we were. I didn't have the energy to double back and locate where their tracks left the trail and Matt wanted to keep moving to get below the wind for a decent lunch stop.

I have thought about those two gentlemen often over the years. I know you'll think I'm crazy but driving home later, my thoughts touched upon the idea that perhaps they were angels. For Matt's part, his very short encounter with these two ghosts who stepped out of the snowy woods was surreal enough as to question his own senses if not for the footprints.

Whether they were angels or not, I will never know on this side of eternity. But when I look at the circumstance of their appearing, along with their message, and then the outcome, one has to wonder. Consider the message and the outcome.

Consider the message.

Their message was for Matt only, therefore I was not visited. I never saw them.

"I come for those who are sick, not for those without need of a physician."

(The physician had healed me 11 years earlier)

The message was stated directly upon their arrival; no beating around the bush.

The obvious message was stated twice (verily verily), "Mister, you need Jesus Christ."

When Matt dissed the messenger by pawning them off to me, the third message was for Matt to listen closer to what I was telling him about Christ. On departure they gave Matt physical directions to become geographically found again.

The messengers departed as quickly as they came, once the message was delivered. It was absolutely clear to me that the reason for this meeting was the message.

I have to say, it sure had the signature of an angel visit. Of the 68 occurrences of angel to man appearances recorded in the Bible, this was their modes operandi. To appear, present the message, exit—job done. No socializing, no negotiating. In the Bible, angels sometimes appeared in angelic form but more often would appear in human form.

Hebrews 13, v2. "Do not forget to entertain (care for, or heed) strangers, for by so doing people have entertained angels without knowing it." So angels *are* among us, testing us all the time. Ever wonder if an angel in the form of a stranger in need was sent to cross your path as a test of your compassion. Help whoever casts needful eyes upon you. I truly believe we have *all* had at least one angel encounter in each of our lives—either as a test to re-run at our judgment, or as in this case, an intervention.

On the way home from that trip, I was musing about a verse I had recently come to understand from the Bible. The verse stated: "My spirit will not always strive with a man", explaining the hardening of an individual's heart towards the truth of Jesus Christ, reaching the point of final rejection of the Savior. I considered how to present this to Matt then jumped in up to my neck. Matt had been enquiring and listening these past 10 years to whatever I could relay about the gift of salvation; his main curiosity being end-time prophecy. Our time together amounted to dozens of hours of add-hock Interstate Highway / Mountain Campfire Bible Studies.

"Matt, I'm going to say something you may not like, but I think it needs to be said."

Our friendship was far past the point of worrying about offending each other.

"There is a point in each of our lives which God can't present Himself any clearer than He has. He uses friends, nature, circumstances, and His word so obviously as to leave no doubt, but still, people will turn away." I hesitated before continuing. "At that point He will no longer present himself to you because your heart has been incurably hardened towards Him." I didn't wait for a reply. "I'm afraid you may be at or approaching that threshold bud," I said, holding my breath, "those two messengers up on the mountain, I don't think that was any coincidence."

Both of us just stared into the night, our headlights illuminating strobing interstate center lines in hypnotic rhythm.

"Yeah, I hear what you're saying. You figure if I understand and haven't surrendered by now, my chances of understanding any better are behind me, so my choosing time is slipping away."

"Exactly," I replied, glad I wouldn't have to explain any further.

"Matt, for the last 10 years I have covered everything Biblically I can tell you; I have nothing more to add. School is out for my part of your education. Now you have strangers walking up to you in the wilderness of West Virginia stating point blank that you need Jesus Christ. I think your decision is now or never."

I didn't mention any possibility of the strangers being angels, I was already considered on the fringe as it was.

"Man, now you've got me worried," he mused nervously as we crossed the Maryland line.

"I'd be worried too, Matt" I agreed, "Choose Christ and ditch the worries" was my matter of fact conclusion.

Now consider the outcome.

Five days later, I received a phone call from Matt shortly after dinner.

"Rich, I understand and have chosen to follow Jesus Christ" came a long breath of relief as if it was the first time he had heard it out of his own mouth, held back for years.

"That's Great News, Matt" I said a bit skeptically, wanting real evidence. "Tell me what happened to convince you."

"Well, I was on my way to work on I95 (at that time he was a maintenance worker for a Philadelphia meat packing plant), listening to Charles Stanley (one of the most unpretentious, Biblically informed, preachers in media today, when most preachers are embarrassing carnival barkers) when it just hit me like a ton of bricks." He paused. "I pulled over and prayed for Jesus Christ to forgive me for my sins and come into my life."

"Then what happened?" I probed further.

"I can't really describe it, but I knew for sure all my sins had been removed, like I was starting my life over again," Matt replied, still holding something back.

"Anything else happen?" I was still looking for final confirmation.

"Well, if you really have to know, I sat there bawling like a baby for the next 10 minutes as 95 traffic whizzed by. I wasn't able to see the road (through his tears), couldn't drive." Searching for an explanation of his crying jag, he added, "It was like the sadness of a whole lifetime had been removed and replaced with something beautiful…."

And *that* my readers, is evidence of true confirmation, not some church ceremony in 3rd grade. It is my experience after hearing hundreds of conversion testimonies that adults who come to Christ will often be overwhelmed with tears of joy in finally understanding who Christ is, what He has done for them, the joy of embracing true unconditional love for the first time and being rid of their sins in trade for the joy of Life everlasting beginning right then. If that moment or soon after doesn't bring tears to a saved person, they just aren't warmed up to 98.6° anymore. For some, it is a public expression but for most, they will try to hold back the tears until alone. Been there, done that. Not only at the time of conversion but throughout a Christian's walk (life) there will be many more times for tearful joy as our Lord brings us along to continually witness His love and nurturing. If this is not the case in your life, I would venture it is time to re-examine where you stand with Jesus Christ. It was after receiving Matt's phone call that I came to believe more strongly the two men on the mountain were an angelic appearance.

Our friendship grew distant over the next few years. Right before Matt's salvation I had moved more than an hour away and was busy getting ready for our third child, working long hours at two jobs. Matt had just fell in love with a fine woman and was planning marriage, so we drifted apart as busy friends often do. I stayed in touch by phone but Matt rarely called me and was avoiding me. Five years later, after Matt was married and had a family of his own, we got together for a three-day backpack reunion in Shenandoah National Park. He apologized for being aloof over the years by explaining he had been struggling with alcoholism since before he was saved. Immediately after being saved, he was battling with the conviction to face his problem but was stumbling, so avoided returning my phone calls, knowing I'd ask how he was doing in his Christian walk. However, now after a successful detox, he was back on his feet and glad to see me. It was a wonderful reunion.

So why three stories about being lost? Because we have all been there or may still be there. It need not happen in the woods.

Story 1:

About three boys thought they knew the way better than their father(s) and follow the wrong path down the wrong side of the mountain. Once they realize they are lost, the only thing that matters to them is to get back to the father who loves them, but they don't know the way. It takes someone else (God puts these people in your life) to set them back on the right path. They choose to listen and return safely to their dads. At the time they found me, they were about to climb back up to the continental divide at midnight and search for their fathers with dead flashlights, searching without Light. That could have been fatal in their state. A dehydrated, underfed, tired mind will make fatal decisions. Spiritually, many of us are trying to find God with dehydrated, under-fed, fatigued spirits, following our own paths using dead flashlights without knowing where to turn. Always remember, Jesus is camped nearby, His camp—a light in the woods waiting for you to call out from the darkness as those boys did, "Is there anyone out there to help us!?"

Story 2:

About a man trying to hide from his sins (his past) by getting lost in the woods where his past won't find him. Your sin will always find you out. Paul and I find him hungry, living off berries, trying to decide whether he should choose his wife or his corrupt career. Even if it wasn't a *corrupt* career, say it was a legitimate career, it's still a choice many people botch by putting career first or second, Christ 4th or 5th if even in the top 10.

Story 3:

Two guys lost in a snowstorm. One receives an unlikely message from two unlikely messengers. "Mister, you need Jesus Christ in your life." The same message received 10 years apart changes the life of both men forever.

The father asked the three crucial questions of Life: "The father started asking Matt cordial questions; where he was *from*, where he was *heading*, why we were camped *here*." Questions we all need to answer or miss the meaning of Life.

Who am I? Why am I here? Where am I going? John 14:6 can show the way.

These stories are included for those who are ready to come out of the woods.

CHAPTER 13

The Final Chapter

One last chapter to wrap it up. Now a bit about religion.

How do you know what religion to follow? Best answer – forget about religions. Religion(s) are diversions from God's truth, but with just enough truth mixed in to keep us wondering. I'm not just talking of religions outside Christianity, I'm also including ALL denominations that declare themselves 'Christian'. To be clearer, that would include Catholicism, all Protestant faiths like Lutheran, Methodist, Baptist, etc., Eastern Orthodox, Zoroastrian, all the way to 21st-century liberal Judaism. Ironically, the true gospel of Jesus Christ still survives within many of these corrupted 'Christian by name' denominations. But since we can't easily discern which congregations within any of these denominations still teach the true gospel and the deity of Christ, and which ones have abandoned it for liberal feel-good teachings, it is better if we just forget about religion until we find Christ. Christ will then guide you through the religion web. The Bible describes Satan as the *Master of Confusion* and you have to admit, the gauntlet of religions facing us is a prime example of that confusion. Satan has done his job well… and he is immeasurably smarter than you and I. So smart, that he is able to totally confuse us about God's plan, then uses our pride to convince us we're not confused and have it all under control. Since we don't know which religion to follow, we tend to be graciously open-minded and say, "If it works for you, then it works you, God bless everyone," and lump *all* religions as different adequate paths to the same God and eternity. This concept, which I call spiritual correctness, is parallel to politically correct.

With that concept in mind—that all religions are adequate paths to the same God, or that different religions have a piece of the truth but no religion has exclusive rights to all the truth —I'm going to step back a bit and take a very broad look at the major religions of the world. But first, let's set up a simple prerequisite which each faith has to pass in order to qualify as legitimate. This qualifier is simple and logical. If a faith teaches a glaring foundational lie, it gets excluded on the basis that God is truth, and can't lie or allow His truth to be removed from our searching. Neither can a perfect God make a mistake. If God *could* make mistakes, why follow Him, believe Him, or trust Him? If He *could* make mistakes, it is only a matter of time before He would fail mankind (you and me).

Who believes what?

The following statistics are from Wikipedia, 2020, Pew Research. I take no safety in numbers and make no conclusions from these statistics. They are just FYI.

Worldwide Affiliation by % of population		Approximate time founded
Christian	29%	1st century AD
Muslim	24%	6th century AD
Non-religious	14%	Shortly after Adam
Hindus	14%	2200 BC
Other	11%	
Buddhists	6%	6th century AD

Worldwide Affiliation by % of population		Approximate time founded
Jewish	*less than 1%*	*4000 BC*

Ex-Communist countries and China claim the highest percentage of non- religious & atheists. However, with the fall of communism, and China opening its borders and policies more liberally, Christianity is rising fast in underground churches.

Islam is on the rise in Europe. This is not due as much to Muslims proselytizing Europeans but because Muslims are moving to Europe for jobs and to escape the Mid-East conflicts, while birthing a lot of little Muslims through traditional large families.

Let's take a very brief look at these major faiths. I'll start with the fourth oldest religion mankind has to offer, Buddhism. Buddha had a lot of great 'life philosophies' which I won't argue with because I agree with many of them; they are just good moral sense on how to treat people for a large part. But he also taught that the Earth rests on the back of a giant turtle who is swimming through the cosmos. That was okay until we went to the moon and didn't see any turtle carrying our planet around. Buddha made that one up. If he got that wrong, should anyone be trusting their life to his philosophies? I mean, he claimed to have been to Nirvana and back, so he should have had the science of how the Earth travels though the cosmos. The Bible test (or even just common-sense test) of a true prophet is 100 per cent accuracy 100 per cent of the time, since the prophecies come from an infallible God. If the prophet errs ONCE, throw him out, his message is not from God. By Jewish law, if a prophet erred once, the people were commanded to stone him to death. They kind of kept budding false prophets to a minimum that way. The myths in Buddhism are so numerous and flagrantly in the face of known observable science that to try to justify them is futile.

"But, Rich", you say, "what about Noah's Ark, the plague of the sea turning red, the parting of the Red Sea, Joshua's trumpets calling down the

329

walls of Jericho, the sun standing still and other Bible whoppers?" Well, I have to take the position that they can't be *dis*-proven. We *do* know that the Earth was once covered by water; that mathematically, all of today's species could easily fit into a ship of dimensions given in Genesis; that Red tides are well understood today, as well as earthquakes. That geo-physicists conclude the Earth has shifted on its axis (sun stands still) every eon or so, causing the magnetic poles to realign with devastating effects which are now being attributed for the latest theories of dinosaur extinction and why we find oil under polar ice caps. Speaking of poles re-aligning, did you know that the sun completely shifts its poles 180° every 11 years? Why not the Earth every 5,000 years? Point is: the turtle story is not even close to the truth, so Buddha fails the truth test.

"But, Rich", you whine again, "Buddha's turtle story was only a way for the people back then to grasp a concept." To which I say: lying as a means does not justify the end. Jesus and the prophets never lied to justify the ends of his messages. And with that, I will stop arguing with myself on your behalf. Besides, I'm always right (or so my wife tells me).

Next, we will blitz thru the third oldest faith, Hinduism and re-incarnation. Hinduism teaches that YOU are a god and with enough lifetimes, you will eventually figure this out and achieve perfection. If you know ANYBODY who knows how to earn their way to anything *approaching* perfection, please point them out to me and I'll concede my argument. Mathematically, reincarnation is impossible. Presently there are seven billion souls on the planet (not including monkeys, cattle, rats, etc.) and the number keeps on growing! Isn't ANYBODY moving on to nirvana? And if they are, why does the human population keep growing? The only way to explain the growth of souls to seven billion is to say some well-behaved plants and turtles got bumped up to homo-sapien status for good behavior (Hindu teaches all life proceeds from previous life). But plants have no brains and, therefore, no choice in their behavior. Does that mean since plants and bugs can't behave badly, they keep on moving up the reincarnation ladder to become humans? If that were the case there would be trillions and bazillions more people on the planet each spring! Especially with all the logging we've done! And I never met a 'bad' turtle, or frog, or butterfly, or even mosquito for that matter. Even the creatures we deem a nuisance are only following instincts for their survival, like a mosquito sucking your blood; it's just doing what it was programmed to do for survival. And so it goes with the whole animal kingdom. Reincarnation teaches that there is a pool of life in constant flux of different forms. Old life returns in new forms or moves on to Nirvana once perfection is achieved. The highest life form is man (but cattle, monkeys, and rats aren't too far behind in the pecking order). According to Hinduism, mankind is divided by birthright into good people and bad people, thus the Hindu caste system. The caste system promotes large-scale continuous unjust treatment of one group of people towards another group of people. The higher caste Brahmans (the ones closest to nirvana) treat the lower cast Untouchables in an unspeakable manner and are actually permitted to burn them to death at will if their shadow fell upon a Brahman! Brahmans would come back as Untouchables just on the basis of how they treated their lower-caste brothers! That would create a never-ending circle of reincarnation since Brahmans could never advance to perfection based on the way they treat the lower caste. And we all have the common sense to know cows and rats are not worthy of our worship, or God would have judged mankind by now for "99 billion served" at McDonald's alone.

As we continue to work our way west, the five pillars of Islam taught by Mohammed in 700 AD confront us as the religion of newspaper headlines this century. Islam seems to be the one religion we in the West attempt to put our stamp of "legitimacy" upon, when it comes to 'believable' faiths. Our tolerance is even willing to look past the factions of radical Islam which teach hatred and blowing up of one's self, along with the thousands of innocents, in the name of Allah. "That's not Islam," we've convinced ourselves. And after all, "Christian" crusaders from Europe were doing the same thing to Arabs 800 years ago. However, once you educate yourself about Mohammed's teachings and history, Islam falls apart. Now, since most of you will never bother to read the Koran or study up on Islam, allow your buddy Rich to walk you through a crude crash course.

After a troubled childhood, Mohammed started having, what he called, evil visions. These visions troubled him to the point of attempted suicide because he believed his visions were from Satan. Mohammed soon married into a very wealthy family. His wife then convinced him his visions were from God, not Satan, and that he needed to start writing down what he was hearing. When having a vision, Mohammed would fall on the ground convulsing as an epileptic would. His followers would throw a carpet over him until he came back into this world again. Once he returned, they or he would write down his visions and instructions.

I think the most important thing to note here is that for years Mohammed *himself* couldn't identify the source of his visions; and his first impulse was that they were Satanic. On the contrary, there are NO Biblical prophets who ever questioned the source of their visions. So you have to wonder if old Mohammed didn't have it right about the source first time around.

How Islam Grew

Islam needed more widespread recognition it wasn't receiving through peaceful methods. Mohammad needed a city and shrine to be the seat of his new-found following; he needed a 'Jerusalem' as a central focus for followers; that would be Medina, the second holiest city of Islam today. Medina was a peaceful mix of Jews, Christians, fractioned groups of those two faiths, and paganism. After unsuccessfully attacking Medina to consolidate (force) its inhabitants under Mohammad's new religion, he agreed to sign a peace treaty with the city fathers who had repulsed his previous attacks. Mohammed recouped to build up his troops, returned one-and-a-half years later, breaking his word, and slaughtering the inhabitants of

Medina who did not bow to Islam, killing thousands of Jews and Christians peacefully dwelling there. Now Islam is rolling, Mohammed has his version of Jerusalem. He then amassed a larger army and continued taking city after city by force for the next six years until he died. Infidels swore allegiance to Islam or took the sword—generally doing the same thing ISIS is doing today. Not exactly the gospel of peace Mohammad claimed Jesus failed in delivering and Mohammed was sent to correct.

There you have it, 27 lines in my dinky book to sum up the rich history of Islam. But hey, if you were really interested you would have read up on it by now. Please take the time to read about it yourself since I have condensed it so rudely here for the sake of time and space. I'm trying to get this book to print before the Second Coming.

According to Islam, there are five steps or pillars that, if obeyed, will get you into their version of heaven.

1. A public declaration of your faith to Allah and his Prophet Mohammed
2. Face Mecca and pray five times a day
3. Pay mandatory alms (10 per cent) to the poor and support of Islam
4. Fasting
5. A pilgrimage to Mecca sometime in your life

They all seem harmless enough but there are more sinister Koranic imperatives that branch off from Pillar #1, like the obligation to participate in a jihad if infidels are starting to spread other teachings in Arab lands. The Koran has very direct instructions with how to deal with non-Muslims trying to live among them. Strangers are permitted to pass through Arab lands and are to be treated as honored guests no matter what their faith, just don't plan on staying. They are also justified in conquering foreign lands to protect their faith (sounds a lot like the US promoting democracy on foreign soil). Such teachings have far-reaching implications, which are bringing the Middle

East to a climactic point on the world stage. By Islamic teachings, Israel is a blight on the land and soul of Islam. Judaism has been purged from all the Mid-east Arab countries; Christianity is currently in the final stages of being purged. Islam believes that the final Imam will not return until all Arab lands are purged of infidels. They believe Israel is Arab land. The Koran teaches its followers to have nothing to do with Jews and Christians, and a dead infidel is a forward step for Islam. The way women are treated is, to be kind here, hardly inspired by God. For example: If a woman for any reason displeases her husband, he has only to declare "I divorce you" three times in a public place with witnesses and walk away from her to dissolve the marriage. She has no recourse and is forbidden to ever marry again. If raped, an Islamic woman must produce four *male* witnesses or don't even bother coming to court. It's pretty wacko, folks. As you know by now, I'm not playing spiritually-correct here.

Judaism & Christianity

All right, let's cover my fellow wackos too. The Old Testament pointed to the coming of Christ for 4,000 years, He came as promised, fulfilled the OT and moved Judaism into the Church Age which has since spread to every corner of the planet. Old Judaism remained, while New Judaism (Christianity) spread. Even while under severe persecution; by 350 AD, Roman census showed 50 per cent of the citizens in all Roman cities throughout the Empire had converted to "Christianity". Different forms and sects of "Christianity" grew for the next 1,600 years. Many were corrupt and many still are, though some segments held true fidelity to the gospel. The truth has always remained intact through God's word, the Bible. So where are post-modern Christians hanging out? Today, most fundamental Christians have left the dying denominations for independent Bible-believing congregations which are thriving. Conversely, there is still a small corps of true born-again Christians who choose to keep the flame burning within the many fragmented and dying branches of the western Christian faiths (*read; old Protestant and Catholic congregations).* That is pretty much the state of the union for true Christianity in the West. Recently, in the mid-20th century (1960s to present) the Church Age has been winding down in the West. Like a stone dropped in a pond 2,000 years ago, true Christianity rippled out from Jerusalem after Christ's resurrection. Today, the ripples are fading out in the West (Americas and Europe), but accelerating in the Far East where the last ripples are still arriving. China and Asia now have the largest fundamental Christian churches in the world. (Korea has churches with tens of thousands filling stadiums each Sunday). The persecuted church in China is the fastest growing faith in Asia and, for that matter, the world. They meet and worship secretly in homes just like the first Christians did.

As far as what Christ taught, we really don't have to review his teachings since most of you either know enough already; or having read this far, you have the fundamental reasons for Christ first coming pretty well covered without repeating myself.

So in the final pages of this writing, I'll move on to his Second Coming. But first there is one very glaring point that separates Christianity from all other world faiths.

One common denominator you will notice about all faiths, excluding true Christianity; *they are all based on a way for **you to earn** your way to heaven / God.* Examples: The **five** pillars of Islam, or the **Ten** Commandments of Judaism, or the **seven** sacraments of Catholicism. The shared 'given' of all world faiths is that we don't deserve heaven because of our sin, so must earn our way there with good living and deeds. But to what degree of obedience to these five-, seven-, 10-step programs is one to satisfy God in order to earn their way to heaven? Does your E for Effort get you in? Is 70 per cent passing or failing in this class?

There is only one doctrine among men which teaches contrary to all the other faiths or "10-Step Programs". All world faiths teach Man reaching **up** to God by earning their way back to Him...except true Christianity, which is God reaching **down** to Man. The true unadulterated message from

Christ, before man altered Christianity to manipulate the political power of Christendom to rule nations, teaches that *we cannot earn our way* into heaven. If we could earn our way to God/Heaven, then sending Christ to the cross to cover our sin with perfect blood was a wasted effort. A personal relationship with Christ does not result from a five-pillar, seven-sacraments, or 10-commandments religious program, it is a deep heart choice to receive the miraculous *free gift* of Life offered from God; no pre-conditions attached, nothing required on our part other than using our free will to accept God's freely given gift. That simple truth sets Christ apart from all religions.

1. Life (Eternal) and Heaven are a *gift* from God. You can't earn it, no matter how good you try to be, or think you are. Your attempts to be good does not remove your sin, only Christ can forgive sin. You simply have to *receive the gift of his forgiveness*. A nicely wrapped gift delivered by UPS doesn't do you any good sitting on your front porch. You have to open the front door, take it into your home (heart), open it, and enjoy it. People tend to think the *gift* is hidden from them, so they resort to logic and try to earn their way to God. The *gift* always stands right in front of you, delivered to your front door, knocking. The *gift* is Jesus Christ, God's physical manifestation of his forgiveness for your sin. Rev. 3:20

2. The 10 commandments were given to us to prove our sin nature. We *can't* earn our way into heaven via the 10 Cs because we can't keep even **one** commandment.

3. *Your* Eternal Life ignites the moment God dwells within you, also called born again or New Life, or receiving the Holy Spirit.

4. All of us have eternal existence, not to be confused with Eternal Life. Life can only come from God. Our eternal existence will either be with God or without Him.

Life is living with God in you, a 100 per cent surrender to His will, after which He will send the Holy Spirit to dwell in you. Life begins. God IS Life.

Without God our eternal existence will be without Eternal (God) Life.

Heaven is the place we will spend our Eternal Life after our bodies fail, but Eternal Life ignition *begins on Earth* the day we trust in God's provision of forgiveness (*the gift*) by removing our sin through Jesus Christ, God in the flesh.

Once you accept the gift, God will convict you from within on how to live for Him. And therein is the rub. Truth is: we are comfortable in our sin, in our own way. People are afraid of how God will change them and so turn away and trust their own moral guidelines. But you, my friend, cannot turn away, for you have read this far and are accountable to Him from this point forward in your life.

If all of this sounds alien to you, it is because you have never come to the point of ignition. "Houston, we have a problem." The engine (heart) has not ignited and your spaceship cannot lift off. Please read the next eight lines very slowly.

The sole purpose of our time on earth is to Live; not just exist, pro-create, and dwell 80 moral years as productive citizens. Contrary to popular belief, Living is not defined as an active appreciation of the accumulated joys and emotions while dwelling on planet Earth. Living is what you have done to reflect God's Life. Remember, we are made in His Image. Life (spiritual Life) comes from God. Living *begins* with spiritual Life. Without Life we are merely alive, passing time until Life begins. Whether *your* Life ever begins, depends on your free will choice. God's Life, Jesus Christ, is waiting for your decision.

I just wrote life or living 11 times, I know it's a spiritual mind twister. Maybe read it over a few times before giving up. Or at least dog-ear the page to come back to it later.

Our sin nature with which we are born kicks into full action at the age of accountability and separates us from our perfect God by the choices we make. Generally, a child's age of accountability falls between the ages of five and 15; note that I said 'generally' and not officially or scripturally. After that time of accountability, they have a full understanding of right and wrong and the consequences. Ever admire the natural innocence in the face of two- year-old? A four-year-old? You're looking into a face that still trusts in a God they don't understand, but He still has them under His wing. You are looking into the face of spiritual innocence.

As parents, we have the awesome responsibility to keep our children (His children) under His wing until old enough to choose or reject Him. Not to scare you, but as parents, God has placed upon us the responsibility to guide our children to Him before their time of accountability. It is a big enough responsibility just to take care of our own spiritual welfare, let alone theirs. As parents, we are blinded into believing our obligation to our children is to merely love them, teach them right from wrong, nurture their physical needs in a safe environment, and point them towards productive careers and mates; putting their spiritual welfare at the bottom of our parental priorities. Or…their spiritual welfare is at the bottom of our priorities because it is at the bottom of your *personal* priority list. Ouch. Or you are content to let your children find their own spiritual way because you never found your own spiritual way. Ouch again.

But alas, help is on the way. Somehow, your life has crossed paths with mine. And believe it or not, God uses dolts like me to get His message out (who says God doesn't have a great sense of humor?) Therefore, this book is in your hands and you have read this far. The purpose of my book was to make you stop your busy life long enough to look at your own spiritual life by writing some short stories that led up to my own point of spiritual ignition. I understand that the only reason you read this book is because you know me and were curious about strange happenings in my early life. However, you have now read about some challenging spiritual matters you may not normally bother to consider. In short, you have been presented with the gospel of Jesus Christ in layman's terms.

The message of this book was in the very beginning, but I never finished that story. If I had, you may not have read any further. On page I of the *Foreword* I described an older gentleman in a car wreck whom I wasn't sure had yet departed his body. I whispered something into his ear before I went around the other side of the car to help his daughter. What I said to him was the same thing I would say to anyone if I only had one last thing to say. I leaned into the old man's ear and told him, "If you are still able to hear, you need to confess your sin and give your heart to Jesus Christ, He is waiting, even now."

Rev 3:20 "Here I am, I stand at the door (to your heart) and knock. He who opens the door I will enter in with and abide (live)...."

Jn 14:6 "I am the Way, the Truth, and the Life; **no man** comes to the Father but by me."

Throughout this book, I have done my best not to quote Bible verses that describe the same truths I have attempted to share. That is because most people don't believe in the inerrancy of the Word of God, so why quote verses from a book people don't believe in? However, let there be no doubt that all of these gospel truths can be backed up by scripture. Instead, I did my best to appeal to the logic of a point to carry through the truth of the matter. If there is one fault I recognize about my effort, it is that I have appealed to logic for a matter that requires the heart for changing. Head knowledge will not bring you to Christ; only a surrendered heart can do that. You can know the history of Christ and *believe* it is all true. You can *believe* the miracles He performed are all true. You can even *believe* He is God come to Earth as a man, but if that head knowledge never translates 18 inches down to the heart, to bring you to the point of surrendering *your* life for *His* Life, then it is empty knowledge, knowledge that was never used for its intended result.

The Challenge:

Now here at the end I will finally return to the heart.

I would ask you to go back to chapter 10, about 7 pages in and read my "To whom it may concern" prayer, which I prayed to the generic God of the universe. Please feel free to pray the exact same words I used right off that page. But do it only if you are truly 100 per cent serious about wanting to know who God is. What you are doing is reciting an oath to follow Him once He proves Himself to you. I promise that if you are dead serious about asking Him to show you His plan for your life; He will gladly honor your request and make Himself tremblingly clear in Christ. Just don't jerk Him around when He keeps His side of your oath. Remember, this IS the God of all existence you're dealing with. Say the prayer and wait a few days, a few weeks, or maybe a few months, and let me know what happens. Who knows? It could be the basis for another book. After saying the prayer, watch closely for who and what circumstances God brings into your life over the next few weeks. When Jesus knocks at your door, let Him in and start to Live.

What do we do about Jesus?

One can only come to two conclusions about Jesus Christ.

Choice #1 – He was a nut. He clearly stated many times through-out the New Testament that He is God, created everything, and raises dead to life. Or, he was a delusional mental case. In which case Christianity is the biggest farce in history ever played on mankind.

Choice #2 – He is who He says He is, God in the flesh, God become man. In which case, it is our responsibility to look as closely at those 33 years as possible, to understand what it means to our lives. Turn the New Testament inside out. Start with the gospel of John, and don't just breeze past that first paragraph.

I know I said "two conclusions" but there are some who claim a third conclusion—that Christ was an enigmatic, charismatic, brilliant, well intended teacher with a very large following who changed the world and *believed* he was God but was not. No, No, No, (shaking my head now). I'm sorry that is not an option. Read Matt 28:18 and you will realize you're back to option #1 & 2. Any man who claims "All Power is given me in heaven and in earth" (meaning universal power) is either God in the flesh, or insane. Following someone who *thinks* they are God but is not, is the same as following the teachings of a Philadelphia street person picking imaginary bugs out of the air to eat for breakfast. They are delusional mad and you are back to option #1.

If it still isn't clear what to do with Jesus, try the Challenge Prayer in Chapter 10. It does not ask Jesus into your heart; it asks God to reveal to you who He is; and that will lead you to Christ. But that prayer is also an oath, my friend; don't use it unless you are serious about honoring your oath when God presents himself. Never make an oath you have no intention of honoring, especially if it is with God.

End-Time Prophecies

(The real final chapter)

Just in case you're not sure if I really popped my cork, allow me to remove all doubt.

I believe from what I have read in the word of God, parallel to daily newspaper headlines and technological advances, that our generation will witness the final days. Earth and mankind are environmentally, politically, economically, militarily, technologically and morally approaching the final meltdown rendezvous at an ever-accelerating pace. I think anyone watching world news today would, in all honesty, agree. If world events are left on their current course, the Bible assessment of the final chapter for Earth is not farfetched at all. And it all revolves around teeny tiny Israel, God's chosen people, go figure. One thing very few people will argue; it is astounding that Israel was re-established after 2,000 years in exile throughout the world; that they have successfully survived repeated, methodic extermination, fought off the entire combined Arab nations (twice) while outnumbered 10:1; and this tiny piece of real estate the size of New Jersey is routinely the focus of world events. America has survival treaties with Israel and is the only world entity standing between Israel and annihilation by her sworn enemies. Once American might has been removed from the world stage, Israel's enemies will move on her. So expect America to be taken out of the picture (politically, economically, or with a few dirty terrorist nukes to extinguish our willpower to fight; who knows how?) before Israel's enemies move on her. Last minute post-script: Add pandemic to above list. Not the one we are in now but a REAL pandemic of 1918 proportions. America is never mentioned in Bible prophecy. The absence of the present world power, America, in prophecy is telling in itself.

According to Bible prophecy, there is nothing else on the world stage that needs to be fulfilled in order for the Great Tribulation to begin, except for the treaty between Israelis and Arabs to re-build the Temple near the site of the Dome of the Rock. All of the nations named as players in the end-time scenario are aligned with each other—the prophesized European Union is in place, China can field the predicted 200 million-man army (a number larger than all Middle-Eastern nations' population at the time it was predicted), Russia is now aligned with Syria and Iran, that power base will expand to a Pan-Arab allegiance, all of the technology is available; we stand at the threshold. I will give a few sobering examples.

The prophets Ezekiel and Daniel prophesied which countries would align against and attack Israel in the end times. In prophesy lingo, it is referred to as 'Ezekiel's War', which occurs before the Battle of Armageddon. He said in the final days Magog would align with Persia, Ethiopia, and Libya to march on Israel (Ez 38; 5-6). "And I will draw you Magog out of the uttermost parts of the North." Draw a line on a map from Jerusalem straight north (uttermost North) and you come to Moscow. Magog was the name used to describe the people to the farthest north of Israel, Moscow is the capital. Syria, Iraq, Iran and Afghanistan are the current names for Persia. When I first studied this stuff in the early 1970s, Iran was aligned with the USA through the pro-Western Shah, Russia was bogged down in a war with Afghanistan, and I wondered how long before those alliances would crumble and reverse 180°. Soon the Shah was overthrown by radical Islam, and today the Russians are building nuclear facilities in Iran while the US is fighting in Afghanistan. Three decades later and what looked highly improbable has stepped right off the pages of Daniel and Ezekiel. Russia is militarily entrenched in Syria's civil war which borders Israel at the Golan Heights. The Arab Spring didn't exactly turn out well for democracy as American leadership declared at the time. A radical Islamic government in Iran, boasting a fledgling nuclear program, is presently setting its sights on Israel. In 2006, China signed a treaty with Saudi Arabia to come to that nation's aide if outside forces invade their country or disrupt oil flow. The Saudis have the same agreement with the US but is widening its base of defense should America's political will fail. All of this revolves around oil revenue and Arab hatred for the Jews, who they vow to wipe off the map. That 2006 treaty provides China an invite to the Middle East it never had before.

The Imam of Iran still reiterates his chant to his nation during *every* Friday Prayer broadcast nationally, and at national unity rallies, "Soon, I promise, Israel will be no more." The more I read about courtship between Iran and Russia, the more I see the beginning of the end. It only takes one fruitcake of a leader to start the ball rolling.

For those of you who remember Ayatollah Khomeini, the revolutionary religious leader of Iran for 20 years, let me quote what he taught a new generation, "The purest joy in Islam is to kill and to be killed for Allah." He spoon fed this hatred to a country where 60 percent of the population is UNDER 35 years old (2012 statistics). Hatred of Israel is part of their culture. So it is no surprise Iran is bent on destroying Israel. However, America is the only obstacle in the way, so America has to be dealt with first. Iran has no intention of fighting a conventional war with a nation they know can't be defeated on a battlefield. But imagine here at home what a few strategic terrorist strikes on power grids could do to shut down our computer-dependent government, military, and manufacturing infrastructure. Without a power grid or computers, the US is back in the Stone Age for 3 months to a year; we couldn't even feed our country one week without computers. I worked in industry and food processing and can tell you our industrial/ agricultural infrastructure is 100 percent computer- and electricity-dependent. Remember what a few squirrels did to the New England power grid for a week in the early 1990s? America is not vulnerable on the battlefield; it is vulnerable at home. There is no lack of Hitlers to start all this rolling; whether nukes are used *is purely speculation on my part* but my point is that Ezekiel said it eventually will come to pass with those nations named, and they are the same nations in the news every week.

Think that is going to go away? Stick your heads in the sand if you must but all of this hatred will eventually come to a boil and spill over; it always does.

The Book of Revelation says a world leader will control the ability of everyone to buy or sell via a number on their hands or forehead. Imagine that, a 1st-century man describing biometric ID. That technology is now available and waiting to be implemented if not for the opposition to one's civil rights. Sweden is on the forefront of testing this technology and already going cashless with bio-implanted chip-commerce. The EU is watching Sweden's results. It is already widespread through credit/debit cards with imbedded ID chips. Once that technology jumps to the next logical step, implanted under the skin of your hand or forehead so no one can steal your Commerce ID, another 2,000-year-old prophesy becomes reality. Not to mention it will eliminate all credit card fraud, tax fraud (no more under the table wages), identity theft, terrorist security problems, black market cash transactions, drug cartels, illegal immigration and numerous other economic/social ills. It would be any government's dream come true. Governments want to implement the cashless technology now but will probably have to wait for another 9/11 on a nuclear scale before even the ACLU pleads "we need to implement this technology, now!" It is coming, and we will all line up. Consider how dead-on simple the prophecy John wrote in Revelation about this "mark" on the hand or forehead. The angel had literally brought John into the future to write down what he sees even though he can't possibly understand it. He is a 1st-century man viewing 21st-century technology. He is told, "Don't try to understand it, just write down what you see." John *isn't* having a dream, he is witnessing the actual future; he's a real Marty McFly! Remember, God is not *constrained* by time, *time* is governed by God. Also, God doesn't deal in fakery; he is showing the real thing to John. He can. Poor John can't understand 21st-century chip technology, but he hits the nail on the head, at least as close as a 1st-century man can. He describes the mark (chip) as a number and what is a computer ID chip? Numbers, 0s and 1s! This number will also have some sort of visible logo in relation to three sixes.

The Old Testament has over 300 prophesies spread across 4000 years foretelling Jesus' First Coming and they all came true. There are twice as many about his Second Coming; I wonder if it will all go down as prophesied. Nahhh,..it's all fairytales, why read the Bible.

And this brings me to my last and final point in my final chapter. The Bible is the record of God's dealings with mankind over a period of 6,000 years; a handful of men recording what God guided them to write. There are writers and there are editors. Prophets, kings, and apostles did the writing; God did the editing *before* it left their pens. If God can breathe our universe into existence, I'm pretty sure He can edit a book. No other book in history has been so well preserved, distributed or examined as the Bible...not even close. Add to that, it is the only major writing which foretells the future with 100 per cent accurate prophesies. No other book can even come close to making that claim. It is the only book that proves out history **before** archeology does...over and over again*.

Until excavations uncovered proof of crucifixions, the Bible contained the *only record* of a crucifixion. Until then, those who disclaimed the Bible said crucifixion was a figment of early Christian's imagination and there is no archeological support for crucifixion.

In June of 1968, bulldozers working north of Jerusalem accidentally laid bare tombs dating from the first century B.C. and the first century A.D. Greek archeologist Vasilius Tzaferis was instructed by the Israeli Department of Antiquities to carefully excavate these tombs. Subsequently, one of the most exciting finds of recent times was unearthed—the first skeletal remains of a crucified man. The most significant factor is its dating to around the time of Christ. Today we take the history of crucifixion for granted; wasn't always that way.

Makes me wonder what may be said if satellite images soon turn up a ship prow jutting out of a glacier on Mt. Ararat.

You'd think in 6,000 years, one of the Bible writers would have slipped up and recorded a false fact about the Earth's natural history like the sun revolves around the Earth, or the Earth rides on the back of a turtle. But instead, science and archeology keep on *proving* the Bible. I recently read a fascinating science journal blurb about DNA tracking. The article said the researchers had traced human DNA back to a bottleneck, when less than 30 individuals were responsible for all DNA known in modern man. And that everyone alive today only has to go back seven generations (before the founding of the western hemisphere and modern mass transportation methods) for DNA proof everyone on the planet is someway related. Jesus also told us that leading up to the end times, earthquakes and natural disasters would increase. Read any science journal concerning earthquake occurrences in the last 40 years. Even conservative numbers say they have increased 300 per cent over the 40 previous years. Jesus also said knowledge would increase greatly. With the advent of the mighty computer and chip technology, we can store on our cell phones more information than all volumes once stored at the famed ancient Library of Alexandria. Call me opinionated, but I think this Bible would be worth looking into, try starting with the book of John. Reading Revelation would be like trying to take Calculus before 4th-grade math.

One last fairytale.

I know, I keep saying "one last" but I am almost done and now you wish I wasn't.

"For as the lightning cometh out of the east, and shineth even unto the west; so shall also the coming of the Son of man be." Mat 24:27

There is an event that the Bible says will preclude the Great Tribulation, and will occur near the start of the seven years of end-time tribulations. It is identified today as The Rapture and only true Bible-believing Christians believe it will occur. Cafeteria Christians, who don't believe in Bible inerrancy, think it is too fantastic a story to believe, even though the verses are as plain as the nose on our face. Personally, I learned 45 years ago not to put a limit on God's power. The Bible says Jesus will descend to the clouds (not to Earth) and call up all Christians who have lived during the 2,000-year church age, those in the grave *and those still living* to join him in the heavens. The Rapture is not the Second Coming of Christ. His Second Coming is at the end of the Tribulation Period "or else all flesh would had destroyed itself". With the true Christians removed, the final seven years of man's rule on Earth, and God's judgments begin.

Born again Christians discuss this subject among themselves as commonly as they would the weather. We expect it in our lifetime, but no one can guess as to when. Here is why I tell you this. Until a few years ago there existed gaps where prophecy had not yet been fulfilled before the Rapture could occur. Today in 2020, all prophecy concerning nation alignments, world events, and technology are in place. But for the grace and patience of God, Christ could return to Rapture his true church tomorrow. The good news is that salvation through Christ is still offered to all, even during the end-time seven years of tribulation. The bad news is that the new world government which comes to power after the Rapture will round up all new believers to be executed for their faith in Christ. Preposterous, you say? What if the new world order is governed by radical Islam or atheist China? Consider: With all Christians raptured, who will jump in, likely by force, to fill that 'religious' void? Revelation teaches that in the final days Satan will establish a one-world government under a one-world religion. Other than salvation still available, there is no other good news until the end of the seven years. In truth, it will be better to die as a post-rapture Christian martyr *ASAP*, than suffer through the tribulations. Welcome back to Roman times. Right about now I'm thinking you may be more interested in Bible verse than earlier. Following are some Rapture verses from Mathew 24.

vs36 No one knows about that day or hour, not even the angels in heaven, nor the Son,[f] but only the Father.

vs37 As it was in the days of Noah, so it will be at the coming of the Son of Man.

(RB Note for vs 37: Just as God removed Noah and his family from the coming judgment on mankind; so it will be with the rapture of Christ own before the tribulations).

vs38 For in the days before the flood, people were eating and drinking, marrying and given in marriage, up to the day Noah entered the ark;

vs39 and they knew nothing about what would happen until the flood came and took them all away. That is how it will be at the coming of the Son of Man.

vs40 Two men will be in the field; one will be taken and the other left.

vs41 Two women will be grinding with a hand mill; one will be taken and the other left.

vs42 Therefore keep watch, because you do not know on what day your Lord will come. vs43 But understand this: If the owner of the house had known at what time of night the thief was coming, he would have kept watch and would not have let his house be broken into.

vs44 So you also must be ready, because the Son of Man will come at an hour when you do not expect him.

In our present day, Christ is slowly stepping back from the world scene as we kick Him out of government, schools, public places, history (which by the way is His-Story), and even liberal churches. At the same time, He is slowly releasing His constraint on the lord of this world, Satan. The world can't see that to ask God to step back is to ask Satan to step up. God is stepping back per man's request and Satan is stepping in. Christ will return for His own before it all comes crashing down to the last days. There is Bible precedence for this: Before God destroyed man, He removed His only followers, Noah and his family. Before He destroyed Sodom and Gomorrah, He removed Abraham, Lot and his family. Before these end times, He will appear in the heavens and with a great shout will call out from the grave and among the living, all true believers.

Think of this: Consider the multitude of miracles that Jesus performed as a testimony to who He said He is. Not particularly the actual miracles themselves, but the focus of the miracles. They were all focused on making our lives better. He healed the sick, fed the hungry, calmed storms to protect those he loved, cast out demons to restore men whole, raised the dead back to life and lastly, willingly gave himself as the Lamb of God to take away the sins of the world. In short, all of His miracles revolved around taking away *our* pain, hunger, sickness, and death to show that He alone has the power to do so because He is God. At the same time, it was within His command to perform such visually earth-shattering events as the world has ever seen and even Hollywood can't think up. But He didn't…yet.

349

Miracles Part II, The Judgment is coming soon to a hometown near you.

Now just for comparison, imagine **you** are Christ 2,000 years ago with all of the power of God at your disposal to impress on mankind that you are God in the flesh. What would **you** do to open mankind's eye to the reason for your coming? I'd probably do the miracles mentioned above as a warm-up act; but then I'd really start blowing minds. I mean, I have all the powers of time and creation at my fingertips to settle the question once and for all concerning my divine authority. For starters, I'd suck the moon to within 3,000 miles of the surface of Israel and suspend it there for a week. I bet within that week I'd have Caesar and all the kings coming to introduce themselves and worship me, and that would pretty much settle it among kings. Then maybe I'd have a few hundred F-35s fly in from the 21st century for a beaucoup ordinance demonstration. After that I'd land the jets and some 747s to boot and watch everyone's face as the pilots and passengers step out of these future birds; ALIENS! To top that, I'd bring down the heavenly host of angels to pass out Manna and Godiva chocolate while singing Heaven's Greatest Hits Vol I—you know, have a real party! Next, level a few mountains...whatever. But he didn't do that sort of stuff the first time around. However, during the seven years and concluding with His Second Coming, the Bible states He will gather the kings of the Earth to fall before Him, draw down the heavens, and bring forth creatures and wonders we have never seen before, none of it to your liking. God has an uncanny way of getting our attention when time is short and we are so stubborn. And mankind has an equally uncanny knack for rejecting Him. All of this revolves around what WE think is better for our lives vs. what He *knows* is better for us. It all comes down to who knows better—loving parent or wayward child? Remember when you thought your parents didn't understand you so you took matters into your own hands? I've bet my life on Christ. What have you bet your life on?

As you have already figured out, I'm not concerned if you think my elevator doesn't go to the top floor. If I was worried about opinions, I never would have written this book. My concern is for all the people I know and love, no matter what they think of me. Jesus already warned me, "Ye know that they (the world) hated me before they hated you." Someone needed to get these truths into your hands and God chose me. So, thank God I'm a nut...and your friend. Mission complete. The whole purpose of this book is for the few who will pray the prayer a few pages in to Chapter 10 and come to Life. Life, what a trip. There is no end.

No End

ABOUT THE BOOK TITLE:

In Philippians 1:21, Paul teaches that you can't live for Christ until you die to self. Once we become true believers, our life is no longer ours, our old sin nature (self) is put to death and we now live through Christ. So the book title is a prayer that we would all die to self and live for Christ. The earlier in your life this happens the better; hope *you* die before you get old. I took the line *Hope I Die Before I Get Old* from The Who's 1966 My Generation, and made it my own personal plea which God answered many years ago.

The most famous of all The Who songs was an anti-establishment anthem memorized by my g-g-g-generation. None of us could imagine at the time we would eventually be on the "old" side of that song title. Now that we see how fast life passes, choose Life so it never passes.

"Talking 'bout *re*-generation" is not a misprint but another play on words from the same song. "Talking 'bout *my* generation" is the refrain following each line verse. I changed it to **re**-generation because in the New Testament, regeneration is the term for New Life (Titus 3:5). The prayer behind my book title is one we all need to pray, "Hope I Die (to self) Before I get Old (too late), talking 'bout regeneration (New Life in Christ)" and see that prayer answered.

Thanks for reading.

Correspondence is welcomed at Rich's email, borealis@ptd.net.

Put "Hope" or "Regeneration" in the subject line so I don't delete as spam if I don't recognize your email address. Don't be afraid of unintentional insulting me, I've heard it all. And don't be afraid to ask that hard question that has kept you from the Bible or a relationship with the living Christ.

ACKNOWLEDGMENTS

Thank you to the following people who reviewed the stories in which they were involved many years ago; to correct or approve for accuracy, and to allow their real names to be used in their associated story(s).

The Mulvena family – for reviewing the car accident story (*Foreword Section*).

Maureen McCarthy – for reviewing the night with officer Bernie Romic at the Optimist Club meeting in her home (*Preface*).

Joe Peca – for reviewing numerous stories, particularly the early ones, and witness to the night I was saved. I could not have a better best friend. (Chapters1–3, 5, 7, 10)

Jay Sadow – for reviewing Devils & Angels. (Chapter 4)

Rob Madonna – for reviewing the Camp Firefly and Nelly Broomall Stories. Also, for reconnecting our friendship after many years. (Chapters 5 & 6)

Tom Harvey - for reviewing the Manoa Lanes stories and the passing of Steve Sisca. I know some of it was difficult to re-visit. Also, for being such a close friend these many years. (Chapters 7–11)

Carl Williams – for reviewing Chapter 12, Lost Part I, and for mentoring me on all things concerning natural history; but mostly for joining me on so many mountains, rivers, swamps and deserts, where no other friends would follow; that such opposites should attract. We are kindred spirits to the end.

Paul Serluco - for reviewing the George *Ural* story, and building the best forts on Glendale Road. (Chapter 12, Lost Part II)

Matt - for reviewing the "Lost" story from somewhere near Haystack Mountain, West Virginia. We will always wonder if you entertained angels. Also, for putting up with Reverend Rich these many years and countless miles. (Chapter 12, Lost Part III)

My lovely wife Lori, who over many years either witnessed some of these events or socially sat with nearly all mentioned and non-mentioned friends to know the stories almost as well as myself; for loving me through my changes.

My Lord & Savior, Jesus Christ for his grace and guidance these last 45 years, and His perfect plan for all our future. REALLY looking forward to meeting you in person!